Intelligence

Intelligence

From Secrets to Policy

Mark M. Lowenthal

CQ PRESS

A Division of Congressional Quarterly Inc.
Washington, D.C.

For
Michael S. Freeman
1946–1999
Historian, Librarian, Friend

CQ Press
A Division of Congressional Quarterly Inc.
1414 22nd Street, N.W.
Washington, DC 20037

(202) 822-1475; (800) 638-1710

www.cqpress.com

Printed and bound in the United States of America

03 02 01 00   5 4 3 2

Cover photo: A Soviet solid rocket motor production plant near Bivsk, USSR. The image was taken by a CORONA intelligence satellite, which was operational from 1960 to 1972. Source: National Reconnaissance Office.

LIBRARY OF CONGRESS CATALOGING-IN-PUBLICATION DATA

Lowenthal, Mark M.
    Intelligence : from secrets to policy / by Mark M. Lowenthal.
        p.   cm.
    Includes bibliographical references and index.
    ISBN 1-56802-512-2 (pbk. : alk. paper)
    1. Intelligence service—United States.   2. Intelligence service.
I. Title.
JK468.I6L65   1999
327.1273—dc21   99-37035

Contents

Figures and Boxes

FIGURES

BOXES

Preface

When academics who teach courses on intelligence get together, one of the first questions they ask one another is, "What are you using for readings?" They ask because there is no standard text on intelligence. Most books are either general histories that will not serve as course texts or academic discussions that are written largely for practitioners and aficionados, not for undergraduate or graduate students. I, like many of my colleagues, have long felt the need for an introductory text. This book is my attempt to fill the gap in intelligence literature.

Intelligence: From Secrets to Policy will not make you a competent spy or even a better analyst. It is designed to give readers a firm understanding of the role that intelligence plays in making national security policy and insight into its strengths and weaknesses. The main theme of the book is that intelligence serves and is subservient to policy and that it works best—both analytically and operationally—when tied to clearly understood policy goals.

Admittedly, this book has a U.S.-centric bias. I am most familiar with the U.S. intelligence establishment, and it is the largest, richest, and most multifaceted intelligence enterprise in the world. At the same time, non-U.S. readers should derive from this book a better understanding of many of the basic issues in intelligence collection, analysis, and covert action and the relationship of intelligence to policy.

This book begins with a discussion of the definition of intelligence and a brief history and overview of the U.S. intelligence community. The core of the book is organized along the lines of the intelligence process as practiced by most intelligence enterprises: requirements, collection, analysis, dissemination, and policy. Each of these aspects is discussed in detail in terms of their role, their strengths, and problems encountered. This structure allows the reader to get a good understanding of both the overall intelligence process and the specific issues encountered in each step of the process. The book also examines covert action and counterintelligence in a similar vein. The last three chapters examine the performance of U.S. intelligence during and after the cold war and the moral and ethical issues that arise in intelligence.

Intelligence: From Secrets to Policy is an outgrowth of two courses that I have taught for many years: "The Role of Intelligence in U.S. Foreign Policy," at the School for International and Public Affairs, Columbia University, and "The History of U.S. Intelligence," at the Elliott School for International Affairs, George Washington University.

As I tell my students, I provide neither a polemic against intelligence nor an apology for it. This volume takes the view that intelligence is a normal function of government: sometimes it works well; sometimes it does not. There is room for both praise and criticism of any intelligence service, including that of the United States.

Intelligence: From Secrets to Policy is an introductory text on intelligence. It is not meant to be the last word on the subject. Rather, it is intended to be a starting point for a serious academic exploration of the issues inherent in intelligence. Each chapter concludes with a list of readings recommended for a deeper examination of relevant issues. Additional bibliographic citations are provided in Appendix 1. Appendix 2 contains four important documents concerning U.S. intelligence.

Several words of thanks are in order: First, to my wife, Cynthia, and children—Sarah and Adam—who have supported my part-time academic career despite the missed dinners it means. Cynthia also reviewed the text incisively and provided me with much help and support throughout the project. Three friends and colleagues—Sam Halpern, Loch Johnson, and Jennifer Sims—reviewed early drafts and made many important improvements. Professors William Green, of California State University at San Bernadino; Patrick Morgan, of the University of California at Irvine; and Donald Snow, of the University of Alabama, also provided extremely helpful comments. Richard Best of the Congressional Research Service helped me keep the bibliographic entries up to date. None of them is in any way responsible for any remaining flaws or for any of the views expressed. I have been most fortunate in the editors I have had at Congressional Quarterly, Charisse Kiino and Jerry Orvedahl. Working with them has been most enjoyable. Finally, thanks to all of my students over the years, whose comments and discussions have greatly enriched my courses and this book.

CHAPTER 1

Introduction—What Is "Intelligence?"

What is intelligence? Why is its definition an issue? Virtually every book written on the subject of intelligence begins with a discussion about what the author believes "intelligence" to mean, or at least how he or she intends to use the term. This editorial fact tells us much about the field of intelligence. If this were a text on any other government function—defense, housing, transportation, diplomacy, agriculture—there would be little or no confusion about, or need to explain, what was being discussed.

Intelligence is different for at least two reasons. First, much of what goes on in intelligence is secret. Intelligence exists because governments seek to hide some information from other governments, which, in turn, seek to discover hidden information by means that they wish to keep secret. All of this secrecy leads some authors to believe that there are issues about which they cannot write or may not know. Thus, they feel the need to describe the limits of their work. Although numerous aspects of intelligence are—and deserve to be—kept secret, their secrecy is not an impediment to describing basic roles, processes, functions, issues, and so on.

The second reason for treating intelligence differently is, in many respects, unique to the United States. The U.S. intelligence community is a relatively recent government phenomenon. Since its creation in 1947, the intelligence community has been the subject of much ambivalence. Some Americans are uncomfortable with the concept that intelligence is a secret entity within an ostensibly open government of checks and balances. Moreover, the intelligence community engages in activities—spying, eavesdropping, covert action—that some people deem to be antithetical to what they believe the United States should be as a nation and as a model for other nations. Some citizens have difficulty reconciling American ideals and goals with the realities of intelligence.

To many people, intelligence seems little different from information, except that it is probably secret. However, it is important to distinguish between the two. Information is anything that can be known, regardless of how it may be discovered. Intelligence refers to information that meets

1

the stated or understood needs of policy makers and has been collected, refined, and narrowed to meet those needs. Intelligence is a subset of the broader category of information; intelligence and the entire process by which it is identified, obtained, and analyzed respond to the needs of policy makers. All intelligence is information; not all information is intelligence.

WHY DO WE HAVE INTELLIGENCE AGENCIES?

The major theme of this book is that intelligence exists solely to support policy makers. Any other activity is either wasteful or illegal. Throughout this book the focus is firmly on the relationship between intelligence, in all of its aspects, and policy making. It is important to understand that the policy maker is not a passive recipient of intelligence, but rather exerts an active influence over all aspects of intelligence. The policy maker's role will also be examined fully. That said, intelligence agencies exist for at least four major reasons.

To Avoid Strategic Surprise.   The foremost goal of any intelligence community must be to keep track of threats, forces, events, and developments that have the ability to threaten the nation's existence. This goal sounds grandiose and far-fetched, but several times in this century alone nations have been subjected to direct military attacks for which they were, at best, inadequately prepared—Russia in 1904, both the Soviet Union and the United States in 1941, Israel in 1973.

Strategic surprise should not be confused with tactical surprise, which is of a different magnitude and, as Professor Richard Betts of Columbia University pointed out in "Analysis, War, and Decision," cannot be wholly avoided. (See box, "Strategic versus Tactical Surprise," p. 3.) Tactical surprise, when it happens, is not of sufficient magnitude and importance to threaten national existence. Repetitive tactical surprise, however, suggests some significant intelligence problems.

To Provide Long-term Expertise.   All senior policy makers are—compared with the permanent bureaucracy—transients. The average time in office for a president of the United States is five years. Secretaries of state and defense serve for less than that, and their senior subordinates—deputy, under, and assistant secretaries—often serve for even less. Even though these individuals enter their respective offices with considerable background in their fields, it is virtually impossible for them to be well-versed in all of the matters and issues with which they will be dealing. Inevitably, they will face issues for which they will have to call upon oth-

Strategic versus Tactical Surprise

The following example puts in perspective the difference between the two types of surprise. There are two partners in a firm, Mr. Smith and Mr. Jones. Every Friday, while Mr. Smith is out at a regular lunch with a client, Mr. Jones helps himself to money from the petty cash.

One afternoon, Mr. Smith comes back from lunch earlier than expected, catching Mr. Jones red-handed. "I'm surprised!" they exclaim simultaneously.

Mr. Jones's surprise is tactical: he knew what he was doing, but did not expect to get caught.

Mr. Smith's surprise is strategic: he had no idea the embezzlement was happening at all.

ers whose knowledge and expertise is longer and deeper. For national security issues, a great deal of knowledge and expertise resides in the intelligence community, where the analytical cadre is relatively stable. Stability tends to be greater in intelligence agencies than in foreign affairs and defense agencies. Also, the higher reaches of the intelligence community tend to be more stable and to have many fewer political appointees than the State and Defense Departments, although these two differences have diminished somewhat over the last decade.

To Support the Policy Process. Policy makers have a constant need for tailored, timely intelligence that will give them background; context; information; warning; and an assessment of risks, benefits, and likely outcomes. Their need is met by the intelligence community.

In the ethos of U.S. intelligence, a strict line exists between intelligence and policy. The two are seen as separate functions. The government is run by and for the policy makers. Intelligence is in a support role and may not cross over into the advocacy of policy choices. Intelligence officers who are dealing with policy makers are expected to maintain a certain objectivity and not lapse into advocacy for specific policies, choices, or outcomes. To do so is seen as threatening the objectivity of the analyses they present. If intelligence officers have a strong preference for a specific policy outcome, their intelligence analysis may display a similar bias. This is what is meant by "politicized intelligence," one of the deepest marks of opprobrium that can be leveled in the U.S. intelligence community.

Policy versus Intelligence: The Great Divide

One way to envision the distinction between policy and intelligence is to see them as two spheres of government activity that are separated by a semipermeable membrane. The membrane is semipermeable because policy makers can and do cross over into the intelligence sphere, but intelligence officials cannot cross over into the policy sphere.

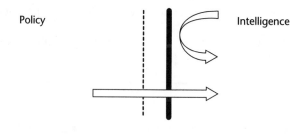

There are three important caveats to add to the distinction between policy and intelligence. First, the idea of intelligence being distinct from policy does not mean that intelligence officers do not care about the outcome and do not influence it. One must draw a distinction between attempting to influence (that is, inform) the process by providing intelligence, which is acceptable, and trying to manipulate intelligence so that policy makers make a certain choice, which is not acceptable. Second, senior policy makers can and do ask senior intelligence officials for their opinions, which are given. Third, this separation works in only one direction, that of intelligence advice to policy. Nothing prevents policy makers from rejecting intelligence out of hand or offering "intelligence" inputs of their own, an action that they will likely see as being different from imposing their views on the intelligence product per se. This also politicizes intelligence, which is an accusation policy makers as well as intelligence officials hope to avoid, because it calls into question the soundness of their policy and the basis on which they have made their decisions. *(See box, "Policy versus Intelligence: The Great Divide," this page.)*

TO MAINTAIN THE SECRECY OF INFORMATION, NEEDS, AND METHODS. Secrecy does make intelligence unique. That others would keep important information from us; that we need certain types of information and wish to keep our needs secret; and that we have means by which to obtain information that we also wish to keep secret are major reasons for having intelligence agencies.

WHAT IS INTELLIGENCE ABOUT?

By the word *intelligence* we are talking largely about issues related to national security—that is, defense and foreign policy and certain aspects of internal security.

The actions, policies, and capabilities of other nations are primary areas of concern. But policy makers and intelligence officers cannot restrict themselves to thinking only about enemies—those powers that are known to be hostile or whose policy goals are in some way inimical. They must also keep track of powers that are rivals, even though they may be neutrals, friends, or even allies. For example, the European Union is made up largely of nations that are U.S. allies. However, in the competition for global resources and markets, many of these same states are our rivals. The same can be said for Japan. Circumstances may also arise in which we would need to keep track of the actions and intentions of friends. Say, for example, an ally is pursuing a course that may involve it in conflict with a third party. Should this not be to our liking—or should it threaten to involve us as well—it would be better to know early on what this ally was doing. Adolf Hitler, for example, might have been better served had he known in advance of Japan's plans to attack the U.S. fleet at Pearl Harbor. In the late twentieth century it has become increasingly important for the United States to keep track of "non-state" actors—terrorists, narcotics traffickers, and others.

We want information about these actors, their likely actions, and their capabilities in a variety of areas—economic, military, societal, and others. The United States built its intelligence organizations in recognition of the fact that some of the information we would like to have is either inaccessible or being actively denied. In other words, the information is secret as far as we are concerned, and those who have the information would like to keep it that way.

The pursuit of secret information is the mainstay of intelligence activity. At the same time, reflecting the political transformation brought about by the end of the cold war, increasing amounts of information that were once secret are now open —especially in those states that were once subject to or allied with the Soviet Union. Indeed, the ratio of open to secret information has likely shifted dramatically. Still, foreign states and actors harbor secrets that the United States must pursue.

Most people tend to think of intelligence in terms of military information—troop movements, weapons capabilities, plans for surprise

---

"And ye shall know the truth ..."

As you enter the old entrance of the CIA headquarters, you see on the left-hand marble wall the following inscription:

"And ye shall know the truth and the truth shall make you free."

John VIII-XXXII

It is a very nice sentiment, but it overstates and misrepresents what is going on in that building or any other intelligence agency.

---

attack. This is an important component of intelligence (in line with the first reason for having intelligence agencies—avoiding surprise attack), but it is not the exclusive type. Political intelligence, economic intelligence, social intelligence, environmental intelligence, and cultural intelligence are all important inputs to analysts. Policy makers and intelligence officials also must think beyond just foreign intelligence. They must consider intelligence activities focused on threats to internal security, such as subversion, espionage, and terrorism.

Other than the internal security threats mentioned above, domestic intelligence, at least in the United States and kindred democracies, is a law-enforcement issue. This fact differentiates the practice of intelligence in Western democracies from that in totalitarian states. The KGB, for example, served a crucial internal secret police function that the CIA does not. Thus, in many respects, the two agencies were not comparable.

What is intelligence *not* about? Intelligence is not about truth! If something were known to be true, states would not need intelligence agencies to collect the information or to analyze it. Truth is such an absolute term that it sets a standard that very little intelligence would be able to achieve. It is better—and more accurate—to think of intelligence as "proximate reality." Intelligence agencies face issues or questions and do their best to come to a firm understanding of what is going on. They can rarely be assured that even their best and most considered analysis is true. Their goals are intelligence products that are reliable, unbiased, and honest (that is, free from politicization). These are all laudable goals, yet they are still different from "truth." (*See box, "And ye shall know the truth," this page.*)

Is intelligence integral to the policy process? The question may seem rhetorical in a book about intelligence, but it is an important question to ask and to answer. To many outside and even within the government, the role of intelligence is not always apparent.

At one level, the answer to the question is "yes." Intelligence should and can provide warning about imminent strategic threats, although several nations have been the subject of strategic surprise. Intelligence officials can also play a useful role as seasoned and experienced advisers. The information that intelligence agencies gather is also of value by virtue of the fact that it might not be available without agencies undertaking secret collection. Therein lies an irony, in that intelligence agencies strive to be more than just collectors of information. They emphasize the value that their analysis adds to their secret information, although equally competent analysts can be found in policy agencies as well. The difference lies in the nature of the work and the outcomes for which the two types of analysts are responsible: intelligence versus policy decisions.

At the same time, intelligence suffers from a number of potential weaknesses that tend to undercut its function in the eyes of policy makers. First, a certain amount of intelligence analysis may be no more sophisticated than current "conventional wisdom" on a given issue. Conventional wisdom is usually—and sometimes mistakenly—dismissed out of hand. But policy makers expect more than that, in part justifiably.

Second, analysis can become so dependent on data that it misses important intangibles. For example, a competent analysis of the likelihood that thirteen small and somewhat disunited colonies would be able to break away from British rule in the 1770s would have concluded that defeat was imminent. After all, Britain was the largest industrial power, it already had trained troops stationed in the colonies, colonial opinion was not united (nor was Britain's), Britain could use the Indians as an added force, and so on. A straightforward political-military analysis would have missed several factors that turned out to be of tremendous importance.

Third, "mirror-imaging," or assuming that other states or individuals will act just the way we do, can undermine analysis. The basis of this problem is fairly understandable. Every day we make innumerable judgments—when we drive, when we walk on a crowded street, when we interact with others in our homes and offices—about how others will react and behave. Indeed, the Golden Rule is based on assumptions of behavior and reaction. These judgments are based on societal norms and rules, etiquette, and experience. It is all too easy for analysts to extend this commonplace thinking to intelligence issues. However, in intelligence it becomes a trap. For example, no U.S. policy maker in 1941 could conceive of Japan starting a war with the United States overtly (rather than continuing its advance while bypassing U.S. territories) given the great disparity in relative strength. In Tokyo, however, those same factors argued compellingly for the necessity of starting war sooner rather than

---

Intelligence—A Working Concept

Intelligence is the process by which specific types of information important to national security are requested, collected, analyzed, and provided to policy makers; the products of that process; the safeguarding of these processes and this information by counterintelligence activities; and the carrying out of operations as requested by lawful authorities.

---

later. The other problem with mirror-imaging is that it assumes a certain level of shared rationality. It leaves no room for the "irrational" actor, a statesman or nation who may be completely irrational or whose rationality has a basis other than our own.

Fourth, and perhaps most important, policy makers are free to reject or to ignore the intelligence they are offered. They may suffer penalties down the road if their policy has bad outcomes, but there is no way to force policy makers to take heed of intelligence. Thus, policy makers can dispense with intelligence at will, and intelligence officers cannot force their way (or their products) back into the process in such cases.

This host of weaknesses seems to overpower the positive aspects listed earlier. It certainly suggests and underscores the fragility of intelligence within the policy process. How, then, can we tell whether intelligence matters? The best way, at least retrospectively, is to ask: Would policy makers have made different choices with or without a given piece of intelligence? If the answer is "yes," or even "maybe," then the intelligence mattered.

What is intelligence? We return to the question with which this chapter began. There are several ways to think about intelligence, all of which will be used throughout this book, sometimes simultaneously:

- Intelligence as process: Intelligence can be thought of as the means by which certain types of information are required and requested, collected, analyzed, and disseminated; and the way in which certain types of covert action are conceived and conducted.
- Intelligence as product: Intelligence can be thought of as the product of these processes, that is, as the analyses and intelligence operations themselves.
- Intelligence as organization: Intelligence can be thought of as the units that carry out its various functions.

FURTHER READINGS

Each of these readings grapples with the definition of intelligence, either by function or by role, in a different way. Some deal with intelligence on is own terms; others attempt to relate it to the larger policy process.

Betts, Richard. "Analysis, War, and Decision: Why Intelligence Failures are Inevitable." *World Politics* 31, no. 1 (October 1978). Reprinted in Klaus Knorr, ed. *Power, Strategy, and Security*. Princeton, N.J.: Princeton University Press, 1983.

Hamilton, Lee. "The Role of Intelligence in the Foreign Policy Process." Essays on Strategy and Diplomacy. Keck Center for International Strategic Studies, Claremont College, 1987.

Herman, Michael. *Intelligence Power in Peace and War.* New York: Cambridge University Press, 1996.

Heymann, Hans. "Intelligence/Policy Relationships." In *Intelligence: Policy and Process,* edited by Alfred C. Maurer. Boulder, Colo.: Westview Press, 1985.

Hilsman, Roger. *Strategic Intelligence and National Decisions.* Glencoe, Ill.: The Free Press, 1958.

Kent, Sherman. *Strategic Intelligence for American Foreign Policy.* Princeton, N.J.: Princeton University Press, 1949.

Laqueur, Walter. *A World of Secrets: The Uses and Limits of Intelligence.* New York: Basic Books, 1985.

Shulsky, Abram N., and Gary J. Schmitt. *Silent Warfare: Understanding the World of Intelligence.* 2d rev. ed. Washington, D.C.: Brasseys, 1993.

Troy, Thomas F. "The 'Correct' Definition of Intelligence." *International Journal of Intelligence and Counterintelligence* 5 (winter 1991–1992).

CHAPTER 2

The Development of the U.S. Intelligence Community

Each nation practices intelligence in ways that are specific—if not peculiar—to that nation alone. This is true even among nations that share a great deal of their intelligence, such as the United States, Britain, Canada, and Australia. A better understanding of how and why the United States practices intelligence as it does is important for much that will be discussed in the following chapters and because the U.S. intelligence system remains the largest and most influential in the world—as model, rival, or target.

This chapter discusses the major themes and the major historical events that shaped the development of U.S. intelligence. This is not intended to be even a brief history of U.S. intelligence in outline form. Rather, these themes and events have been chosen because they played a significant role in forging U.S. intelligence and in determining how it continues to function.

A brief word is in order about the phrase "intelligence community," which is used throughout the book, as it is in most other discussions of U.S. intelligence. The word "community" is particularly apt in describing U.S. intelligence. The community comprises agencies and offices whose work is often related and sometimes combined, but who work for different customers and under various lines of authority and control. The intelligence community grew out of a set of evolving demands and without a master plan. It is highly functional and sometimes dysfunctional. One director of central intelligence, Richard Helms (1966–1973), testified cogently before Congress that, despite all of the criticisms of the structure and functioning of the intelligence community, if one were to create it from scratch, much the same community would likely emerge. Helms's focus is not the structure of the community, but the fact that the services it provides are multiple, varied, and not under one individual's complete authority. It is an approach to intelligence that is unique to the United States, although others have copied facets of it since.

MAJOR THEMES

THE NOVELTY OF U.S. INTELLIGENCE.   Of the major powers of the twentieth century, the United States has the briefest history of significant intelligence beyond wartime emergencies. British intelligence dates from the reign of Elizabeth I (1558–1603); French intelligence from the sway of Cardinal Richelieu (1624–1642); and Russian intelligence from the reign of Ivan the Terrible (1553–1584). Even taking into account the fact that the United States came into being only in 1776, its intelligence experience is brief. Not until 1940 was there the first glimmer of what might be called a national intelligence enterprise. Although permanent and specific naval and military intelligence units date from the late nineteenth century, a broader U.S. national intelligence capability began to arise only with the creation of the Coordinator of Information, the predecessor of the World War II–era Office of Strategic Services (OSS).

How do we explain this nearly 170-year absence of organized U.S. intelligence? For most of its history, the United States did not have very strong foreign policy interests. The success of the Monroe Doctrine, articulated in 1823, abetted by the acquiescence and tacit support of Britain, solved the basic security interests of the United States and its broader foreign policy interests. The need for better intelligence became apparent only after the rise of the United States to world power status and its involvement in broader international issues at the end of the nineteenth century.

Furthermore, the United States faced no threat to its security from its neighbors, from powers outside the Western Hemisphere, or—with the exception of the Civil War—from large-scale internal dissent that was inimical to the form of government. This benign environment—so unlike that faced by all European states—undercut any perceived need for national intelligence.

The United States—until the cold war—had a well-established tradition of severely limiting expenditures on defense and related activities during peacetime. Intelligence, already under-appreciated for the reasons noted above, fell into this category. (Historians of intelligence have noted, though, that intelligence absorbed a remarkable and anomalous 12 percent of the federal budget under President Washington. This was the high-water mark of intelligence spending as a percent of the federal budget, a level that was never approached again. In 1999 intelligence accounted for roughly 1.6 percent of the federal budget, using figures declassified by the director of central intelligence.)

Intelligence was a novelty in the 1940s. Policy makers in both the executive branch and Congress viewed intelligence as a "newcomer" to national security. Even within the Army and Navy, intelligence developed relatively late and was far from robust until well into the twentieth century. As a result, intelligence did not have long-established patrons in the government, but it did have many rivals among departments, particularly the military and the FBI, which were not willing to share their sources of information. Another result of its novelty was that intelligence did not have well-established traditions or modes of operation and thus was forced to establish these during two periods of extreme pressure: World War II and the cold war.

A THREAT-BASED FOREIGN POLICY.   With the promulgation of the Monroe Doctrine, the United States assumed a vested interest in the international status quo. This interest became even more pronounced after the Spanish-American War in 1898. With the acquisition of a small colonial empire, the United States achieved a very satisfactory international position—largely self-sufficient and largely unthreatened. However, the twentieth century saw the repeated rise of powers whose foreign policies were direct threats to the status quo: Kaiserine Germany in World War I, the Axis in World War II, and then the Soviet Union.

Responding to these threats to the international status quo became the mainstay of U.S. national security policy. The threats also gave focus to much of the operational side of U.S. intelligence, from its initial experience in the OSS during World War II to its broader covert actions in the cold war. Intelligence operations were one way in which the United States countered these threats.

THE INFLUENCE OF THE COLD WAR.   Historians of intelligence often debate whether the United States would have had a large-scale intelligence capability had there been no cold war. The view here is that the answer is "yes." As will be discussed below, Pearl Harbor was the necessary cause of the U.S. intelligence community, not the cold war.

That said, the prosecution of the cold war became the major defining factor in the development of most of the basic forms and practices of the U.S. intelligence community. The cold war was, until the collapse of the Soviet Union, the predominant national security issue, taking up to half of the intelligence budget, according to former director of central intelligence Robert Gates (1991–1993). Moreover, the fact that the Soviet Union and its subject allies were largely closed targets had a major effect on U.S. intelligence, forcing it to resort to a variety of largely remote technical systems to collect the required intelligence. Unable to get close to the Soviet intelligence target, the U.S. learned to collect intelligence from a distance.

THE GLOBAL SCOPE OF INTELLIGENCE INTERESTS.   The cold war quickly shifted from a struggle for predominance in postwar Europe to a global struggle in which virtually any nation or region could be a pawn between the two sides. Although some areas always remained more important than others, none could be written off entirely. Thus, U.S. intelligence became global, collecting and analyzing information about and stationing intelligence personnel in every region.

A WITTINGLY REDUNDANT ANALYTICAL STRUCTURE.   Intelligence can be divided into four broad activities: collection, analysis, covert action, and counterintelligence. The United States developed unique entities to handle the various types of collection (imagery, signals, espionage) and covert action; counterintelligence is a function that is found in virtually every intelligence agency. But in analysis, U.S. policy makers purposely created three agencies whose functions appear to overlap: the CIA's Directorate of Intelligence, the State Department's Bureau of Intelligence and Research, and the Defense Intelligence Agency. Each of these agencies is considered an "all-source" analytical agency—that is, they have access to the full range of collected intelligence, and each works on virtually the same issues as the others.

There are two major reasons for this redundancy, and they are fundamental to how the United States conducts analysis. The first is the recognition that different consumers of intelligence—policy makers—have different intelligence needs. The president, the secretary of state, the secretary of defense, and the chairman of the Joint Chiefs of Staff have intelligence needs that are different from one another and from other policy makers. Even when they are working on the same issue, each has different operational responsibilities. The United States developed analytical centers to serve each of their specific and unique needs. Also, admittedly, each agency wanted to be assured of a stream of intelligence that was dedicated to its needs.

Second, the United States developed the concept of competitive analysis. This concept holds that by having analysts with different backgrounds and views come to bear on an issue, parochial views are more likely to be countered—if not weeded out—and "proximate reality" is more likely to be achieved. Competitive analysis should, in theory, be an antidote to "groupthink" and forced consensus, although this is not always the case in practice. Competitive analysis is not possible without multiple analytical agencies.

CONSUMER-PRODUCER RELATIONS.   The distinct line that is drawn between policy and intelligence leads to questions about how intelligence producers and consumers should relate to each other. The nub of the issue is the degree of proximity that is desirable.

There have been two schools of thought in this debate in the United States. The "distance" school argued that the intelligence establishment should keep some distance between itself and the policy makers so as to avoid running the risk of providing intelligence that lacks objectivity and favors or opposes one policy choice over others. Adherents of the distance school also feared that policy makers could interfere with intelligence in order to receive analysis that supported or opposed specific policies. This group believed that too close a relationship increased the risk of "politicizing" intelligence.

The "proximate" group argued that too great a distance raised the risk that the intelligence community would be less aware of policy makers' needs and would produce intelligence that was less useful. This group felt that proper training and internal reviews could avoid politicization of intelligence.

By the late 1950s to early 1960s the "proximate" school became the preferred model for U.S. intelligence. But the debate was significant in that it underscored the early and persistent fears about intelligence becoming politicized.

In the late 1990s some people perceived two subtle shifts in the policy–intelligence relationship. The first was a greatly increased emphasis on "support to military operations," which some believed gave too much priority to this sector—at a time when threats to national security had decreased—at the expense of other intelligence consumers. The second was the feeling among some analysts that they were being torn between operational customers (see the next issue) and analytical customers.

THE RELATIONSHIP BETWEEN ANALYSIS AND COLLECTION AND COVERT ACTION.   Parallel to the debate over producer-consumer relations, factions have waged a similar debate over the proper relationship between intelligence analysis, on the one hand, and intelligence collection and covert action, on the other.

The issue has centered largely over the structure of the CIA, which houses both analytical and operational components: the Directorate of Intelligence (DI) and the Directorate of Operations (DO); the latter is responsible for both espionage and covert action.

Again, "distance" and "proximate" schools took form. The distance school has argued that analysis and the two operational functions are largely distinct and that housing them together runs risks, for the security of human sources and methods and for analysis. They have raised concerns about the ability of the DI to provide objective analysis where the DO is concurrently running a major covert action. Will there not be pressure, either overt or subliminal, to have analysis support the covert action? This is not an abstract question. Such stresses existed between some analytical components of the intelligence community and support-ers of the contras in Nicaragua in the 1980s, for example. Some analysts questioned whether the contras would ever be victorious, which was seen as "unsupportive" by some of those who were involved in support-ing the contras.

The proximate school has argued that separating the two functions deprives both analysis and operations of the benefits of a close relation-ship. Analysts gain a better appreciation of operational goals and reali-ties, which they can factor into their work, and also a better sense of the value of sources developed in espionage. Operators gain a better appre-ciation of the analyses they receive, which they can factor into their own planning.

Although critics of the current structure have repeatedly suggested separating the two functions, the proximate school has prevailed. Indeed, in the mid-1990s the DI and DO entered what they called a "partnership," in which their front offices and various regional offices were located together.

THE DEBATE OVER COVERT ACTION.   Covert action has always gen-erated uneasiness in some quarters in the United States concerned about its propriety or acceptability as a facet of U.S. policy. Within that debate, another debate emerged, over the use of paramilitary operations—the training and equipping of large military units, such as the contras. Other than assassination, paramilitary operations have been among the most controversial aspects of covert action, and they have a very uneven record.

THE CONTINUITY OF INTELLIGENCE POLICY.   For most of the cold war there was no difference between Democratic and Republican intelli-gence policies. The cold war consensus on the need for a continuing pol-icy of containment vis-à-vis the Soviet Union transcended politics until the Vietnam War, at which point a difference emerged between the two parties that was in many respects more rhetorical than real. For example, both Jimmy Carter and Ronald Reagan made intelligence policy aspects of their campaigns for the presidency. Carter, in 1976, lumped revelations about the CIA and other agencies' misconduct with Watergate and Viet-nam; Reagan, in 1980, spoke of "restoring" the CIA, along with the rest of U.S. national security. Although the ways in which they supported and used intelligence differed greatly, it would be wrong to suggest that one was "anti-intelligence" and the other "pro-intelligence."

HEAVY RELIANCE ON TECHNOLOGY.   The United States has, since the creation of the modern intelligence community in the 1940s, relied very heavily on technology as the mainstay of its collection capabilities, for several reasons. First, a technological response to a problem is not unique to intelligence; it also describes how the United States has waged war, beginning as early as the Civil War in the 1860s. Second, the closed nature of the major intelligence target, the Soviet Union, required remote technical means to collect information.

The reliance on technology is significant beyond the collection capabilities it engendered, because it had a major effect on the structure of the intelligence community and how it functioned. Some people maintain that the reliance on technology has resulted in an insufficient use of human intelligence collection (espionage). There are no empirical data to support this view, yet it has persisted since at least the 1970s. The main argument, which tends to arise when intelligence is perceived to have performed less than optimally, is that human intelligence can collect certain types of information (intentions, plans) that technical collection cannot. There is little disagreement about the strengths and weaknesses of the various types of collection, but such an assessment does not necessarily support the view that espionage always suffers vis-à-vis technical collection. The persistence of the debate reflects an underlying concern about intelligence collection that has never been adequately addressed, that is, the proper balance—if one can be constructed—between technical and human collection.

SECRECY VERSUS OPENNESS.   The openness that is an inherent part of a representative democratic government clashes with the secrecy within which intelligence must operate. No democratic government with a significant intelligence community has spent more time debating and worrying about this clash than has the United States. The issue cannot be settled with finality, but the United States has made an ongoing series of compromises between its values—as a government and as an international leader—and the requirements for some level of intelligence activity as it has continued to explore the boundaries of this issue.

THE ROLE OF OVERSIGHT.   For the first twenty-eight years of its existence, the intelligence community operated with a minimal amount of oversight from Congress. One reason was the cold war consensus noted above. Another was a willingness on the part of Congress to abdicate rigorous oversight. Secrecy was also a factor, which appeared to impose procedural difficulties in handling sensitive issues between the two branches. After 1975, as will be discussed below, congressional oversight changed suddenly and dramatically, increasing to the point where Congress became a full participant in the intelligence process and a major consumer of intelligence.

MAJOR HISTORICAL DEVELOPMENTS

In addition to the themes that have run through much of the history of the intelligence community, several specific events played pivotal roles in the shaping and functioning of U.S. intelligence.

THE CREATION OF COI AND OSS (1940–1941).   As noted above, until 1940 the United States did not have anything approaching a national intelligence establishment. The successive creations of the Coordinator of Information (COI) and the Office of Strategic Services (OSS) by President Franklin Roosevelt were important precedents. Both the COI and OSS were headed by William Donovan. In addition to being the first steps toward the creation of a national intelligence capability, COI and OSS were important for two other reasons. First, both organizations were heavily influenced by British intelligence practices, particularly the British emphasis on what we would now call covert action—guerrillas, operations with resistance groups behind enemy lines, sabotage, and so on. For Britain this wartime emphasis on operations came as a natural result of being one of the few ways Britain could strike back at Nazi Germany in Europe until the Allied invasions of Italy and France. These covert actions, which had little effect on the outcome of the war, became the main historical legacy of the OSS.

Second, although OSS operations played little role in the Allied victory in World War II, they served as a training ground—both technically and in terms of esprit—for many of the people who helped establish the postwar intelligence community, particularly the CIA.

PEARL HARBOR (1941).   The surprise attack by Japan was a classic intelligence failure. The United States overlooked a variety of signals; U.S. processes and procedures were deeply flawed; and mirror-imaging blinded U.S. policy makers to a very different assessment in Tokyo. But, for U.S. intelligence, the attack on Pearl Harbor was most important as the raison d'être for the community that was established after World War II. Its fundamental mission was to prevent a recurrence of a strategic surprise of this magnitude, especially in an age of nuclear-armed missiles.

MAGIC AND ULTRA (1941–1945).   One of the Allies' major advantages in World War II was their superior signals intelligence, that is, their ability to intercept and decode Axis communications. MAGIC refers to U.S. intercepts of Japanese communications; ULTRA refers to British, and later British-U.S., interceptions of German communications. This wartime experience showed the tremendous importance of this specific type of intelligence; it was perhaps the most important type of intelligence during the war. Also, it helped solidify U.S.-British intelligence cooperation, which continued long after the war. Moreover, in the United States MAGIC and ULTRA were controlled by the military, not by OSS. This underscored the friction between the military and OSS. It also secured a major intelligence function, signals intelligence, for the military, which continues to this day in the National Security Agency.

THE NATIONAL SECURITY ACT (1947).   The National Security Act gave a legal basis to the intelligence community, creating the position of director of central intelligence (DCI) and a CIA under the director. The act signaled the new importance of intelligence in the nascent cold war and also made the intelligence function permanent, a step away from the previous U.S. practice of reducing the national security apparatus in peacetime. Implicitly, the act made the existence and functioning of the intelligence community a part of the cold war consensus.

Several aspects of the act are worth noting. Although the DCI could be a military officer, the CIA was not placed under military control. Nor was the CIA to have any domestic role or police powers. The legislation does not mention any of the activities that came to be most commonly associated with the CIA—espionage, covert action, even analysis. Its stated job, and President Harry S. Truman's main concern at the time, was to coordinate the intelligence being produced by various agencies.

KOREA (1950).   The unexpected invasion of South Korea had two major effects on U.S. intelligence. First, the failure to predict the invasion led DCI Walter Bedell Smith (1950–1953) to make some dramatic changes, including putting increased emphasis on national intelligence estimates (NIEs). Second, the Korean War made the cold war global. Having previously been confined to a struggle for dominance in Europe, the cold war now spread to Asia and, implicitly, to the rest of the world as well. This broadened the scope and responsibilities of intelligence.

THE COUP IN IRAN (1953).   In 1953 the United States staged a series of "popular" demonstrations in Iran that overthrew the government of Premier Mohammad Mossadegh and restored the rule of the shah, who was more friendly to Western interests. The success and ease of this operation made covert action an increasingly attractive tool for U.S. policy makers, especially under the tenure of DCI Allen Dulles (1953–1961).

THE GUATEMALA COUP (1954).   In 1954 the United States overthrew the leftist government of Guatemalan president Jacobo Arbenz Guzmán out of concern that it might prove sympathetic to the Soviet Union. The United States provided a clandestine opposition radio station and air support for rebel officers. The Guatemala coup "proved" that the success in Iran was not unique, thus further elevating the appeal of this type of action for U.S. policy makers.

THE "MISSILE GAP" (1959–1961).   In the late 1950s some in the United States were concerned that the apparent Soviet lead in the "race for space" also meant a Soviet lead in missile-based strategic weaponry. The main critics were Democratic aspirants for the 1960 presidential nomination, including Sens. John F. Kennedy and Stuart Symington. The Eisenhower administration knew, by virtue of the U.S. reconnaissance program, that the accusations were untrue, but it did not respond to the charges so as to safeguard the sources of the intelligence. When the Kennedy administration took office, it discovered the charges to be untrue, but the new secretary of defense, Robert McNamara, came to believe that intelligence had inflated the Soviet threat to safeguard the defense budget. This was an early example of intelligence becoming a political issue, raised primarily by the party out of power.

The way in which the missile gap is customarily portrayed in intelligence history is incorrect. The "legend" is that the intelligence community, perhaps for base and selfish motives, overestimated the number of Soviet strategic missiles. This is incorrect on several grounds. The overestimate came largely from political critics of the Eisenhower administration, not the intelligence agencies. In reality, critics overestimated the number of strategic-range Soviet missiles, and the intelligence community underestimated the number of medium- and intermediate-range missiles that the Soviets were building to cover their main concern, Europe. McNamara's distrust over what he saw as self-serving Air Force parochialism moved him to create the Defense Intelligence Agency.

THE BAY OF PIGS (1961).   The abysmal failure of the attempt to overthrow Fidel Castro by CIA-trained Cuban exiles showed the limits of large-scale paramilitary operations in terms of their effectiveness and the United States's ability to mask its role in them.

THE CUBAN MISSILE CRISIS (1962).   Although widely seen now as a success, in terms of intelligence the confrontation with the Soviet Union over its planned deployment of missiles in Cuba was initially a failure. It was a failure in that all analysts, with the notable exception of DCI John McCone (1961–1965), argued that Soviet premier Nikita Khrushchev would not be so bold or rash as to place missiles in Cuba. The missile crisis was also a success, in that U.S. intelligence discovered the missile sites before they were complete, giving President Kennedy sufficient time to deal with the situation without resort to force. U.S. intelligence was also able to give President Kennedy firm assessments of Soviet strategic and conventional force capabilities, which bolstered his ability to make difficult decisions. Finally, the intelligence community's performance went a long way toward rehabilitating its reputation after the Bay of Pigs.

THE VIETNAM WAR (1964–1975).   The war in Vietnam had three important effects on U.S. intelligence. First, during the war concerns grew that frustrated policy makers were politicizing intelligence to be supportive of policy. The Tet offensive in 1968 is a case in point. Faced with intelligence indicating preparations for a large-scale Viet Cong offensive, President Johnson had two unpalatable choices. He could prepare the public for the event, but then face questions as to how this was possible if the United States was winning the war. Alternatively, he could attempt to ride it out, confident that the attack would be defeated. Johnson took the second choice. The Viet Cong were defeated militarily in Tet, but the surprise effect of the attack and the scale of military operations that the United States undertook to defeat them turned a successful intelligence warning and a military victory into a major political defeat. Unfortunately, many assumed that the attack was a surprise.

Often-heated debates took place between military and nonmilitary intelligence analysts about the progress of the war. This was seen most sharply in the "order of battle" debate, which centered on how many enemy units were in the field. Third, and more long-lasting and important, the war severely undercut the cold war consensus under which intelligence operated.

THE ABM TREATY AND SALT I ACCORD (1972).   These initial strategic arms control agreements between the United States and the Soviet Union explicitly recognized and legitimized the use of "national technical means" (that is, a variety of satellites and other technical collectors) by both parties to collect needed intelligence, and they prohibited overt interference with national technical means. Furthermore, these agreements created the new issue of verification—the ability to ascertain whether treaty obligations were being met. (Monitoring, or keeping track of Soviet activities, had been under way since the inception of the intelligence community, even before arms control.) U.S. intelligence inevitably was dragged into these activities, with new accusations by some that intelligence was being politicized. Those concerned that the Soviets were cheating held that cheating was either going undetected or being ignored. Arms control advocates argued that the Soviets were not cheating or that the cheating was so small as to be inconsequential, regardless of the terms of the agreements, or that some amount of cheating was preferable to unchecked strategic competition. Either way, the intelligence community found itself to be a fundamental part of the debate.

INTELLIGENCE INVESTIGATIONS (1975–1976).   In the wake of revelations that the CIA had violated its charter by spying on U.S. citizens, a series of investigations examined the entire intelligence community. A panel chaired by Vice President Nelson Rockefeller concluded that violations of law had occurred. Investigations by House and Senate special committees went deeper, discovering a much wider range of abuses.

Coming so soon after the Watergate scandal and the loss of South Vietnam, these intelligence hearings further undermined the public's faith in government institutions, in particular the intelligence community, which had been largely sacrosanct. Since these investigations, intelligence has never regained the latitude it once enjoyed and has had to learn to operate with much more openness and more scrutiny. Also, Congress faced the fact of its own lax oversight. Both the Senate and House created permanent intelligence oversight committees, which have taken on much more vigorous oversight of intelligence and are now major consumers of intelligence themselves.

IRAN (1979).   In 1979 Ayatollah Ruhollah Khomeini's revolution forced the shah of Iran from his throne and into exile. U.S. intelligence, due in part to policy decisions made by several administrations that severely limited collection, was largely blind to the growing likelihood of this turn of events. Nevertheless, the intelligence community took much of the blame for the result. Some even saw the shah's fall as the inevitable result of the 1953 coup that had restored him to power.

IRAN-CONTRA (1986–1987).   The administration of Ronald Reagan botched its attempt to use proceeds from missile sales to Iran (which not only contradicted the administration's own policy of not dealing with terrorists but also violated a law) to sustain the contras in Nicaragua—despite congressional restrictions on such aid. The project provoked a constitutional crisis and congressional investigations. The affair highlighted a series of problems, including the limits of oversight in both the executive branch and Congress; the ability of executive officials to ignore Congress's intent; and the disaster that can result when two distinct and disparate covert actions became intertwined. The affair also undid much of President Reagan's efforts to rebuild and restore intelligence capabilities.

THE FALL OF THE SOVIET UNION (1989–1991).   Beginning with the collapse of the Soviet satellite empire in 1989 and culminating with the dissolution of the Soviet Union itself in 1991, the United States witnessed the triumph of its long-held policy of containment. The collapse was so swift and so stunning that few can be said to have anticipated it.

Critics of the intelligence community argued that this was the ultimate intelligence failure, given the centrality of the Soviet Union as an intelligence community issue. Some even felt that this "failure" justified radically reducing and altering the intelligence community. Defenders of U.S. intelligence argued that the community had portrayed much of the inner rot that led to the Soviet collapse.

This debate has not concluded; significant questions remain not only about U.S. intelligence capabilities but also about intelligence in general and what can reasonably be expected from it (see chapter 11 for a detailed discussion).

THE AMES SPY SCANDAL (1994).   The arrest and conviction of Aldrich Ames, a CIA employee, on charges of spying for the Soviet Union and for post-Soviet Russia for almost ten years shook U.S. intelligence. Espionage scandals had broken before; in the "year of the spy" (1985), several cases came to light—the Walker family, Ron Pelton, Larry Wu-tai Chin.

Ames's unsuspected treachery was, in many respects, more searing. Russian espionage continued, despite the end of the cold war. Ames's career revealed significant shortcomings in CIA personnel practices (Ames was a marginal officer with a well-known alcohol problem), in CIA counter-espionage and counter-intelligence, and in CIA–FBI liaison to deal with these issues. The affair also revealed continuing shortcomings in how the executive branch shared information bearing on intelligence matters with Congress.

A FINAL NOTE

Again, this list is not exhaustive and is not meant to be so. Indeed, a good argument can be provoked among practitioners and students of intelligence by such an exercise. Still, this list delineates trends and events that have played a major role in shaping the U.S. intelligence community.

KEY TERMS

competitive analysis
monitoring
national intelligence

national technical means (NTM)
politicized intelligence
verification

FURTHER READINGS

Most histories of U.S. intelligence tend to be CIA-centric, and these readings are no exception to that generalization. Nonetheless, these readings still offer some of the best discussions of the events and issues discussed in this chapter.

Ambrose, Stephen E., with Richard H. Immerman. *Ike's Spies: Eisenhower and the Espionage Establishment*. Garden City, N.Y.: Doubleday, 1981.

Brugioni, Dino A. *Eyeball to Eyeball: The Inside Story of the Cuban Missile Crisis*, edited by Robert F. McCort. New York: Random House, 1990.

Colby, William E., and Peter Forbath. *Honorable Men: My Life in the CIA*. New York: Simon and Schuster, 1978.

Draper, Theodore. *A Very Thin Line: The Iran-Contra Affair.* New York: Hill and Wang, 1991.

Gates, Robert M. *From the Shadows*. New York: Simon and Schuster, 1996.

Hersh, Seymour. "Huge CIA Operations Reported in U.S. Against Anti-War Forces, Other Dissidents in Nixon Years." *The New York Times*, December 22, 1974.

Houston, Lawrence R. "The CIA's Legislative Base." *International Journal of Intelligence and Counterintelligence* 5 (winter 1991–1992).

Jeffreys-Jones, Rhodri. *The CIA and American Democracy*. New Haven, Conn.: Yale University Press, 1989.

Lowenthal, Mark M. *U.S. Intelligence: Evolution and Anatomy*. 2d edition. Westport, Conn.: Praeger Publishers, 1992.

Montague, Ludwell Lee. *General Walter Bedell Smith as Director of Central Intelligence: October 1950-February 1953*. University Park: Pennsylvania State University Press, 1992.

Moynihan, Daniel Patrick. *Secrecy: The American Experience*. New Haven, Conn.: Yale University Press, 1998.

Persico, Joseph. *Casey: From the OSS to the CIA*. New York: Viking, 1990.

Powers, Thomas. *The Man Who Kept the Secrets: Richard Helms and the CIA*. New York: Alfred A. Knopf, 1979.

Ranelagh, John. *The Rise and Decline of the CIA*. New York: Touchstone Books, 1987.

Troy, Thomas F. *Donovan and the CIA: A History of the Establishment of the Central Intelligence Agency*. Frederick, Md.: University Publications of America, 1981.

U.S. Senate. Select Committee to Study Governmental Operations with Respect to Intelligence Activities [The Church Committee]. Final Report, Book IV: *Supplementary Detailed Staff Reports on Foreign and Military Intelligence*. 94th Congress, 2d session, 1976. [Also known as the Karalekas report, after its author, Anne Karalekas.]

Wohlstetter, Roberta. *Pearl Harbor: Warning and Decision*. Stanford, Calif.: Stanford University Press, 1962.

Wyden, Peter. *Bay of Pigs: The Untold Story*. New York: Simon and Schuster, 1979.

CHAPTER 3

The U.S. Intelligence Community

This chapter describes the structure and functioning of the U.S. intelligence community and offers alternative ways of thinking about them.

THE STANDARD VIEW OF THE INTELLIGENCE COMMUNITY

The standard view of the U.S. intelligence community is hierarchical and bureaucratic, emphasizing vertical lines of authority. Figure 3-1 offers such a view but also categorizes agencies by intelligence budget sectors: National Foreign Intelligence Program (NFIP), Joint Military Intelligence Program (JMIP), and Tactical Intelligence and Related Activities (TIARA).

The CIA, unlike the Bureau of Intelligence and Research (INR) at State or the Defense Intelligence Agency (DIA) in Defense, has no cabinet-level patron. The CIA's main customers are the president and the National Security Council (NSC). This relationship has both benefits and problems. On the one hand, it gives the CIA access to the ultimate decision maker. On the other hand, the president—unlike the secretaries of state and defense or the chairman of the Joint Chiefs of Staff—has other responsibilities beyond national security. Moreover, it is more difficult to engage the president in intelligence turf issues than it is to engage the other cabinet-level officers. The director of central intelligence (DCI) must engage on his own, perhaps to his ultimate bureaucratic disadvantage. The DCI comes under the control of the NSC.

The secretary of defense controls much more of the intelligence community on a day-to-day basis than does the DCI. The panoply of agencies that belong to the Department of Defense (DOD)—National Security Agency, Defense Intelligence Agency, National Imagery and Mapping Agency, Defense airborne reconnaissance programs, the service intelligence units—vastly outnumber, in people and dollars, the CIA. At the

FIGURE 3-1   The Intelligence Community: An Organizational View

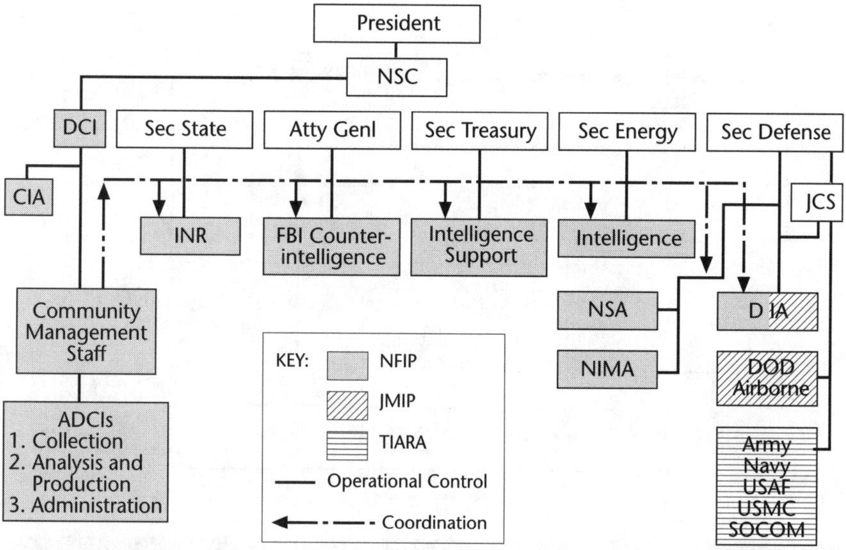

Source: U.S. House Permanent Select Committee on Intelligence, *IC21: The Intelligence Community in the 21st Century.* 104th Congress, 2d session, 1996.

same time, the secretary of defense is unlikely to have the same level of interest in intelligence as the DCI. In fact, much responsibility within DOD for intelligence is customarily delegated to the deputy secretary of defense.

Figure 3-1 is somewhat deficient in that it does not describe the variety of functions of the agencies, which are central to their relationships. Indeed, there are several different ways of looking at the U.S. intelligence community in order to get a better appreciation of what it does and how it works.

ALTERNATIVE WAYS OF LOOKING AT THE INTELLIGENCE COMMUNITY

It is useful, before examining the structure of the intelligence community further, to look at its basic functions.

There are, in effect, two broad functional areas: management and execution. Within each of these two areas are many specific tasks. Management encompasses the management of requirements, resources, col-

FIGURE 3-2   Alternative Ways of Looking at the Intelligence Community:
A Functional Flow View

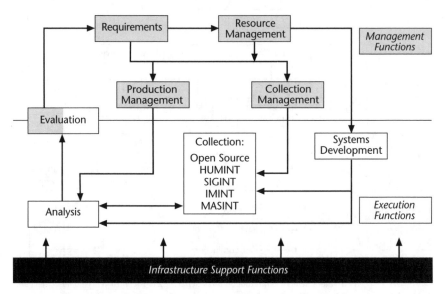

Source: U.S. House Permanent Select Committee on Intelligence, *IC21: The Intelligence Community in the 21st Century.* 104th Congress, 2d session, 1996.

lection, and production. Execution comprises the development of collection systems, the actual collection and production of intelligence, and maintenance of the infrastructure support base. Figure 3-2 divides management and execution by a horizontal rule, but one function straddles the rule: evaluation. Evaluation is not one of the strongest functions of the intelligence community. Relating intelligence means (resources: budgets, people) to intelligence ends (outcomes: analyses, operations) is extremely difficult. The intelligence community does not take on the task with great relish. Yet it is a very important task and one that, if it were done more systematically and more broadly, might yield dividends to intelligence managers.

The flow suggested by Figure 3-2 is admittedly idealized, but it gives a very good idea of how the main managerial and execution concerns relate to one another. The flow is circular, going in endless loops. If one were to suggest starting at some point, that point would be requirements. Without requirements, very little that happens afterward makes sense. Given their proper role, requirements should drive everything else.

The "Simplicity" of Intelligence

In the baseball movie "Bull Durham," a manager tries to explain to his somewhat hapless players the simplicity of the game they are supposed to be playing: "You throw the ball; you hit the ball; you catch the ball."

Intelligence has a similar deceptive simplicity: you ask a question; you collect information; you answer the question.

In both cases, there are many devils in the details.

The various aspects of collection—systems development and collection itself—occupy much more of the figure than does analysis. This reflects the realities of the intelligence community, whether desirable or not.

THE MANY DIFFERENT INTELLIGENCE COMMUNITIES

Within the U.S. intelligence community lie many different intelligence communities. Figure 3-3 gives a better sense of what these various communities are by showing what each agency or subagency component does, while still preserving the sense of hierarchy. The vertical lines should be thought of as flowing from the topmost organizations through each of the agencies or components below.

At the top of the hierarchy are the individuals who are major intelligence managers, major customers, or both. The president is the major customer but is not an intelligence manager. The various cabinet secretaries are all customers, and two of them—the secretaries of state and defense—control significant intelligence assets. State has INR; DOD has the entire panoply of defense intelligence organizations, which respond to a broad range of needs. DOD organizations participate in national-level intelligence processes and products, providing indications and warning of impending attack (see chapter 6) and intelligence support for military operations at all levels—from theater (broad regional commands) down to tactical (small units engaged in operations or combat). The attorney general has control over the FBI; Energy has a small intelligence office devoted to its specific concerns; and Commerce controls the commercial attachés, who are assigned to embassies and serve an overt intelligence function. The DCI is manager of the CIA and, through the Community

FIGURE 3-3   Alternative Ways of Looking at the Intelligence Community:
A Functional View

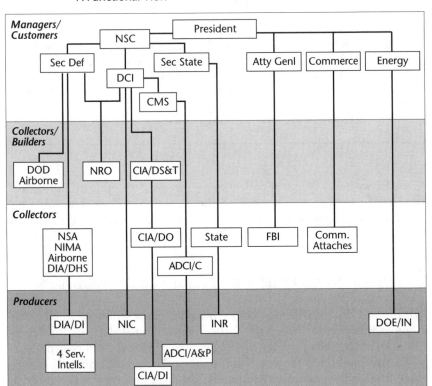

Management Staff (CMS), coordinator of the larger national intelligence effort.

At the next level down are the builders of various types of technical collection systems. The main one is the National Reconnaissance Office (NRO), which is responsible for the design, building, and (via the Air Force or NASA) the launch of satellite collection systems. DOD also has an airborne reconnaissance responsibility for "airbreathing" systems such as unmanned aerial vehicles (UAVs) or drones, which are of increasing importance on the battlefield for tactical collection. Finally, the CIA's Directorate of Science and Technology (DS&T) has a role in some technical collection programs.

A variety of offices are responsible for the collection (including processing and exploitation) of intelligence. Within DOD are the National Security Agency (NSA), which collects signals intelligence (SIGINT); the

National Imagery and Mapping Agency (NIMA), which processes and exploits imagery (IMINT); the Defense airborne systems; and the Defense HUMINT Service (DHS) of DIA, whose duties are reflected in its name. The CIA is responsible for espionage (human intelligence—HUMINT) collection via the Directorate of Operations (DO). State collects for itself and for others via its array of embassies and Foreign Service officers, although its activities are not "tasked intelligence"—that is, they are not undertaken in response to a specific requirement—as are the others listed here; Commerce collects via the commercial attachés. The FBI collects counter-intelligence information via its National Security Division and has legal attachés posted in many U.S. embassies overseas. Congress created the position of assistant DCI for collection in 1996. This ADCI assists the DCI in his community-wide role by helping coordinate collection activities under the CMS, although many of the specifics remain to be worked out.

The most important of the producers of finished intelligence are the three agencies responsible for producing "all-source" intelligence: CIA's Directorate of Intelligence (DI); DIA's Directorate of Intelligence (DI); and State's INR. Within DOD, the four service intelligence offices also produce finished intelligence. Energy has the intelligence office noted above. The DCI controls the National Intelligence Council (NIC), comprising the national intelligence officers (NIOs) and responsible for national intelligence estimates (NIEs) and some other analyses. The position of assistant DCI for analysis and production was created in 1996 to assist the DCI in his community-wide role by helping analysis and intelligence production activities under the CMS.

The basic relationships, strengths, and weaknesses noted in the first figure are still evident here, but it is easier from Figure 3-3 to discern functions as well.

INTELLIGENCE COMMUNITY
RELATIONSHIPS THAT MATTER

All "wiring" diagrams, no matter how sophisticated, are deceptive. They portray where agencies sit in relationship to one another, but they cannot portray how they interact and which relationships matter and why. Moreover, as loathe as we are to admit it, personalities matter. As much as we like to think of government as one of laws and institutions, the personalities and relationships of the people filling these important positions also affect agency working relations.

The DCI's relationships. The relationship between the DCI and the president is key for the institutional well-being of the intelligence community. The DCI is the embodiment of the intelligence community, and the president is the ultimate policy consumer. DCI Richard Helms (1966–1973) put it succinctly when he observed that the DCI's authority derives directly from the perception that he has access to the president. If the DCI does not have regular access to the president and is not included in meetings where intelligence should be a contributor, there are several ramifications. For the DCI, the problem is personal and professional; for the intelligence community, the poor relationship means it is being left out of the process; in the perception of others who become aware of the problem, the role of the DCI is diminished. DCI John McCone (1961–1965) enjoyed good access to President John F. Kennedy and, initially, to Lyndon Johnson, but Johnson began to exclude McCone when the DCI disagreed with Johnson's incremental approach to the war in Vietnam. After a short period of frustration, McCone resigned. Similarly, DCI James Woolsey (1993-1995), after his resignation, made no secret of the fact the he had little access to President Clinton.

How close should the relationship between the DCI and the president be? Some observers worry that if it is too close, the DCI may lose some of the intelligence objectivity that he or she should be bringing to the policy process. Policy makers must be able to rely upon the professionalism of the DCI. Still, if the intelligence community were forced to choose between the two extremes, an overly close relationship would probably be preferable to a very distant one.

One indication of the closeness of the relationship between the DCI, the president, and other senior officers is "cabinet rank." By law, the members of the cabinet are the secretaries of the executive departments. Presidents have accorded cabinet rank to other top officials, such as the ambassador to the United Nations, as a courtesy and a sign of their enhanced status. The designation has little meaning, since the United States does not have government by cabinet as does the United Kingdom. In 1981 President Reagan gave DCI William Casey (1981–1987) cabinet rank, largely as a consolation for not having chosen Casey to be secretary of state. Some criticized the move, arguing that the cabinet is a policy-making body and the DCI is not a policy maker but an adviser to policy makers, similar to the DCI's status on the NSC. Casey's successor, Judge William Webster (1987–1991), made it clear that he did not want this designation and would refuse it.

Some have suggested that the DCI, like the director of the FBI, be appointed to a fixed term of office—the FBI director now serves for ten years. The main argument in favor of a fixed term is that it would make the DCI a more professional and less political appointment. (Politicization was always possible but arose in reality only in 1977, when President Jimmy Carter asked for the resignation of DCI George Bush.) A second argument in favor is that it would allow DCIs to serve under presidents who had not appointed them, thus increasing the chances for objectivity. The main argument against it, and one that has been voiced by several former DCIs, goes back to the personal nature of the DCI–president relationship. The concern is that, under a fixed DCI term that overlapped the cycle of elections, the president would inherit a DCI not of his choosing and with whom he or she might not have any rapport—thus increasing the chance that the DCI's access would diminish.

The secretary of state is the chief foreign policy officer below the president; the DCI should be an arm of foreign policy. At least two issues are important in the relationship between the secretary of state and the DCI: coordinating proposed intelligence operations with foreign policy goals; and using the State Department (that is, the Foreign Service) as cover for clandestine intelligence officers overseas. Inevitably, tension arises between the bureaucracies under these two officials. Few DCIs and secretaries of state enjoy the warm relationship that Allen Dulles and his brother John Foster Dulles had. More often, there is a slight edge to the relationship, if not outright competition.

Overseas, there is a long tradition of tension between U.S. ambassadors and their senior CIA officers, usually called chiefs of station. The ambassador is in charge of the entire "country team"—all U.S. personnel assigned to his or her embassy, regardless of their parent organization. But chiefs of station do not always keep the ambassador—whether career Foreign Service or political appointee—apprised of their intelligence activities. Despite repeated efforts to address the problem, it still recurs.

As has been noted, on a day-to-day basis, the secretary of defense controls more of the intelligence community (NSA, DIA, NIMA, the service intelligence units) than does the DCI (CIA, NIC). The secretary of defense also represents the vast majority of the intelligence customer base (some have suggested as much as 80 percent), because of the broad range of defense intelligence requirements. Moreover, the intelligence budget is hidden within the defense budget and, in many ways, is beholden to it. Therefore, the relationship between the secretary of defense and DCI is very important. No matter how collegial the relationship may appear, it is not one of equals.

Much of the secretary of defense's authority for intelligence usually devolves to the deputy, who becomes, in effect, the chief operating officer for defense intelligence. Thus, many of the issues that arise between DOD and the DCI are worked out by the DCI and deputy secretary of defense.

There are three key components to the relationship between the DCI and Congress. The first is the power of the purse. Congress not only funds the intelligence community (and the rest of the government) but can, through its funding decisions, affect intelligence programs. Although Congress is usually thought of as reducing presidential budget requests,

Congress has in many instances championed programs and funded them despite opposition from the executive.

The second component to the Congress–DCI relationship is, again, personal. DCIs have occasionally not gotten along with their overseers, to the ultimate detriment of the DCIs and the intelligence community. William Casey was fairly contemptuous of the oversight process, which cost him support—even among his political allies. James Woolsey ended up in a constant public squabble with the chairman of the Senate Intelligence Committee, Dennis DeConcini (D, Ariz.). John Deutch (1995–1997) had a difficult relationship with the House Intelligence Committee. The question of the rights and wrongs in each of these cases is irrelevant. Simply put, the DCI can only lose in the end.

The third component of the relationship between Congress and the DCI is the public perception of intelligence and support for it. Because of the secrecy surrounding intelligence, many of the glimpses that citizens have into intelligence come from congressional activities. Even without knowing the details of hearings, the fact that a congressional committee is investigating an intelligence issue affects media and public perceptions. And, as is usually the case, bad news tends to get reported more often than good news. After all, if the intelligence community is doing its job, why have a hearing or investigation?

The deputy DCI for community management's relationship with the Office of the Secretary of Defense. Congress created this second deputy DCI position in 1996 to give the DCI better support in his community-wide role. The main day-to-day interaction between intelligence and DOD occurs at the level of the deputy DCI for community management (DDCI/CM) and the Office of the Secretary of Defense (OSD). DOD tends to look at the intelligence community warily, worrying about whether the community managers are looking after DOD needs and are not assuming too much power over defense intelligence. The key to this relationship is the credibility of the DDCI/CM with OSD, that is, that the DDCI has a working knowledge of defense intelligence programs and needs and of the defense budget process. Theirs is an unbalanced relationship, with OSD the stronger partner. If officials in OSD have the sense that the DDCI/CM is not paying adequate attention to DOD needs and privileges, they can stymie much that the DDCI/CM and the CMS reporting to this DDCI want to do.

OSD/C3I and its relationship with Congress. OSD/C3I stands for Office of the Secretary of Defense/Command, Control, Communications, and Intelligence; it is the civilian side of defense intelligence, with a deputy assistant secretary of defense acting as a full-time intelligence manager. This office is one of two main conduits through which defense intelligence issues reach Congress, the other being DIA itself. But given the principle of civilian control of the military, C3I is more powerful and more important than DIA. Indeed, C3I has jurisdiction over defense intelligence requirements, the various defense intelligence agencies (NSA, DIA, NIMA, and some others), and some defense collection programs—the "airbreathers." OSD/C3I deals with the House and Senate Armed Services Committees.

INR and the secretary of state. State's Bureau of Intelligence and Research (INR) is the smallest of the three all-source analytical components (compared with CIA and DIA) and is often thought of as the weakest. A great deal of INR's ability to get things done, both in its own department and as a player in the intelligence community, depends on the relationship between the INR assistant secretary and the secretary of state and one or two other senior State officials, often referred to collectively as "the 7th floor." In some respects, the relationship among these State officials parallels that between the DCI and the president. If INR has access to the 7th floor, then it plays a greater role and has greater bureaucratic support when needed. But it is a highly variable relationship, depending on the preferences of the secretary and key subordinates. To cite two contrasting examples, Secretary of State George Shultz (1982–1989) met with all of his assistant secretaries regularly; Secretary of State James Baker (1989–1992) did not, preferring to meet with a few very senior subordinates who then dealt with the rest of the department. Thus, under Shultz, INR had more opportunities to gain access; under Baker, most of INR's customers were other bureaus, but less so the vaunted 7th floor.

In recent years INR has taken a number of steps to increase its visibility in the State Department and to involve other bureaus more actively in setting intelligence requirements. The goal has been to increase the bureaus' appreciation of the role of intelligence and of INR, thus making them potential sources of support. The degree to which these steps have improved INR's position in its department remains to be seen.

Congressional relationships. The relationship of the two intelligence committees with each other and with the other House and Senate committees with which they must work form another important set of relationships. The oversight responsibilities of the House and Senate Intelligence Committees are not identical, and this fact helps outline their differing sets of relations. The Senate Intelligence Committee has sole jurisdiction over only the DCI, the CIA, the CMS, and the NIC. The Senate Armed Services Committee has always jealously guarded its oversight over all aspects of defense intelligence. The relationship between Senate Intelligence and Senate Armed Services has been stand-offish at best and sometimes hostile. Outbreaks of hostility have usually stemmed from the Senate Armed Services Committee's reactions to real or imagined efforts by Senate Intelligence to step beyond its carefully circumscribed turf. Sen-

ate Armed Services has usually responded with punitive actions of varying degrees (such as delaying action on the intelligence authorization
bill).

House Intelligence has exclusive jurisdiction over the entire NFIP—
all programs that transcend the bounds of any one agency or are non-
defense—as well as shared jurisdiction over the defense intelligence programs. This arrangement has fostered a better working relationship
between House Intelligence and House Armed Services than exists
between their Senate counterparts. This is not to suggest that moments of
friction do not arise, but the overall relationship between the House committees has not approached the hostility exhibited in the Senate.

The relationships between the two intelligence committees and the
House and Senate Defense Appropriations subcommittees are important
for avoiding disjunctures between authorized programs and appropriated
funds. All appropriators tend to resent (and would sometimes like to
ignore) all authorizers. Once again, the relationship between intelligence
authorizers and appropriators has been smoother in the House than in the
Senate.

State Department activities are overseen by the House Foreign Affairs
and Senate Foreign Relations Committees, but their relationship with
their respective Intelligence Committees tends to be less fractious than
the relationship between the Intelligence and Appropriations Committees. Finally, the two Judiciary Committees oversee the FBI.

The two intelligence committees themselves have an important relationship. As noted, the House committee's jurisdiction is broader than the
Senate's. On the other hand, the Senate Intelligence Committee has the
exclusive and important authority to confirm the nominations of the DCI
and the two deputy DCIs. The two committees often choose to work on
different issues during the course of a Congress, apart from their work on
the intelligence authorization bills. Despite differences of style and of
emphasis, hostility or rancor has rarely intruded, even when they held
strong differences of viewpoint.

THE INTELLIGENCE BUDGET PROCESS

Money is not only the root of all evil, but also the root of all government.
How much gets spent and who makes those decisions are two of the most
fundamental questions before the state. The intelligence budget is somewhat complex. It is divided into three components, whose shares of the
total intelligence budget are on the order suggested here, but with some
year-to-year variance. These three programs offer yet another way to view
the intelligence community.

FIGURE 3-4   Alternative Ways of Looking at the Intelligence Community:
A Budgetary View

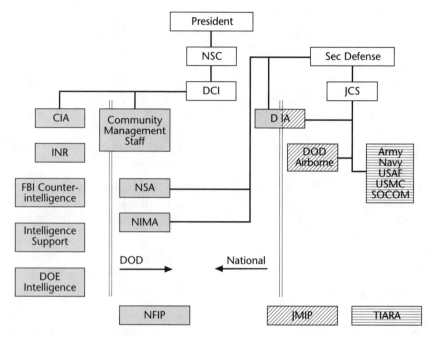

The NFIP, as its name implies, consists of programs that either transcend the bounds of an agency or are non-defense programs. The NFIP comprises over half of the intelligence budget and is made up of the following:

Civilian Programs
CIA
State/INR
FBI/Counterintelligence
Treasury/Office of Intelligence
  Support
CIA Retirement and Disability
  System (CIARDS)
Defense Programs
General Defense Intelligence
  Program (GDIP)

Consolidated Cryptographic
  Program (CCP)
DOD Foreign Counter-
  intelligence Program (FCIP)
National Imagery and Mapping
  Program
National Reconnaissance
  Program (NRP)
Community-wide Program
Community Management
  Account (CMA)

JMIP is made up of programs within the Defense Department that transcend the bounds of any one military service. As the titles of some

JMIP programs indicate, many of these programs parallel NFIP categories. The JMIP comprises over a tenth of the intelligence budget and is made up of the following programs:

Defense Cryptologic Program (DCP)

Defense Imagery and Mapping Program

Defense General Intelligence Applications Program (DGIAP)

Defense Intelligence Tactical Program (DITP)

Defense Intelligence Special Technologies Program (DISTP)

Defense Airborne Reconnaissance Program (DARP)

Defense Space Reconnaissance Program (DSRP)

Defense Intelligence Counterdrug Program (DICP)

TIARA is made up of the four service intelligence programs and intelligence for the Special Operations Command. TIARA comprises about one-third of the intelligence budget and is made up of the following programs:

Army intelligence

Navy intelligence

Air Force intelligence

Marine intelligence

Special Operations Command (SOCOM)

This budgetary view of the intelligence community indicates its complexity. Figure 3-4 arranges the various components of the intelligence community by budget sectors; not all of the agencies within a budget sector are controlled by the same authority. The solid lines denote direct control. The two double vertical lines show which part of the budget and agencies are national and which are DOD. There is an overlap, as some agencies are both national and Defense, even if they fall into NFIP or JMIP. DIA straddles the line, containing both NFIP and several of the JMIP programs. Figure 3-4 also indicates the preponderance of control that the secretary of defense exercises over intelligence community resources.

The process by which the intelligence budget is shaped is complex and long. The budget-building process within the executive branch takes more than a year, beginning with the DCI providing guidance around November to the intelligence program managers. The "crosswalks" between CIA and Defense, meaning efforts at various working levels to coordinate programs and to make difficult choices between programs, are major facets of the budget process. Crosswalks can take place at the program level or below and can go as high as the DCI and the secretary or deputy secretary of defense. The executive process ends the following

FIGURE 3-5   The Intelligence Budget: Four Phases over Three Years

It takes about three years to develop a budget and then spend the money, beginning in March of any year and continuing until September two and a half years later. The figure shows the activity for each phase and the time during which it happens.

Year 1:	Mar–Sept	Oct ⟶		
Year 2:		Aug	Aug ⟶	
Year 3:			Sept	Oct ⟶
Year 4:				Sept
Activity:	**Planning**	**Programming**	**Budgeting**	**Execution**
	Guidance:	*Request and Review:*	*Build and Submit:*	*Obligate and Spend:*
	Establishes broad guidelines of planning, programming, and budgeting.	Program resources are projected for future year requirements for dollar and manpower resources—a *multiyear* request.	Money or authority available to purchase goods and services or to hire people—for *1* or *2* years.	Committing and spending the money on authorized programs.

December, thirteen months after it began, with the DCI sending a final intelligence budget to the president for final approval.

The following February, the president's budget goes to Congress, where a new, eight-month process begins. This consists of hearings in the various authorization and appropriations committees, committee mark-ups of the bills, floor action, conference committees between the House and Senate to work out differences—since both houses must pass identical bills—and final passage, after which the bill goes to the president for signature. By this point, the executive branch is already working on the next budget.

This seemingly endless process points up another important aspect of the intelligence budget. At any given point during the year, as many as eight different fiscal year (October 1–September 30) budgets are in some form of use or development. *(See box, "Eight Simultaneous Fiscal Years," p. 38.)* Two past fiscal year budgets are still in use, if we take into account the actual spending of the funds that have been appropriated, in addition to the budget for the current year. Although funds for salaries and similar expenses are spent in a single fiscal year, other funds—such as those to build highly complex technical collection systems—are spent over several years.

The budget for the following fiscal year is going through the political processes. The budget for the year after that is going through its year-long build in the executive branch. Finally, there are two future years in various states of somewhat imprecise planning.

Eight Simultaneous Fiscal Years

Over the course of a fiscal year (October to the end of the following September), eight concurrent fiscal years are in some state of being. This shows the situation during FY 1998:

FYs 1996, 1997: past fiscal years, some funds still being spent
FY 1998: current fiscal year, funds being spent
FY 1999: budget being developed by executive branch and Congress
FY 2000: program nearing completion in executive branch
FY 2001: in early development in executive branch
FYs 2002, 2003: in long-range planning in executive branch

A great deal of influence accrues to those individuals in both branches of government who can master the process and the details of the budget.

KEY TERMS

ADCI/A&P Assistant director of central intelligence for analysis & production
ADCI/C Assistant director of central intelligence for collection
CIA Central Intelligence Agency
CMS Community Management Staff
C3I Command, control, communications, and intelligence
DCI Director of central intelligence
DDCI Deputy director of central intelligence
DDCI/CM Deputy director of central intelligence for community management
DHS Defense HUMINT (human intelligence) Service
DI Directorate of Intelligence (both CIA and DIA)
DIA Defense Intelligence Agency
DO Directorate of Operations (CIA)
DOD Department of Defense
DOE Department of Energy
DS&T Directorate of Science and Technology (CIA)
FBI Federal Bureau of Investigation

HUMINT Human intelligence
IMINT Imagery intelligence
INR Bureau of Intelligence and Research, State Dept.
JCS Joint Chiefs of Staff
JMIP Joint Military Intelligence Program
NFIP National Foreign Intelligence Program
NIC National Intelligence Council
NIE National intelligence estimate
NIMA National Imagery and Mapping Agency
NIO National intelligence officer
NRO National Reconnaissance Office
NSA National Security Agency
NSC National Security Council
OSD Office of the Secretary of Defense
SIGINT Signals intelligence
SOCOM Special Operations Command
TIARA Tactical intelligence & related activities
UAV Unmanned aerial vehicles (drones)

FURTHER READINGS

The following readings give background on the current organization and structure of the U.S. intelligence community and also include some studies of proposed changes to enable the intelligence community to deal better with the challenges it will face in the future.

Elkins, Dan. *An Intelligence Resource Manager's Guide.* Washington, D.C.: Joint Military Intelligence Training Center, Defense Intelligence Agency, 1997.

Johnson, Loch K. *Secret Agencies: U.S. Intelligence in a Hostile World.* New Haven, Conn.: Yale University Press, 1996.

Lowenthal, Mark M. *U.S. Intelligence: Evolution and Anatomy.* 2d ed. Westport, Conn.: Praeger Publishers, 1992.

Richelson, Jeffrey T. *The U.S. Intelligence Community.* 4th ed. Boulder, Colo.: Westview, 1999.

U.S. Commission on the Roles and Responsibilities of the United States Intelligence Community. *Preparing for the 21st Century: An Appraisal of U.S. Intelligence.* Washington, D.C., 1996.

U.S. House Permanent Select Committee on Intelligence. *IC21: The Intelligence Community in the 21st Century.* Staff study, 104th Congress, 2d session, 1996.

CHAPTER 4

The Intelligence Process— A Macro Look: Who Does What for Whom?

The term *intelligence process* refers to the various steps or stages in intelligence from policy makers perceiving a need for information to the community's delivery of an analytical intelligence product to them. This chapter offers a macro overview of the entire intelligence process and introduces some of the key issues in each phase. Succeeding chapters deal in greater detail with the major phases.

Intelligence, as practiced in the United States, is commonly thought of as having five steps, to which this book adds two more. The seven phases of the intelligence process are identifying requirements; collection; processing and exploitation; analysis and production; dissemination; consumption; and feedback.

Identifying requirements means defining those policy issues or areas to which intelligence is expected to make a contribution. It may also mean specifying the collection of certain types of intelligence. The impulse is to say that all policy areas have intelligence requirements, which they do. However, intelligence capabilities are always limited, and so priorities must be set among these requirements, with some getting more attention, some getting less, and some perhaps getting little or none at all. The key issues are: Who sets these requirements and priorities and then conveys them to the intelligence community? What happens, or should happen, if policy makers fail to set these requirements on their own?

Once requirements and priorities have been established, the necessary intelligence must be collected. Some requirements will be better met by specific types of collection; some may require that several collection types be brought to bear. Making these decisions among always-constrained collection capabilities is a key issue, as is the question of how much can or should be collected to meet each requirement.

As was examined in chapter 1, collection produces information, not intelligence. The information that is collected must be processed and exploited before it can be considered to be intelligence and before it can be given to analysts. In the United States, there is constant tension over the allocation of resources between collection on the one hand and processing and exploitation on the other, with collection inevitably coming out the winner, to the point where much more is collected than can be processed or exploited.

The previous processes are meaningless unless the intelligence is turned over to analysts who are expert in their respective fields and can turn the various types of collected intelligence into a variety of reports that will, one hopes, respond to the needs of the policy makers. The types of products chosen, the quality of the analysis, and the continuous tension between current intelligence products and longer range products are key issues.

The issue of moving the analysis to the policy makers stems directly from the multitude of analytical vehicles available for disseminating intelligence. How widely intelligence should be distributed and how urgently it should be passed or flagged for the policy maker's attention are key issues in dissemination.

Most discussions of the intelligence process end here, with the intelligence having reached the policy makers whose requirements first set everything in motion. However, two important phases remain: consumption and feedback.

Policy makers are not "blank slates" or automatons who are impelled to action by intelligence. Indeed, how the policy makers consume intelligence—whether written or oral briefings—and the degree to which they do or do not use the intelligence are important issues.

Although feedback does not occur nearly as often as the intelligence community might desire, there should be a dialogue between intelligence consumers and producers after the intelligence has been received. Policy makers should give the intelligence community some sense of the degree to which the intelligence requirements are being met and should discuss any adjustments that the intelligence community can make to any parts of the process. Ideally, this should happen while the issue or topic is still relevant, so that improvements and adjustments can be made. Failing that, even an ex post facto review can be tremendously helpful.

The following sections give a better sense of the key questions and issues that are involved in each phase of the intelligence process.

REQUIREMENTS

Each nation has a wide variety of national security and foreign policy interests. Some nations have more than others. Of these various interests, the primacy of some is self-evident: those that deal with large and known threats; those that deal with neighboring or proximate states; those that are more severe. But the international arena is dynamic and fluid. So even among the agreed-upon key interests there are likely to be occasional readjustments of priorities.

Given that intelligence should be an adjunct to policy and not a policy maker in its own right, intelligence priorities should reflect policy priorities. Ideally, policy makers should have well-considered and well-established views of their own priorities and should convey these clearly to their intelligence apparatus. Some of the requirements may be obvious or so long-standing as not to need discussion. The cold war concentration on the Soviet Union was one of these.

But what happens if the policy makers do not decide, find that they cannot decide, or fail to convey their priorities to the intelligence community? Who sets intelligence priorities then? The question is neither frivolous nor hypothetical. Senior policy makers often assume that their intelligence needs are known by their intelligence providers. After all, the key issues are apparent. A former secretary of defense once told the author exactly that. When asked if he ever considered giving his intelligence officers a more precise definition of his needs, he said, "No. I assumed they knew what I was working on." There is strong reason to believe that his view was not unique.

An obvious way to fill the requirements gap left by policy makers would be for the intelligence community to fill the gap on its own. However, in a system like that of the United States, where a strict line divides policy and intelligence, this solution may not be possible. Intelligence officials may feel that the limits on their role preclude their making the decision; policy makers may see intelligence officials who seek to fill the void as a threat to their function and may even react hostilely.

The intelligence community faces two unpalatable choices. The first is to fill the requirements vacuum, running the risk of being wrong or being accused of having overstepped into the realm of policy. The second choice is for intelligence officials to overlook the absence of defined requirements and to continue collection and the phases that follow based on the last known priorities and the intelligence community's sense of priorities, knowing that they run the risk of being accused of failing to meet important priorities. In short, there is no good choice when such a gap occurs.

Some intelligence managers might take issue with this definition of their choices. They would note, correctly, that one function of intelligence is to look ahead, to identify issues that are not high priority at present but may be so in the future. But, as important as this function is, it is difficult to get policy makers to focus on issues that are far off or only may become important. They are hard pressed to work on the issues demanding attention now. Thus, the requirements conundrum remains.

Conflicting or competing priorities are also an issue. Although some sense of order may be easily imposed over certain issues, others may end up claiming equal primacy. Again, in the ideal situation the policy makers should make the difficult choices. In reality, most governments are large enough as to have various competing sectors of interest either between or within departments or ministries. The end result is that, once again, the intelligence community may be left to its own devices. In an intelligence community like that of the United States, parts of the intelligence community may reflect the preferences of the policy makers to whom they are most closely tied. In some cases, there may be no final adjudicating authority, leaving the intelligence community to do the best it can. The DCI should be the final adjudicator, but the director's ability to impose priorities on a day-to-day basis across the entire intelligence community remains limited. All issues tend to get shorter shrift when too many are competing for attention.

The hidden factor that drives priorities is resources. It is impossible to cover everything. The United States, for example, has long had interests in every part of the globe, although some are more significant and more central than others. For decades, the U.S. intelligence community has used a variety of processes to set priorities. The most recent, used here as an example, is Presidential Decision Directive 35 (PDD-35), signed by President Bill Clinton in 1995.

PDD-35 divides issues with two schemes. Intelligence issues are divided into "hard targets" and "global coverage." Hard targets are the so-called rogue states (Cuba, Iran, Iraq, Libya, North Korea) and the transnational issues (weapons proliferation, narcotics, international crime, terrorism). Global coverage is everything else. Although PDD-35 was conceived of as a way to parcel out resources across the board, the lion's share of collection and other assets, of necessity, go to the hard targets.

PDD-35 also gives support to military operations (known as SMO) one of the highest priorities. Although everyone would agree that supporting the military is important, some have argued that the emphasis on SMO has led to an increasing "militarization" of intelligence, to the detriment of other intelligence consumers in the civil national security agencies.

The second scheme within PDD-35 for dividing issues is that of tiers. The several tiers connote the relative priority of the issues. Issues can and do move up and down in the tier system. The problem is that issues do not receive significant attention until after they have begun moving up to the higher priority tiers, at which point they must compete with the issues already in that bracket.

This underscores the problem with any intelligence requirements system. Such a system is, of necessity, static. Even if the requirements are reviewed and re-ranked periodically, they remain "snapshots" in time. Policy makers or intelligence officials must decide at some point as to the requirements and the resources that will be applied to them. However, the nature of international relations is such that unexpected issues will inevitably crop up with little or no warning. Thus, the system that preserves a modicum of flexibility or a modest reserve capability will be more responsive to the realities of intelligence requirements.

Moreover, if a requirement cannot be met with current collection systems, then developing the technical systems or the human sources to meet the requirement will take time. Thus, uncertainty about requirements or lower priorities for some requirements will affect the development of collection capabilities.

COLLECTION

Collection derives directly from requirements. It is also the first—and perhaps the most important—facet of intelligence where budgets and resources come into play. Technical collection is extremely expensive, and, given that different types of systems offer different benefits and capabilities, the administration and Congress must make difficult budget choices. Also, the needs of agencies vary, further complicating collection choices.

How much information should be collected? Or, put another way: Does more collection mean better intelligence? The answer to these questions is ambiguous. On one hand, the more information that is collected, the more likely that required intelligence will be part of it. On the other hand, not everything that is collected is of equal value. Some collected information may have little or no value at all. Analysts must wade through the material that is collected—to process and to exploit it—to find the intelligence that is really needed. This is often referred to as the "wheat versus chaff" problem. In other words, increased collection also increases the task of finding the truly important intelligence.

An interesting phenomenon, found in at least the U.S. intelligence community, is that different analytical groups may prefer different types of intelligence. For example, the CIA may put greater store in clandestine human intelligence (espionage), in part because it is a product of CIA activities. Other "all-source" analysts, on the other hand, have sometimes shown less regard for clandestine human sources than has the CIA and have given greater emphasis to signals intelligence, for example.

PROCESSING AND EXPLOITATION

Intelligence collected by technical means—imagery, signals, test data, and so on—does not arrive in ready-to-use form. It must be processed and exploited, that is, processed from complex signals into images or intercepts. These then must be exploited—analyzed if they are images, perhaps decoded and probably translated if they are signals. Processing and exploitation are key steps in converting technically collected information into intelligence.

As noted above, in the United States collection always outruns processing and exploitation. We collect much more than we can ever process and exploit. Technical collection systems have always found greater favor in the executive branch and Congress. They have an appeal that the systems and personnel required for processing and exploitation do not. One of the reasons for the appeal of technical collection systems is emotional and is perhaps best explained by reviewing an analogous situation in the defense budget. Les Aspin, chairman of the House Armed Services Committee (1985–1993) and later the secretary of defense (1993–1994), once observed that both Congress and the executive branch favored procurement (buying new weapons) over operations and maintenance (keeping already purchased systems functioning). Buying new systems was more appealing to the decision makers in both branches and to the more important defense contractors. Operations and maintenance, although important, are less exciting and less glamorous. Collection is akin to procurement and is much more appealing than processing and exploitation.

Collection advocates argue, usually successfully, that collection is the bedrock of intelligence, that without collection the entire enterprise has little meaning. Collection also has support among the companies (prime contractors and their numerous subcontractors) who build the technical collection systems and who lobby for follow-on systems. Processing and exploitation, on the other hand, are "in-house" intelligence community activities. Although these "downstream activities" (that is, the steps that follow collection) are also dependent on technology, the technology is not in the same league, in terms of contractor profit, as collection systems.

However, the large and still growing disparity between collection and processing/exploitation results in a great amount of collected material never being used. It simply dies "on the cutting room floor." Thus, advocates of processing and exploitation counter-argue that the image or signal that is not processed and not exploited is identical to the one that is not collected—it has no effect at all.

There is no "proper" ratio between collection and processing/-exploitation. In part, the ratio will depend on the issue, on available resources, and on policy-maker demands. But many who are familiar with the U.S. intelligence community believe that the relationship between these two phases is badly out of balance.

ANALYSIS AND PRODUCTION

There is major, often daily tension between current intelligence and long-term intelligence. Current intelligence focuses on issues that are at the forefront of the policy makers' agenda, the things they are working on right now. Long-term intelligence deals with trends and issues that may not be at the forefront now but are important and may come to the forefront, especially if they do not receive some attention now. The skills for preparing the two types of intelligence are not identical, nor are the intelligence products that can or should be used to disseminate them to policy makers. But a subtle relationship exists between current and long-term intelligence. Like collection versus process/exploitation, a proper balance—not necessarily 50/50—should be the goal.

The U.S. system of competitive analysis—that is, having the same issue addressed by several different analytical groups— entails some analytical costs. Although the goal is to bring disparate points of view to bear on an issue, intelligence community products written within this system run the risk of succumbing to "group think," with lowest-common-denominator language resulting from intellectual compromises. Alternatively, agencies can indulge themselves in endless and—at least to the policy consumers—meaningless "footnote wars," whose only goal is to maintain a separate point of view regardless of the salience of the issue at stake.

Analysts should have a key role in helping determine collection priorities. Although the United States has instituted a series of offices and programs to improve the relationship between analysts and the collection systems on which they are dependent, the connection between the two has never been particularly strong or responsive.

The training and the mindsets of analysts are important. Analysts must often deal with intelligence that is contradictory, both internally and when viewed against their strongly held professional beliefs and perhaps their own past work. The way in which analysts deal with these contradictions depends on their training and the nature of the broader analytical system, including the review process.

Finally, it is important to recognize that analysts are not intellectual ciphers. They are likely to have ambitions and will want their issues to receive a certain degree of high-level attention. This is not meant to suggest that they will resort to intellectually dishonest means to gain attention, but that is a possibility that their superiors within the intelligence community and policy makers must keep in mind.

DISSEMINATION AND CONSUMPTION

The process of moving the intelligence from the producers to the consumers is largely standardized. The intelligence community has a set "product line" to cover the types of reports and customers with which it must deal. The product line ranges from bulletins on fast-breaking and important events to studies that may take a year or more to complete.

Following are descriptions of some of the better known intelligence products.

President's Daily Briefing. The PDB is delivered every morning to the president and some of the most senior presidential advisers by the PDB staff at the CIA. The PDB changes in format to suit the preferences of each president.

Senior Executive Intelligence Brief. The SEIB—for decades known as the National Intelligence Daily—is an early morning intelligence newspaper prepared by the CIA, in coordination with the other intelligence producers, for several hundred senior officials in Washington. Copies are distributed throughout the executive branch as well as to the intelligence oversight committees in Congress.

The Secretary's Morning Summary (SMS) and Military Intelligence Digest (MID). Unlike the SEIB, which is theoretically a product of the entire intelligence community, the SMS is prepared by INR; the MID is prepared by DIA. Although the primary customers of each of these are the policy makers within their own departments, the SMS and MID are also circulated elsewhere in the executive branch. Thus, in the sense of offering a different array of issues and perhaps different analyses, the SMS and the MID are counterparts to the SEIB. On any given day, the SEIB, SMS, and MID will cover some of the same issues and will also cover issues that are of particular interest to their primary readers alone.

National Intelligence Estimates. NIEs are the responsibility of national intelligence officers (NIOs), who are members of the National Intelligence Council, which reports directly to the DCI. NIEs represent the considered opinion of the entire intelligence community and, once completed and agreed to, are signed by the DCI for presentation to the president and other senior officials. The drafting of NIEs can take anywhere from a few months to a year or more. Special NIEs, or SNIEs (pronounced "sneeze") are written on more urgent issues and on a fast-track basis.

The PDB, SEIB, SMS, and MID are all current intelligence products, focusing on events of the past day or two at most and on issues that are being dealt with at present or will be dealt with over the next few days. NIEs are long-term intelligence products that attempt to "estimate" (not "predict") the likely direction an issue will take in the future. Ideally, NIEs should be anticipatory, focusing on issues that are likely to be important in the near future and for which there is sufficient time to arrive at a community-wide judgment. This ideal is not always met, and some NIEs are drafted on issues that are already on policy makers' agendas. If these same issues demand current analysis, it will be distributed through other analytical vehicles or via a SNIE.

The following are among the issues that must be dealt with in dissemination:

- Among the large mass of material being collected and analyzed each day, what is important enough to report?
- To which policy makers should it be reported—the most senior, or lower ranking ones? To many or to just a few?
- How quickly should it be reported? Is it so urgent as to require immediate delivery, or can it wait for one of the reports that senior policy makers receive the next morning?
- How much detail should be reported to the various intelligence consumers? How long should the report be?
- What is the best vehicle for reporting it—one of the products mentioned above, a memo, a briefing?

The intelligence community customarily makes these decisions. They entail a number of factors and occasional trade-offs between conflicting goals. Ideally, the community uses a "layered approach," in which it uses a variety of intelligence products to convey the same intelligence—in different formats and degrees of detail—to a broad array of policy makers. Its decisions should also reflect an understanding of the needs and preferences of the policy makers and should be adjusted as administrations change.

Most discussions of the intelligence process do not include the consumption phase, since the intelligence is complete and has been delivered. However, this approach ignores the key role played by the policy community throughout the entire intelligence process.

FEEDBACK

Communications between the policy community and the intelligence community are at best imperfect throughout the intelligence process. One area where this is most noticeable is after intelligence has been transmit-

FIGURE 4-1   The Intelligence Process: A CIA View

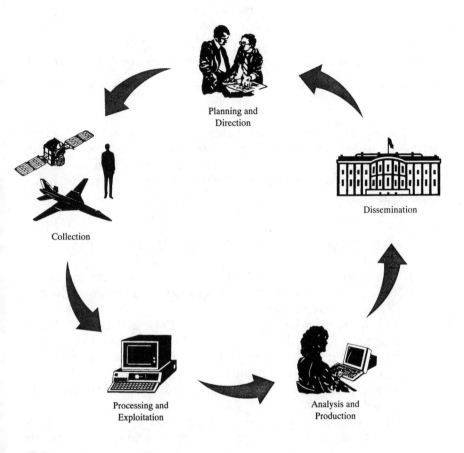

Planning and
Direction

Dissemination

Collection

Processing and
Exploitation

Analysis and
Production

Source: Central Intelligence Agency, *A Consumer's Handbook to Intelligence,* September 1993.

ted. Ideally, the policy makers would be giving their intelligence producers feedback continually on what they have received—what has been useful, what has not, which areas need continuing or increased emphasis,
which can be reduced, and so on.

    In reality, the community receives feedback less often than it desires,
and it certainly does not receive feedback in any systematic manner, for
several reasons. First, few people in the policy community have the time
to think about or to convey this sort of reaction. They work from issue to
issue with little time to reflect on what went right or wrong before push-

FIGURE 4-2   The Intelligence Process: A Schematic

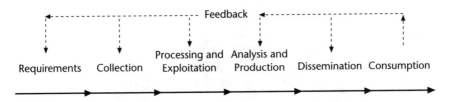

ing on to the next issue. Also, few policy makers think feedback is necessary. Even when the intelligence they are receiving may not be exactly what they need, they usually do not bother to inform their intelligence producers. The failure to provide feedback is the analog to the policy makers' inability or refusal to help define requirements.

THINKING ABOUT THE INTELLIGENCE PROCESS

Given the importance of the intelligence process as both a concept and an organizing principle, it is worth thinking about how the process works and how best to conceptualize it.

Figure 4-1 is published by the CIA in *A Consumer's Guide to Intelligence*. It presents the intelligence cycle (as the guide calls it) as a perfect circle. Beginning at the top, policy makers provide planning and direction, and the intelligence community collects intelligence, which is then processed and exploited, analyzed and produced, and disseminated to the policy makers.

Although meant to be little more than a quick schematic presentation, the CIA diagram misrepresents some aspects and misses many others. First, it is overly simple. It has an end-to-end completeness that misses many of the vagaries in the process noted above. It is also oddly unidimensional. A policy maker asks questions and, after a few steps, gets an answer. There is no feedback, nor does the diagram convey that the process might not be completed in one cycle.

A more realistic diagram would show that at any stage in the process it is possible—and sometimes necessary—to go back to an earlier step. Initial collection may prove unsatisfactory and may lead policy makers to change the requirements; processing and exploitation or analysis may reveal gaps, resulting in new collection requirements; consumers may change their needs or ask for more intelligence. And, on occasion, intelligence officers may receive feedback.

FIGURE 4-3   The Intelligence Process: Multilayered

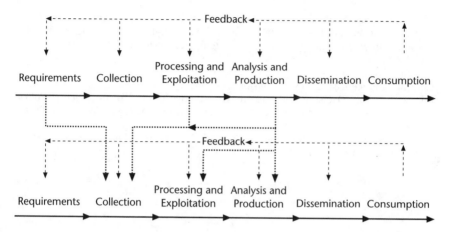

This admittedly imperfect process can be portrayed as in Figure 4-2. This diagram, although better than the CIA's, remains somewhat unidimensional. A still better portrayal would capture the more than occasional need to go back to an earlier part of the process in order to meet unfulfilled or changing requirements, collection needs, and so on.

Figure 4-3 shows how in any one intelligence process issues will likely arise (the need for more collection, uncertainties in processing, results of analysis, changing requirements) that will cause a second or even third intelligence process to take place. Ultimately, one could repeat the process lines over and over to portray continuing changes in any of the various parts of the process and the fact that policy issues are rarely resolved in a single neat cycle. This diagram is a bit more complex, but it also gives a much better sense of how the intelligence process operates in reality, being linear, circular, and open-ended all at the same time.

KEY TERMS

analysis and production
collection
consumption
dissemination

downstream activities
feedback
footnote wars
processing and exploitation

FURTHER READINGS

The intelligence process in the United States has become so routinized in its basic steps and forms that it is not often written about analytically as an organic whole. These readings are among the few that attempt to examine the process on some broader basis.

Central Intelligence Agency. *A Consumer's Guide to Intelligence.* Langley, Va., 1993.
Johnson, Loch. "Decision Costs in the Intelligence Cycle." In *Intelligence: Policy and Process,* edited by Alfred C. Maurer, et al. Boulder, Colo.: Westview Press, 1985.
———. "Making the Intelligence 'Cycle' Work." *International Journal of Intelligence and Counterintelligence* 1 (winter 1986–1987).

CHAPTER 5

The Intelligence Process—Collection and the Collection Disciplines

Collection is the bedrock of intelligence. Indeed, intelligence collection has been written about since the Biblical references to spies in the Book of Joshua. Without collection, intelligence is little more than guesswork—perhaps educated guesswork, but guesswork nonetheless. The United States and several other nations use multiple means of collecting the intelligence they require. The means are driven by two factors: the nature of the intelligence being sought and the ability to get at it in various ways. In the United States the various means of collecting intelligence are sometimes referred to as "collection disciplines" or "INTs." This chapter discusses the overarching themes that affect all collection means, then addresses what the various INTs provide as well as their strengths and weaknesses.

OVERARCHING THEMES

Several themes or issues cut across the various collection disciplines and tend to drive many of the debates about and decisions on intelligence collection. These themes are important because they point out that collection is more than the questions of "What can we collect?" or "Should we collect this?" Collection is a highly complex government activity that is subject to numerous decisions and stress points.

BUDGET.   Technical collection systems, many of which are based on satellites, are very expensive. These systems and programs are a major cost within the U.S. intelligence budget. Thus, the ability to operate large number of collection systems at the same time will always be constrained by costs. Moreover, since different types of satellites are employed for different types of collection (imagery versus signals), policy makers have to make difficult trade-offs. Significant costs are also associated with launching the satellites. The larger the satellite, the larger the rocket required to put it into orbit. Finally, the costs of processing and exploitation (P&E), without which collection is meaningless, should be factored into total cost. Builders of collection systems often ignore this last cost as part of their estimates for collection.

During the cold war, cost issues rarely surfaced. The sense of threat, coupled with the fact that there was no better way to collect intelligence on the Soviet Union, tended to support the high costs of the systems. Also, decision makers placed greater emphasis on collection systems than on the processing and exploitation needed to deal with the intelligence collected. In the post–cold war period, given the absence of any large and potentially overwhelming threat, these collection costs have become more vulnerable politically.

The budget is also important because it is a major means by which Congress influences and even controls intelligence activities. As noted, Congress tended to be supportive of collection requirements through the cold war, but it also tended to support the disparity between collection and the less favored processing and exploitation. Some changes began to appear in the mid-1990s. The House Intelligence Committee, for example, advocated the use of some smaller imagery satellites, both for greater flexibility and to save on building and launching costs. This committee also tried to redress the collection/P&E balance.

COLLECTION SYNERGY.   One of the major advantages of having multiple means of collection is that one system or discipline can provide tips or clues that can be further collected against by other systems. On major requirements, no one type of collection is used alone; the collectors are designed to be cooperative, when the system is working correctly. The goal of the U.S. intelligence community is to produce all-source intelligence or fusion intelligence, that is, intelligence based on as many collection sources as possible so as to compensate for the shortcomings of each and to get a greater sum from their strengths. All-source intelligence reflects collection in depth. At the same time, the multiple array also allows collection managers to increase collection in breadth, that is, to increase the number of issues being covered, albeit with less depth for any issue.

An excellent example of collection synergy is the Cuban missile crisis of 1962. Although analysts were slow to understand that Soviet premier Nikita Khrushchev was willing to make such a risky move as deploying medium- and intermediate-range missiles in Cuba, the intelligence community brought a variety of collection means to bear. Anti-Castro Cubans still on the island provided some of the first reliable evidence that missiles were being deployed. A human source provided the data that targeted the U-2 flights over a trapezoid bounded by four towns in western Cuba. Imagery then provided crucial intelligence about the status of the missile sites and the approximate time before completion, as did Soviet technical manuals provided to the United States by Col. Oleg Penkovsky, a spy in the employ of the United States and Britain. Imagery and naval units gave the locations of Soviet ships bringing the missiles to the almost-completed sites. Finally, Penkovsky also provided the United States with excellent, authoritative information on the state of Soviet strategic forces—indicating overwhelming U.S. superiority.

THE VACUUM CLEANER PROBLEM.   Those familiar with U.S. technical collection systems often note that they are vacuum cleaners, not microscopes. These collectors sweep up a great deal of information, within which *may* be the intelligence actually being sought. This problem is sometimes referred to as "wheat versus chaff." Roberta Wohlstetter, in her classic study *Pearl Harbor: Warning and Decision,* refers to this problem as "noise versus signals," noting that the signals one wishes to receive and to know are often imbedded in a great deal of surrounding noise.

No matter which metaphor one uses, the issue remains the same: collection is less than precise. Indeed, this problem underscores the importance of processing and exploitation.

The issue then becomes how to extract the intelligence from the mountain of information. One answer would be to increase the number of analysts who deal with the incoming intelligence, but that raises further demands on the budget. Another possible response, even less palatable, would be to collect less. But, even then, there would be no assurance that the "wheat" remained in the smaller volume still being collected.

COMPETING COLLECTION PRIORITIES.   Since the number of collection platforms, or spies, is limited, policy makers must make choices among competing collection requirements. As noted above, they use various systems to set priorities, but some issues inevitably get shorter shrift, or may be ignored altogether, in favor of those that are seen as more pressing.

Both policy makers and the intelligence officers acting on their behalf request increased collection on certain issues. However, their requests are made within a system that is inelastic in both technical and human collectors. Every collection request that is fulfilled means another collection issue or request goes wanting; it is a zero-sum game. That is why a priority system is necessary in the first place. Moreover, the system has little or no "surge" capacity; few collection systems (airplanes, drones, and ship-based systems) or spies are waiting in reserve for an emergency. Even if additional satellites have already been built, launching them requires a ready rocket of the appropriate size, an available launch pad,

The Indian Nuclear Test, 1998

In May 1998 the newly elected government of India—as it had promised in its election campaign—resumed testing nuclear weapons. The U.S. intelligence community did not detect the test preparations.

As a result, retired admiral David Jeremiah was asked by the DCI to review the intelligence community's performance on this "hard target" issue—preventing the proliferation of nuclear weapons.

Jeremiah reported several findings, including the fact that—given the Indian government's avowed intention to test, which required no clandestine collection at all—intelligence performance could have been better. But he also noted that collection assets that might have picked up indications of the impending test were focused on the Korean demilitarized zone (DMZ), at the request of the commander of U.S. forces in Korea.

No one will deny the importance of the Korean DMZ. As one director of the National Security Agency put it, the Korean DMZ is the only place in the world in the late 1990s where someone else can decide if the United States will go to war. The Korean DMZ is a constant concern. It could be argued that, for a brief period in May 1998, Indian test activities should have been accorded a higher priority.

and other resources. Similarly, one does not simply tap a spy and send him or her off to a new assignment. Cover stories need to be created, along with the inevitable paraphernalia; training may be necessary; and a host of other preparations must be made. Inelasticity of resources makes the priorities system difficult at best.

If an emergency arises, collection resources will be shifted away from lower priority issues, which can result in difficult—and sometimes mistaken—choices. *(See box, "The Indian Nuclear Test, 1998," this page.)*

PROTECTING SOURCES AND METHODS.   The details of collection capabilities—and even the existence of some capabilities—are among the most highly classified secrets of any state. In U.S. parlance, classification is referred to as the protection of sources and methods. It is one of the primary concerns of the entire intelligence community and a task specifically assigned to the director of central intelligence by law.

Several levels of classification are in use, reflecting the sensitivity of the intelligence or intelligence means. *(See box, "Why Classify?" p. 57.)* The security classifications are driven by concerns that the disclosure of

Why Classify?

Numerous critics of the U.S. classification system have argued—not incorrectly—that classification is used too freely and sometimes for the sake of denying information to others who have a legitimate need for it.

However, there is a rationale and some sense to the way in which classification is intended to be used. Classification derives from the damage that would be done if the information were revealed. Thus, classification related to intelligence collection underscores both the importance of the information and the fragility of its source—something that would be very difficult to replace if revealed.

The most common classification is SECRET (CONFIDENTIAL is rarely used any longer), followed by TOP SECRET. Within TOP SECRET are numerous TOP SECRET/CODEWORD compartments—meaning specific bodies of intelligence based on their sources. Admission to any level of classification or compartment is driven by an individual's certified "need to know" that specific type of information.

Each classification level is defined; current definitions are found in Executive Order 12958, of April 17, 1995 (italics added):

- CONFIDENTIAL: information whose unauthorized disclosure "could be expected to cause *damage* to the national security."
- SECRET: information whose unauthorized disclosure "could be expected to cause *serious damage* to the national security."
- TOP SECRET: information whose unauthorized disclosure "could be expected to cause *exceptionally grave damage* to the national security."

Higher levels of access are useful bureaucratic levers for use by those who have them against those who do not.

capabilities will allow those nations that are collection targets to take steps to prevent collection, thus effectively negating the collection systems.

However, the levels of classification also impose costs. Some are financial. The physical costs of security—guards, safes, and special means of transmitting intelligence—are high. Added to these are the costs of security checks for those individuals who are to be entrusted with classified information (see chapter 7 for details).

Some argue that the classifications impose still other costs. Critics maintain that the classification system is used inappropriately and even promiscuously, classifying material either too highly or in cases where it should not be classified at all. Critics are also concerned that the system can be abused to allow the intelligence community to hide mistakes, failures, or even crimes.

Beyond the costs of the classification system and its potential abuse, the need to conceal sources and methods limits the use of intelligence as a policy tool. For example, in the late 1950s Khrushchev broke a nuclear test moratorium and blustered about the Soviet Union's growing strategic nuclear forces. President Dwight Eisenhower, bolstered by the first U.S. images of the Soviet Union, knew that the United States enjoyed a strong strategic superiority. But, in order to protect sources and methods, Eisenhower did not reply to Khrushchev's false boasts. What might have been the results had the United States released some imagery to counter the Soviet claims? Would the release have spurred the Soviets to greater weapons-building efforts? Would it have severely undercut Soviet foreign policy? Would it have affected U.S. intelligence capabilities, even though the Soviets already knew they were being overflown by satellites and by U-2s? These questions are not answerable, but they give a good feel for the nature of the problem.

More recently, the U.S. intelligence community has grown concerned about protecting intelligence sources and methods during post-cold war military operations that involve cooperation with nations that are not U.S. allies. Even among allies the United States employs gradations of intelligence sharing, with Britain enjoying the deepest intelligence-sharing relationship with the United States, followed closely by Australia and Canada. Intelligence relations with other NATO allies are close, albeit less so than with the "English-speaking cousins." But some recent operations, such as in Bosnia, have involved military operations with nations about which the United States still harbors lingering suspicion—such as Russia or Ukraine. In these cases the need to protect intelligence sources and methods must be balanced against the need to share intelligence—not only for the sake of the operation but to ensure that military partners in the operation are not put in a position where their actions or inactions prove to be dangerous to U.S. troops.

LIMITATIONS OF SATELLITES.   All satellites are limited by the laws of physics. Most orbiting systems can spend only a limited time over any target. On each successive orbit the satellites will shift to a slightly different coverage pattern. Moreover, orbiting satellites travel in predictable orbits. Potential targets of a satellite can derive the orbit from basic knowledge about its launch and initial orbit. Unfortunately, some individuals and organizations attempt to make this information available, for a variety of reasons. This information enables nations to take steps to avoid collection—in part by timing activities that they wish to keep secret so that they occur when satellites are not overhead.

Satellites that are in geosynchronous orbit stay over the same spot on Earth at all times. But to do this they must be 22,000 miles above the Earth. The great distance between the collectors and their targets raises the problem of transmitting collected information back to Earth. Collection can be precise only up to a point, thus explaining the "vacuum cleaner" problem noted above.

THE "STOVEPIPES" PROBLEM.   Intelligence practitioners often refer to collection "stovepipes." This term refers to two characteristics of intelligence collection. First, each of the technical collection disciplines— imagery (IMINT); signals intelligence (SIGINT); and measurement and signatures intelligence (MASINT)—and the nontechnical human intelligence, or espionage (HUMINT), have end-to-end processes from collection through dissemination. (Open-source intelligence—OSINT—does not.) Thus, there is a "pipeline" from beginning to end. Second, the collection disciplines are separate from one another. They are often competitors. The various INTs sometimes vie with one another to respond to requests for intelligence—largely as a means of assuring continuing funding levels—regardless of which INT is best suited to provide the required intelligence. Often, several of the INTs respond, regardless of their applicability to the problem. Within the U.S. intelligence system no one is in charge of coordinating the various INTs. So, the "stovepipes" are complete but quite individual and separate processes.

RECONNAISSANCE GAMES.   In an obverse to the problem noted above—in which a target uses knowledge about the collection capabilities of an opponent to avoid collection (known as "denial")—the target can use the same knowledge to transmit information to a collector. This information can be either true or false (if the latter, it is called "deception"). For example, a nation can display an array of weapons as a means of deterring attack. Such a display may reveal actual capabilities or may be staged so as to present a false image of strength. A classic example of this behavior was the Soviet Union's sending its limited number of strategic bombers in large loops around Moscow during parades so they could be repeatedly counted by U.S. personnel in attendance, thus inflating Soviet air strength. The use of decoys or dummies to fool imagery, or false communications to fool SIGINT, also fall into this category. The Allies exploited these techniques prior to D-Day to raise German concerns about an invasion in the Pas de Calais rather than Normandy. The Allies created a nonexistent invasion force, replete with inflatable dummy tanks and streams of false radio traffic, and all under the supposed command of Gen. George S. Patton.

RECONNAISSANCE IN THE POST-COLD WAR WORLD.   The U.S. collection array was largely built to respond to the difficulties of penetrating the Soviet target—a closed society with a vast land mass, frequent bad weather, and a long-standing tradition of secrecy and deception.

Does the United States require the same extensive array to deal with post-cold war intelligence issues? On the one hand, the threat to the United States has lessened. On the other hand, intelligence targets are more diffuse and more geographically disparate than before. Also, some of the leading intelligence issues—the so-called transnational issues such as narcotics, terrorism, and crime—may be less susceptible to the technical collection capabilities built to deal with the Soviet Union or other "classic" political-military intelligence problems. Now, many of the collection targets are "nonstate" actors with no fixed geographic location and no vast infrastructure that offers collection opportunities. These transnational issues may require greater human intelligence, albeit in geographic regions where the United States has fewer capabilities.

Overhead imagery capabilities have gone commercial. LANDSAT, SPOT, and other satellites have ended the U.S. and Russian monopoly on overhead imagery. Any nation—or transnational group—can order imagery from commercial vendors. They may even do so through false fronts to mask their identity. This commercial capability remains so new that its implications have not been completely thought out by those building the commercial systems and by intelligence agencies. On the positive side, commercial imagery offers opportunities, freeing classified collection systems for the truly hard targets. On the negative side, it may offer hostile states or terrorists access to useful imagery via false fronts— buyers who serve to mask the ultimate users of the imagery. "Shutter control"—who controls what the satellites will photograph—is already an issue between those in the U.S. government who seek to limit photography of Israel and those who own the satellites.

Finally, open-source information (OSINT) is growing rapidly. The collapse of a number of closed, Soviet-dominated societies drastically reduced the "denied targets" area. One intelligence veteran observed that during the cold war 80 percent of the information about the Soviet Union was secret and 20 percent was open, but in the post-cold war period the ratio had more than reversed for Russia. Theoretically, the greater availability of open-source intelligence should make the intelligence community's job easier. However, the intelligence community was created to collect secrets; collecting open-source information is not a wholly analogous activity. The intelligence community has had difficulties assimilating open-source information into its collection stream. Moreover, the intelligence community harbors some institutional prejudice against open-source intelligence, since it seems to run counter to the very purposes for which the intelligence community was created. (It is worth noting that the OSS had an overt branch—Research and Analysis—but it apparently had little legacy in the postwar intelligence community.)

THE COLLECTION DISCIPLINES: STRENGTHS AND WEAKNESSES

Each of the collection disciplines has strengths and weaknesses. But when evaluating them—especially the weaknesses—it is important to remember that the goal is to bring as many collection disciplines as possible to bear on the major issues. The use of multiple disciplines should allow the collectors to gain advantages from mutual reinforcement and from individual capabilities that can make up for shortcomings in the others.

IMAGERY. IMINT is also referred to as PHOTINT (photo intelligence). It is a direct descendant of the brief practice of sending soldiers up in balloons during the U.S. Civil War. In World Wars I and II both sides used airplanes to obtain photos. Airplanes are still employed, but several nations now employ imagery satellites. In the United States the National Reconnaissance Office (NRO) develops these satellites. The National Imagery and Mapping Agency (NIMA) is responsible for processing and exploiting imagery. Some imagery also comes via the Defense Department's airborne systems, such as unmanned aerial vehicles (UAVs), or drones.

The term *imagery* is somewhat misleading in that it makes most people think of a picture produced by an optical system akin to a camera. Some imagery is produced by optical systems, usually referred to as electro-optical (EO) systems. Early satellites contained film that was jettisoned in capsules and recovered. Modern satellites transmit their images as signals, or data streams, that are received and reconstructed as images.

Infrared imagery (IR) produces an image based on the heat reflected by the surfaces being recorded. IR provides the ability to detect "warm" objects (for example, engines on tanks or planes inside hangars). Imagery can also be produced by radar, which has the ability to "see" through cloud cover. Some systems, referred to as multispectral or hyperspectral imagery (MSI and HSI), derive "images" from spectral analysis. These images are not photographic per se but are built by reflections from several bands across the spectrum of light, some visible, some invisible. They are usually referred to as measurement and signals intelligence (MASINT).

How Much Resolution Is Enough?

The degree of resolution that analysts desire depends on the nature of the target and the type of intelligence that is being sought. For example, one-meter resolution will allow fairly detailed analysis of man-made objects or subtle changes to terrain. Ten-meter resolution will lose some detail but still will allow the identification of buildings by type or allow surveillance of large installations and associated activity. Twenty- to thirty-meter resolution will cover a much larger area but still will allow the identification of large complexes such as airports, factories, and bases.

Thus, the degree of resolution has to be appropriate to the analyst's need. Sometimes high resolution is the correct choice, sometimes it is not.

The level of detail provided by imagery is called "resolution." Resolution refers to the smallest object that can be distinguished in an image, expressed in size—one meter, ten meters, and so on. Designers of imagery systems must make a trade-off between the resolution and the size of the scene being imaged. The better the resolution, the smaller the scene. (*See box, "How Much Resolution Is Enough?" this page.*)

During the cold war it was often popular to refer to the ability to "read the license plates in the Kremlin parking lot"—a wholly irrelevant parameter. Different collection needs have different resolution requirements. For example, keeping track of large-scale troop deployments requires much less detail than tracking the shipment of military weapons. Indeed, the U.S. intelligence community developed the science of "crateology," by which analysts were able to track Soviet arms shipments based on the size and shape of crates being loaded or unloaded from Soviet-bloc cargo vessels. (This analytical practice was subject to deception by the simple act of using purposely mis-sized crates to mask the nature of the shipments.)

Imagery offers a number of advantages over other collection means. First, it is sometimes graphic and compelling. When put before policy makers, an easily interpreted image often is worth a thousand words. Second, imagery is easily understood much of the time by policy makers. Even though few, if any, policy makers are trained imagery analysts, all of them are quite accustomed to seeing and interpreting images. From family photos, to newspapers and magazines, to news broadcasts, we all spend an unnoticed part of our day not only looking at images but also interpreting them. Imagery is also easy to use with policy makers in that

The Need for Photo Interpreters—
Two Cases in Point

Two incidents underscore the difficulty of interpreting even not-so-subtle images.

One of the signs of planned Soviet missile deployments in Cuba in 1962 was an image of a peculiar road pattern called "the Star of David" for its resemblance to that symbol. To the untrained eye it would look like an odd road interchange, but trained U.S. photo interpreters recognized it as a pattern they had seen before—in Soviet missile fields. But, to run into a senior policy maker's office exulting about a Star of David road pattern without explaining it, and perhaps bringing along samples from imagery of the Soviet Union, might lead to ridicule. Interpreters also found soccer fields—a sign of non-Cuban activity.

In the late 1970s and early 1980s, when Cuba was sending expeditionary forces to various parts of the Third World, one of the signatures of their arrival was newly constructed baseball fields. Cuban troops play baseball for recreation. Again, to inform an official that the Cubans must be in Angola or Ethiopia because we have seen baseball fields is almost ludicrous. Some supporting analysis is required, perhaps including a note that only the United States, Cuba, Mexico, Canada, Japan, and Nicaragua take baseball this seriously, and we can eliminate all of the others as unlikely to have large troop concentrations in these regions.

little or no interpretation is necessary as to how it was acquired. Although the process by which images are taken from space, transmitted to earth, and processed is more complex than using a 35-mm camera, policy customers have enough sense of the process to take it for granted.

Another advantage of imagery is that many of the targets make themselves available. Most nations' militaries exercise on regular cycles and at predictable locations, making them highly susceptible to IMINT. Finally, an image of a certain site will often provide information not just about one activity, but about some ancillary ones as well.

Imagery suffers a number of disadvantages as well. The very graphic quality that is an advantage is also a disadvantage. An image can be too compelling, leading to hasty or ill-formed decisions or to the exclusion of other, more subtle intelligence that may be contradictory. Also, the intelligence on an image may not be self-evident; it may require interpretation by trained photo interpreters who can "see" things on the image that the untrained person cannot. At times, the policy makers must take on faith that the skilled analysts are correct. *(See box, "The Need for Photo Inter-preters—Two Cases," p. 63.)*

Another disadvantage of imagery is that it is, quite literally, a snap-shot, a picture of a particular place at a particular time. This is sometimes referred to as the "where and when" phenomenon. Imagery is a static piece of intelligence, telling you something about where and when it was taken but nothing about what happened before or after the image was taken. Analysts can perform a "negation search," looking at past imagery to determine when an activity commenced. The site can be revisited to watch for further activity. But a single image will not tell you all of this.

Details about U.S. imagery capabilities have become better known. Using this knowledge, states can take steps to deceive collection—through the use of camouflage, dummies—or to preclude collection—by conducting certain activities at times when they are less likely or unlike-ly to be observed.

SIGNALS INTELLIGENCE.   SIGINT is a twentieth-century phenome-non. British intelligence pioneered the field during World War I, success-fully intercepting German communications by tapping underwater cables. The most famous product of this work was the Zimmermann Telegram, a German offer to Mexico of an anti-U.S. alliance that Britain made avail-able to the United States without revealing how it was obtained. With the advent of radio communications, cable taps were augmented by the abil-ity to "pluck" signals from the air. The United States also developed a suc-cessful signals intercept capability that survived World War I. Prior to World War II the United States broke Japan's Purple code; Britain, via ULTRA, read German codes.

Today, signals intelligence can be gathered by earth-based collec-tors—ships; planes; or ground sites such as the large Russian facility still functioning in Cuba—or by satellites. Again, U.S. satellites are built by the NRO. The National Security Agency (NSA) is responsible for both carrying out U.S. signals intelligence activities and for protecting the United States against hostile SIGINT.

SIGINT actually comprises several different types of intercepts. The term is often used to refer to the interception of communications between two parties, which is also known as communications intelligence (COMINT). SIGINT can also refer to the pickup of data relayed by weapons during tests, which is sometimes called telemetry intelligence (TELINT). Finally, SIGINT can refer to the pickup of electronic emissions from modern weapons and tracking systems (military and civil), which are useful means of gauging their capabilities, such as range and frequen-cies on which systems operate. This is sometimes referred to as electron-ic intelligence (ELINT).

The ability to intercept communications is highly important, since it gives insight into what is being said, planned, and even considered. This is as close as one can come, from a distance, to "reading the other side's mind," a goal that cannot be achieved by imagery. Tracking communications also gives a good "indication and warning." As with imagery, COMINT relies to some degree on regular behavior by those being watched, especially among military units. Messages may be sent at regular hours or regular intervals using known frequencies. Changes in those patterns—either increases or decreases—may be indicative of a larger change in activity. Monitoring changes in communications is known as "traffic analysis," which has more to do with the volume and pattern of communications than the content. (*See box, "SIGINT versus IMINT," p. 66.*)

COMINT also has some weaknesses. First and foremost, it depends on there being communications that can be intercepted. If the target goes silent or opts to communicate via secure landlines rather than through the air, then the ability to undertake COMINT ceases to exist. It might be possible to tap the landlines, but this is obviously a more difficult task than remote interception from a ground site or satellite. The target also can begin to encrypt—or code—its communications. Within the offensive/defensive struggle over SIGINT is a second struggle between encoders and codebreakers or cryptographers. "Crypies," as they are known, like to boast that any code that can be constructed can also be solved. But we are far removed from the Elizabethan age of relatively simple ciphers. Computers greatly increase the ability to construct complex, one-time use codes. At the same time, computers also increase the ability to attack these same codes. Finally, the target can use false transmissions as a means of creating less compromising patterns or as a means of subsuming important communications amid a flood of meaningless ones—in effect, increasing the ratio of noise to signals.

TELINT and ELINT offer valuable information on weapons capabilities that would otherwise be unknown or would require far more risky human intelligence operations. However, as the United States learned from its efforts to monitor Soviet arms, the weapons tester can employ many techniques to maintain secrecy. Like communications, test data can be encrypted. Test data can also be encapsulated—that is, recorded within the weapon being tested and released in a self-contained capsule that will be recovered—so that the data are never transmitted as a signal that would be susceptible to interception. If the data are transmitted, they can be sent in a single "burst" rather than throughout the test, greatly increasing the difficulty of intercepting and reading the data. Or, the data can be transmitted via a "spread spectrum," that is, using a series of frequencies through which the data will move at irregular intervals. Receivers can be

---

SIGINT versus IMINT

A director of the National Security Agency once made the following distinction between imagery and signals intelligence: "IMINT tells you what has happened; SIGINT tells you what will happen."

It is a bit of an exaggeration—and was said tongue in cheek—but it captures an important difference between the two INTs.

---

programmed to match the frequency changes, but this will greatly increase the difficulty of intercepting the full data stream.

MEASUREMENT AND SIGNATURES INTELLIGENCE.   TELINT and ELINT are both major contributors to a little understood branch of intelligence known as measurement and signatures intelligence (MASINT). This type of intelligence refers to weapons capabilities and industrial activities. Multispectral and hyperspectral imagery (MSI and HSI), discussed above, also contribute to MASINT.

An arcane debate rages between those who see MASINT as a separate collection discipline and those who see it as simply a product, or even a by-product, of SIGINT and other collection capabilities. For our purposes, it is sufficient to understand that MASINT exists and that, in a world increasingly concerned about such issues as proliferation of weapons of mass destruction, it is of increasing importance. For example, MASINT can help identify the types of gases or waste leaving a factory, which can be extremely important in chemical weapons identification. It can also help identify other specific characteristics (composition, material content) of weapons systems.

MASINT has suffered as a collection discipline because of its relative novelty and its dependence on the other technical INTs for its products. Often analysts or policy makers look at a MASINT product without knowing it. MASINT is a potentially important INT still struggling for recognition. It is also more arcane and requires analysts with more technical training to be able to use it fully. At present, policy makers are less familiar with it—and probably less comfortable—than they are with IMINT or SIGINT.

HUMAN INTELLIGENCE   HUMINT is espionage—spying—and is sometimes referred to as the world's second-oldest profession. It is as old as the Bible. Joshua sent two spies into Canaan before leading the Jewish people across the Jordan River. Spying is what most people think about when they hear the word "intelligence," whether they conjure famous spies from history such as Nathan Hale or Mata Hari (both failures) or the many fictional spies such as James Bond. In the United States HUMINT is largely the responsibility of the CIA, through its Directorate of Operations (DO). DIA also has a HUMINT capability with the Defense HUMINT Service (DHS).

HUMINT largely involves sending agents to foreign countries where they attempt to recruit foreign nationals to spy. Agents must identify individuals who have access to the information that we may desire; gain their confidence and assess their weaknesses and susceptibility to being recruited; and make a "pitch" to them suggesting a relationship. Sources may accept a pitch for a variety of reasons: money, disaffection with their own government, blackmail, thrills. Once the pitch has been accepted, the agent must meet with his or her sources regularly to receive information, holding meetings in such a way and in such places so as not to be caught and then transmitting the information back home.

In addition to gaining the skills required for this activity, agents have to maintain their "cover" stories—the overt lives that give them a plausible reason for being in that foreign nation. There are two types of "cover": official and nonofficial. Agents with official cover hold another government job, usually posted out of the embassy. Official cover makes it easier for the agent to maintain contact with his or her superiors but raises the risk of being suspected as an agent. Nonofficial cover (called NOC—pronounced "knock") avoids any overt connection between the agent and his or her government but can make it more difficult to keep in contact.

In addition to recruiting foreign nationals, HUMINT agents may undertake more direct spying, such as stealing documents or planting sensors. Some of their information may come through direct observation of activity. Thus, HUMINT involves more than just espionage.

Espionage provides a very small part of the intelligence that is collected. IMINT and SIGINT produce a greater volume of intelligence. But HUMINT, like SIGINT, has the major advantage of affording access to what is being said, planned, and thought. Moreover, clandestine human access to another government also may offer opportunities to influence that government by feeding it false or deceptive information. For intelligence targets where the technical infrastructure may be irrelevant as a fruitful target—such as terrorism, narcotics, or international crime, where the "signature" of activities is rather small—HUMINT may be the only available source.

HUMINT also has disadvantages. First, it cannot be done remotely, as the various types of technical collection can be. It requires proximity and access and therefore must contend with the counterintelligence capabilities of the other side. It is also far riskier, since it puts individuals at risk, and, if they are caught, has political ramifications that are less likely to occur with technical collectors.

HUMINT is far less expensive than the various technical collectors, although it still involves costs for training, special equipment, and the accoutrements spies need to build successful cover stories.

Like all the other collection INTs, HUMINT is susceptible to deception. Some critics argue that HUMINT is the most susceptible to deception. The "bona fides" of human sources will always be subject to question initially and, in some cases, may never be wholly resolved. Many questions will arise and linger. Why is this person offering to pass information—ideology, money, vengeance? Of course, he or she will claim to have good access to valuable information, but how good is it? Is it consistent, or is this a single event? How good is the information? Is this person a "dangle," that is, offered as a means of passing information that the other side wants to have passed—either because it is false or because it will have a specific effect? Is this person a double agent who will be collecting information on your HUMINT techniques and capabilities even as he or she passes information to you?

HUMINT agents must walk a fine line between prudent caution and the possibility that too much caution will lead them to deter or reject a promising HUMINT source. Deception is particularly difficult to deal with, because people naturally find it difficult to accept the fact that they are being deceived. On the other hand, people might slip into a position where they trust no one, which can result in turning away sources who might have been very valuable.

Another issue to be considered with HUMINT is its unique sources and methods. HUMINT sources are considered to be extremely fragile, since good human penetrations take so long to develop and risk the lives of the case officers, their sources, and perhaps even the sources' families. Therefore, the intelligence analysts who receive HUMINT reports may not be told the details of the source or sources. Analysts are not told, for example, "this report comes from a first secretary in the Fredonian Foreign Ministry." Instead, the report will include information on the access of the source, the past reliability of the source, or variations on this concept. Sometimes several sources may be blended together in a single report. Although the masking of HUMINT sources promotes their preservation, it may have the unintended effect of devaluing the reports for analysts, who may not have a full appreciation of the value of the source and the information.

In the United States there is constant tension between HUMINT and the other collection disciplines. The dominance of technical collection periodically gives rise to calls for a greater emphasis on HUMINT. So-called intelligence failures, such as the fall of the shah in 1979 and the unexpected Indian nuclear tests in 1998, also lead to demands for more HUMINT.

Again, there is no "right balance" between HUMINT and the other collection disciplines. Indeed, such an idea runs counter to the concept of an all-source intelligence process that seeks to apply as many collection disciplines as possible to a given intelligence need. But not every collection INT will make an equal or even similar contribution to every issue. Clearly, it is better to have a collection system that is strong and flexible and can be modulated to the intelligence requirement at hand than to have one that swings between apparently opposed fashions of technical and human collection.

OPEN-SOURCE INTELLIGENCE   To some, OSINT may seem like a contradiction in terms. How can information that is openly available be considered intelligence? This question reflects the misconception discussed in chapter 1 that intelligence must inevitably be about secrets. A great deal of intelligence is about secrets, but not to the exclusion of openly available information. As noted above, even during the height of the cold war, according to one senior intelligence official, at least 20 percent of the intelligence about the Soviet Union came from open sources.

OSINT includes a wide variety of information and sources:

- Media: newspapers, magazines, radio, television, and computer-based information
- Public data: government reports, official data such as budgets and demographics, hearings, legislative debates, press conferences, speeches
- Professional and academic: conferences, symposia, professional associations, academic papers, and experts

One of the hallmarks of the post-cold war world is the increase in the availability of OSINT. In the post-cold war period the ratio of open source to classified intelligence on Russia has more than reversed from its 20:80 ratio during the cold war. The number of closed societies and "denied areas" have decreased dramatically. Some of the former Warsaw Pact states are now NATO allies. This does not mean that classified collection disciplines are no longer needed, but that the areas in which OSINT is available have expanded.

The major advantage of OSINT is its accessibility. It is readily available, although it still requires collection. OSINT requires less processing and exploitation than the technical INTs or HUMINT, but it still requires some P&E. Given the diversity of OSINT, it may be more difficult to manipulate so as to deceive than the other INTs. OSINT is also useful for helping put the secret information into a wider context, which can be extremely valuable.

The main disadvantage of OSINT is its volume. In many ways, it represents the worst "wheat and chaff" problem. Some argue that the so-called information revolution has made OSINT more difficult without a corresponding increase in usable intelligence. Computers have increased the ability to manipulate information; however, the amount of derived intelligence has not increased apace.

Popular misconceptions about OSINT, even within the intelligence community, persist. OSINT is not free. Buying print media costs the intelligence community money, as does a variety of services that are useful—if not essential—to help analysts manage, sort, and sift large amounts of data more efficiently. Another misconception is that the Internet is the main fount of OSINT. Experienced intelligence practitioners discover that the Internet—meaning searches among various sites—yields no more than 3–5 percent of the total OSINT "take."

Despite the fact that OSINT has always been used, it remains undervalued by significant segments of the intelligence community. This attitude derives from the fact that the intelligence community was created to discover secrets. If the United States's national security needs could be largely met with OSINT, then the intelligence community would look very different. Some people in the intelligence community have mistakenly equated the degree of difficulty involved in obtaining information with its ultimate value to analysts and policy makers. Contributing to this pervasive bias is the fact that OSINT has always been handled differently by the intelligence community. All of the other INTs have dedicated collectors, processors, and exploiters. With the exception of the Foreign Broadcast Information Service (FBIS), which monitors foreign media broadcasts, OSINT does not have dedicated collectors, processors, and exploiters. Instead, analysts are largely expected to act as their own OSINT collectors, a concept that would be seen as ludicrous with any other INT. This is unfortunate, since OSINT is the perfect place to start any intelligence collection. By first determining what material is available from open sources, intelligence managers could focus their clandestine collectors on those issues where such means were really needed. Thus, properly used, OSINT could be a very good intelligence collection resource manager.

PIZZINT: Some Intelligence Humor

In addition to IMINT, SIGINT, HUMINT, OSINT, and MASINT, intelligence officers, in their lighter moments, speak of some other INTs. One of the most famous is PIZZINT—pizza intelligence. This refers to the belief that Soviet officials based in Washington would keep watch for large numbers of pizza delivery trucks going late in the evening to the CIA, the White House, the Defense Department, and the State Department as an indication that a crisis was brewing somewhere. The notion was that they would see numerous pizza trucks making deliveries and then hurry back to the Soviet embassy to alert Moscow that something must be going on somewhere.

Some other INTs that intelligence officers talk about with tongue firmly in cheek are:

LAVINT: I heard it in the men's room (lavatory intelligence).
RUMINT: rumor.
REVINT: revelation intelligence.
DIVINT: divine intelligence.

COLLECTION—CONCLUSION

Each collection discipline offers unique advantages that are well-suited to some types of intelligence requirements but brings with it certain disadvantages as well. (*See Figure 5-1, "A Comparison of the Collection Disciplines," p. 72.*) By deploying a broad and varied array of collection techniques, the United States derives two advantages: it is able to exploit the advantages of each type of INT, which, ideally, will compensate for the shortcomings of the others; it is able to apply more than one collection INT to an issue, which enhances the likelihood of meeting the collection requirements for that issue. However, the intelligence community cannot provide answers to every question that is asked, nor does it have the capability to meet all possible requirements at any given time. The collection system is simultaneously powerful and limited.

The cost of collection was rarely an issue during the cold war because of the broad political agreement on the need to stay informed about the Soviet threat. In the post-cold war world, the absence of any overwhelming strategic threat makes the cost of collection systems more difficult to justify, and it leads some to question whether the United States needs the same level of collection capability that it did during the cold war. On the one hand, the threat to U.S. national security has greatly

FIGURE 5-1 A Comparison of the Collection Disciplines

INT	Advantages	Disadvantages
IMINT	Graphic and compelling	Perhaps overly graphic and compelling
	Use seems familiar to policy makers	Still requires interpretation
	Ready availability of some targets—particularly military exercises	Literally a "snapshot" of a moment in time; very static
	Can be done remotely	Subject to problems of weather, spoofing
		Expensive
SIGINT	Offers insights into plans, intentions	Signals may be encrypted or encoded—requiring them to be "broken"
	Voluminous material	Voluminous material
	Military targets tend to communicate in regular patterns	May encounter communications silence, use of secure lines, "spoofing" via phony traffic
	Can be done remotely	Expensive
HUMINT	Offers insights into plans, intentions	Riskier in terms of lives, political fallout
	Relatively inexpensive	Requires more time to acquire and validate sources
		Problems of dangles, false feeds, double agents
MASINT	Extremely useful for issues such as proliferation	Expensive
	Can be done remotely	Little understood by most users
		Requires a great deal of processing and exploitation
OSINT	More readily available	Voluminous
	Extremely useful as a place to start all collection	Less likely to offer insights available from clandestine INTs

diminished. On the other hand, the problems that remain are more diverse and diffuse to collect against than was the largely unitary Soviet problem. Ultimately, there is no yardstick for measuring national security problems against a collection array in order to determine how much collection is enough.

KEY TERMS

all-source intelligence
collection disciplines
communications intelligence
   (COMINT)
cryptographers
deception
denial
denied areas
denied targets
electronic intelligence (ELINT)
encryption
espionage
geosynchronous orbit
human intelligence (HUMINT)
imagery intelligence (IMINT)
indications and warning
INTs

measurement and signatures
   intelligence (MASINT)
negation search
noise versus signals
nonofficial cover (NOC)
official cover
open-source intelligence (OSINT)
photo intelligence (PHOTINT)
pitch
resolution
signals intelligence (SIGINT)
sources and methods
spies
telemetry intelligence (TELINT)
traffic analysis
wheat versus chaff

FURTHER READINGS

For ease of use, these readings are grouped by activity. For all of the books by spies and about spying, there are very few good discussions of the tradecraft of espionage and the role it plays, as opposed to its supposed derring-do aspects.

General Sources on Collection

Burrows, William. *Deep Black: Space Espionage and National Security.* New York: Random House, 1986.
Wohlstetter, Roberta. *Pearl Harbor: Warning and Decision.* Stanford, Calif.: Stanford University Press, 1962.

Espionage

Burgstaller, Eugen F. "Human Collection Requirements in the 1980's." In *Intelligence Requirements for the 1980's: Clandestine Collection,* edited by Roy F. Godson. Washington, D.C.: National Strategy Information Center, 1982.
Phillips, David Atlee. *Careers in Secret Operations: How to Be a Federal Intelligence Officer.* Frederick, Md.: Stone Trail Press, 1984.

Imagery

Brugioni, Dino A. *Eyeball to Eyeball: The Inside Story of the Cuban Missile Crisis,* edited by Robert F. McCort. New York: Random House, 1990.
————. *From Balloons to Blackbirds: Reconnaissance, Surveillance and Imagery Intelligence—How It Evolved.* McLean, Va.: Association of Former Intelligence Officers, 1993.
Central Intelligence Agency. *CORONA: America's First Satellite Program,* edited by Kevin C. Ruffner. Washington, D.C.: CIA, 1995.
Day, Dwayne A., et al., eds. *Eye in the Sky: The Story of the Corona Spy Satellites.* Washington, D.C.: Smithsonian Institution Press, 1998.
Peebles, Christopher. *The Corona Project: America's First Spy Satellite.* Annapolis, Md.: U.S. Naval Institute Press, 1997.
Richelson, Jeffrey T. *America's Secret Eyes in Space: The U.S. Keyhole Spy Satellite Program.* New York: Harper and Row, 1990.
————. "High Flyin' Spies." *Bulletin of the Atomic Scientists* 52 (September–October 1996): 48–54.
Shulman, Seth. "Code Name CORONA." *Technology Review* 99 (October 1996): 23–25, 28–32.
SPOT Image Corporation. "Satellite Imagery: An Objective Guide." Reston, Va.: SPOT, 1998.

Open-Source Intelligence

Lowenthal, Mark M. "Open Source Intelligence: New Myths, New Realities." *Defense Daily News,* November 1998. [http://www.defensedaily.com/reports; http://www.defensedaily.com/reports/osintmyths.htm]

Satellites

Klass, Philip. *Secret Sentries in Space.* New York: Random House, 1971.

Secrecy

Moynihan, Daniel Patrick. *Secrecy: The American Experience.* New Haven, Conn.: Yale University Press, 1998.
Secrecy. Report of the Commission on Protecting and Reducing Government Secrecy. Washington, D.C., 1997.

Signals Intelligence

Bamford, James. *The Puzzle Palace: A Report on America's Most Secret Agency.* Boston: Viking, 1982.
Brownell, George A. *The Origin and Development of the National Security Agency.* Laguna Hills, Calif.: Aegean Park Press, 1981.
Kahn, David. *The Codebreakers.* Rev. ed. New York: Scribner, 1996.
National Security Agency and Central Intelligence Agency. *VENONA: Soviet Espionage and the American Response, 1939–1957,* edited by Robert Louis Benson and Michael Warner. Washington, D.C.: NSA and CIA, 1996.
Warner, Michael, and Robert Louis Benson. "Venona and Beyond: Thoughts on Work Undone." *Intelligence and National Security* 12, no. 3 (July 1996): 1–13.

CHAPTER 6

The Intelligence Process—Analysis

Despite all of the attention lavished on the operational side (collection and covert action) of intelligence, analysis is the mainstay of the process, providing civil and military policy makers with information directly related to the issues they face and the decisions they have to make. As the discussion of dissemination in chapter 4 indicated, intelligence products do not arrive once or twice a day, but in a steady stream throughout the day. Certain documents, particularly the daily intelligence products, arrive first thing in the morning, but other intelligence reports can be delivered when they are ready or held for delivery at a specific time.

Although not all intelligence practitioners will agree, the ongoing production and delivery of intelligence can have a numbing effect on policy makers. Intelligence analysis can become part of the daily flood of information—intelligence products; commercially provided news; reports from policy offices, embassies, and military commands; and so on. One of the challenges for intelligence is to make itself stand out from this steady stream.

This goal can be achieved in two ways. One is to emphasize the unique nature of the intelligence sources. But this is not the preferred choice of intelligence officials, since they believe that they are much more than just conduits for their sources. Intelligence officials believe that their analysis adds value to the intelligence they collect. The other way for intelligence to achieve prominence is to produce analysis that stands out from the steady information stream on its own merits, to add value. The value added includes the timeliness of intelligence products, the ability of the community to tailor products to specific policy makers' needs, and the objectivity of the analysis. But the fact that value-added is discussed as often as it is within the intelligence community suggests that this goal is not achieved as often as desired.

MAJOR THEMES

It is very difficult to prescribe how to produce value-added intelligence—or to measure the frequency with which it is produced—head-on because there is no agreement among intelligence officers and their policy customers as to what adds value. Indeed, for policy customers, value-added is a very idiosyncratic and personal attribute. Therefore, this chapter discusses the several issues that have been problems for intelligence analysis for many years. Analysis is much more than sitting down with the collected material, sifting and sorting it, and coming up with a brilliant piece of prose that makes sense of it all. The themes addressed here reflect major decisions that analysts have to make in the analytical process and areas of controversy that have proved to be resilient or recurrent.

FORMAL REQUIREMENTS—DO THEY MATTER?   In the ideal intelligence-process model, policy makers give some thought to their main intelligence requirements and then communicate them to the intelligence managers. This formal process often does not happen, leaving intelligence managers to make educated guesses, many of which are either obvious or well-grounded.

Some argue that this less formal process is, in reality, much better than the ideal one, since most of the requirements are fairly well-known and do not need to be defined through a formal process. For example, most people, if asked to name the main U.S. intelligence priorities during the cold war, would have mentioned a number of Soviet-related issues. Even in the less clear post-cold war period, a similar exercise would yield such obvious answers as narcotics, terrorism, proliferation, Russia's reform and stability, and the various regional trouble-spots of the moment, such as the Balkans, the Middle East, and North Korea. Interestingly, this list parallels the U.S. intelligence priorities as stated in the Clinton administration's Presidential Decision Directive 35.

The real importance of the requirements process may be not in defining the issues that need coverage but in giving the intelligence community some sense of priority among the requirements. Assigning priorities is especially important and difficult in the absence of a single overwhelming issue, as has been the case since the early 1990s. The real problem is that when several issues are considered to be roughly equal in importance, no one of them truly has priority.

CURRENT VERSUS LONG-TERM INTELLIGENCE.   This is one of the perennial analytical issues. Current intelligence—reports and analysis on issues that may not stretch more than a week or two into the future—is the mainstay of the intelligence community. In many respects, current intelligence "pays the rent" for the intelligence community. Current intelligence is the product most often requested and seen by policy makers.

But many intelligence analysts find themselves frustrated by the emphasis on current intelligence. Having developed expertise in an area and analytical skills, they wish to write longer range analyses that look beyond current demands. However, few policy makers are likely to read papers with longer horizons—not for lack of interest but for lack of time and lack of the ability to pull away, even briefly, from the current pressing issues. Thus, a conflict arises between what the policy makers need to read and what many analysts wish to produce.

A middle ground exists by virtue of the fact that the intelligence community does not make a stark choice between one type of product and another. In the course of any given day, a range of intelligence analysis is produced. But the fact remains that the current intelligence products predominate in terms of resources and the way policy makers perceive the intelligence community.

CRISES VERSUS THE NORM.   One of the ways in which requirements are set is in response to crises. Crisis-driven requirements also represent the ultimate victory of current over long-range intelligence needs.

Given the limited nature of collection and analytical resources, certain issues inevitably receive short shrift or even no attention at all. And just as inevitably, annual requirements planning fails to predict which of the seemingly less important issues will erupt into a crisis at some point during the year. Thus, the planning exercises are to some degree self-fulfilling—or self-denying—prophecies.

Analytical managers must find a way to create or preserve some minimal amount of expertise against the moment when a less important issue erupts and suddenly moves to the top of policy makers' concerns. The intelligence community has only a small collection reserve, no analytical reserve, and a limited capacity to move assets to previously uncovered but now important topics. Assets therefore move from hot topic to hot topic, with other topics receiving little or no coverage.

Despite the problem of defining requirements and the vagaries of international relations, the intelligence community is on the spot when it "misses" an issue—fails to be alert to its eventuality or is unprepared to deal with it when it occurs. In part, the high expectations are deserved, since one of the functions of intelligence is strategic warning. But strategic warning is usually taken to mean advance notice on issues that would pose a threat to national security, not regional crises that might require some level of involvement. Such crises strain the image of the intelligence community as well as its resources, since policy makers in both branches and the media tend to be harsh—sometimes fairly, sometimes not—in their view of "misses."

THE WHEAT VERSUS CHAFF PROBLEM.   This problem, already discussed as part of collection, ultimately becomes an analytical issue. Although much that is collected does not get processed and exploited, the amount that does is still formidable. Even in the age of computers, few technical shortcuts have been found to help analysts deal with this problem. To a very large degree, the analysts' daily task of sifting through the incoming intelligence germane to their portfolio remains a grind, whether done electronically or on paper. Sifting is not just a matter of getting through the accumulated imagery, signals, open-source reporting, and so on. It is also the much more important matter of seeing this mass of material in its entirety, of being able to perceive patterns from day to day and reports that are anomalous. To repeat, there are no shortcuts. Sifting requires training and experience. Although some intelligence practitioners think of analysts as the "human in the loop," the analysts' expertise should be an integral part of collection sorting as well.

ANALYST TRAINING.   Unfortunately, the intelligence community does not spend a significant amount of time on analyst training. Much that an analyst learns comes through on-the-job training. Analysts arrive with certain skills learned in college or at the graduate level and then assimilate into their specific intelligence agency or unit. They learn basic processes, basic requirements, the daily schedule of work, and preferred means of expression—all of which vary from agency to agency. They become familiar with the types of intelligence with which they will be working.

The minimum skills for all analysts are knowledge of one or more specific fields, appropriate language skills, and a very basic ability to express themselves in writing. *(See box, "Choosing Good Analysts," p. 79.)* But these are basic skills, a foundation upon which better skills must be built. Some of the new skills to be mastered are parochial. Each intelligence agency has its own corporate style that must be learned. More important, analysts must learn to cope with the wheat versus chaff problem and to write as succinctly as possible. These two skills reflect the demands of current intelligence and the fact that policy makers are busy and prefer economies of style. The bureaucratic truism remains that shorter papers will usually best longer papers in the competition for policy makers' attention.

Another important skill that analysts must learn is objectivity. Although intelligence analysts can and often do have strong personal views about the issues they are covering, their views have no place in

Choosing Good Analysts

Napoleon reportedly asked new officers on his staff one question: "Are you lucky?" Napoleon understood that luck in battle, although intangible, was a useful attribute.

A senior intelligence official used to ask his subordinates two questions about new analysts they wished to hire: "Do they think interesting thoughts? Do they write well?" This official believed that, with these two talents in hand, all else would follow with training and experience.

their intelligence products. Analysts will be listened to because of their accumulated expertise, not the forcefulness of their views. Indeed, presenting personal views would cross the line between intelligence and policy. Still, analysts need training to learn how to filter out their views, especially when their views run counter to the intelligence at hand or the policies being considered.

A more subtle and very difficult skill to master is cultivating the intelligence consumer without politicizing the intelligence as a means of currying favor.

Finally, there is the question of how far training (or experience) can take a given analyst. Any reasonably intelligent individual with the right skills and education can be taught to be an effective analyst. But the truly gifted analyst—like the truly gifted athlete or musician or scientist—is inherently better at his or her job by virtue of inborn talents. In all fields, such individuals are rare. They must be nurtured. But the benefits they derive from training are different from those that less-gifted analysts derive.

MANAGING ANALYSTS.   Managing intelligence analysts presents a number of unique problems. A major concern is developing career tracks. Analysts need time to develop true expertise in their fields, but intellectual stagnation can set in if an analyst is left to cover the same issue for too long. Rotating analysts among assignments quickly helps them avoid stagnation and allows them to learn more than one area. But this career pattern raises the possibility that analysts will never gain real expertise in any one area, becoming instead intelligence "generalists." Ideally, managers seek to create some middle ground—providing analysts with assignments that are long enough for them to gain expertise and substantive knowledge while also providing sufficient opportunities to shift assignments and maintain intellectual freshness. Nor is there any specific time frame for assignments; the length of an assignment depends on the individual analyst and on the demands generated by intelligence requirements at the time.

The criteria for promotion are another management issue. As government employees, intelligence analysts generally are assured of promotions up to a level that can be described as "high middle." The criteria for promotion through these grades are not overly rigorous. Ideally, promotions should come as a result of merit, not time served. But what criteria should a manager consider in evaluating an intelligence analyst for merit promotion: accuracy of analysis over the past year; writing skills; increased competence in foreign languages and foreign area knowledge; participation in a specific number of major studies? And how should a manager weight the various criteria?

The competition is stronger for more senior assignments than for lower level assignments, and the criteria for selection are different. The qualities that first merit promotion—keen analytical abilities—are the ticket to management positions, where responsibilities and pay are greater. Ironically, or perhaps sadly, analytical skills have little to do with, and are little indication of the ability to carry out, managerial duties. But, with few exceptions, management positions are the only route to senior promotion.

ANALYSTS' MIND-SETS.   Analysts, as a group, exhibit a set of behaviors that can affect their work. Obviously, not all analysts exhibit each of these characteristics all of the time, and some analysts may never exhibit any of them. Still, many of these traits are common among the analytic population.

Mirror imaging is one of the most frequent flaws of analysts; it is the assumption that other leaders, states, groups, and so on share motivations or goals similar to those most familiar to the analyst. (See box, "Mirror Imaging," p. 81.) "They're just like us," is the quintessential expression of this view. The prevalence of mirror imaging is not difficult to understand. We learn, from an early age, to expect certain behavior of others. The Golden Rule is based on this concept of reciprocal motives and behavior. Unfortunately, as an analytical tool, mirror imaging fails to take into account differences of motivation, perception, or action based on national differences, subtle differences of circumstance, different rationales, the absence of any rationale, and so forth.

A classic example of mirror imaging was the U.S. analysis of Japan's likely actions in 1941. Although many U.S. analysts and policy makers expected Japan to attack somewhere, they ruled out a direct attack on the United States largely because, if put in a similar position, they would not

Mirror Imaging: Political Analysis

Here are two examples of how mirror imaging can affect analysis. During the cold war, some Kremlinologists and Sovietologists would talk about Soviet "hawks" and "doves" or try to assess which Soviet leaders belonged to which group. No empirical evidence existed to suggest that there were Soviet hawks and doves. Instead, the fact that the U.S. political spectrum included hawks and doves led to the facile assumption that the Soviet system must have them as well.

Second, during the late 1980s some analysts working on Iran spoke of Iranian "extremists" and Iranian "moderates." When pressed by skeptical peers as to their evidence for the existence of "moderates," the analysts argued: if there are extremists, there must be moderates. Again, they were reflecting other political systems they knew, as well as making a faulty assumption. Some of their colleagues argued that Iranian politics might comprise "extremists" and "ultra extremists."

---

have attacked a nation so much more powerful in terms of war-making potential. But in Tokyo, the steady decline in Japanese potential dictated a different answer, a direct attack on the most formidable foe.

To avoid mirror-imaging, managers must train analysts to recognize it when it intrudes in their work and must establish a review process above the analyst that is alert to this analytical tendency.

Clientism is a flaw that occurs when analysts become so imbued with their subjects—usually after they have been working on an issue for too long—that they lose their ability to view issues with the necessary criticality. (In the State Department this phenomenon is usually called "clientitis," which actually means "an inflammation of the client," although it is used to convey someone who has "gone native" in his or her thinking.) Analysts can spend time apologizing for the actions of the nations they cover rather than analyzing them. The same safeguards that analysts and their managers put in place to avoid mirror imaging are required to avoid clientism.

"ON THE GROUND KNOWLEDGE." The degree to which analysts have direct knowledge about the nations on which they write varies greatly. During the cold war, U.S. analysts had difficulty spending significant amounts of time in the Soviet Union or its satellites, nor were they able to travel widely in these nations. Similarly, intelligence analysts may have less contact with the senior foreign officials about whom they write than do the U.S. officials who must deal with these foreigners. Their distance from the subjects they analyze can occasionally be costly to analysts, in terms of how their policy consumers view the intelligence they receive. Indeed, some policy customers may have more "in-country" experience or direct contact with foreign leaders than do the intelligence analysts.

Analysts, like everyone else, are proud of their accomplishments. Once they have mastered a body of knowledge, they may look for opportunities—no matter how inappropriate—to display their knowledge in detail. Analysts can have difficulty limiting their writing to just those facts and analyses that may be necessary for a specific consumer need. The analyst may want the consumer to have some greater appreciation for where the issues being discussed fit in some wider pattern; the analyst may want to share (or show off) some larger part of his or her knowledge. Unfortunately—and perhaps too frequently—the policy customer wants to know "only about the miracles, and not the lives of all the saints who made them happen." Analysts require training, maturity, and supervision to cure this behavior. Some analysts get the message sooner than others; some never get it at all and produce analysis that requires greater editing to get it down to the essential message, which can cause resentment on the part of the edited analyst. On the other hand, the intelligence provider may lose the attention of the policy customer if he or she gives too much material, large portions of which do not seem entirely relevant to the policy maker's immediate needs.

Just as analysts want to show the depth of their knowledge, so too they want to be perceived as experienced—perhaps far beyond what is true. Again, this is a common human failing. Professionals in almost any field, when surrounded by peers and facing a situation that is new to them but not to the others, will be tempted to assert their familiarity, whether genuine or not. Given the choice between appearing jaded ("been there, done that") and naïve ("Wow! I've never seen that before!"), analysts usually choose to appear jaded. (See box, "Jaded versus Naïve," p. 83.) The risk of being caught seems small enough, and it is preferable to being put down by someone else who displays greater experience ("The same thing happened in Bessarabia in 1958. I thought you knew that.").

Unfortunately, the jaded approach carries costs. First, it represents intellectual dishonesty, something all analysts should avoid. Second, it proceeds from the false assumption that each incident is much like others, which may be true at some superficial level but also may be false at very fundamental levels. Finally, being jaded closes the analyst's thinking, regardless of his or her level of experience, to the possibility that an incident or issue may be entirely new, requiring wholly new types of analysis.

Jaded versus Naïve—a Cautionary Example

In April 1986 the operators of the Chernobyl nuclear reactor caused an explosion by running an unauthorized experiment on a Sunday evening. On Monday afternoon, Sweden reported, with some concern, higher than normal radioactive traces in their air monitors, which they had placed in many cities.

In the United States an intelligence manager asked one of his senior analysts what he made of the Swedish complaints. The analyst downplayed them, saying the Swedes were always concerned about their air and often made such complaints for the smallest amounts of radiation. The issue was forgotten and everyone went home at a decent hour. The next day the truth became known, and analysts spent a frantic day of catching up with the facts at Chernobyl.

How could this have been handled differently? At a minimum, inquiries could have been made in Sweden regarding the types of radiation. The answer would have identified the source as a reactor rather than a weapon. The prevailing winds over Sweden could have been surveyed to identify the source. But the jaded approach precluded all of this.

Some years later the intelligence manager had an opportunity to meet with some of his Swedish counterparts. They had analyzed the radiation and checked the winds and concluded, initially, that a reactor at nearby Ignalina, across the Baltic Sea in Soviet territory, was leaking. They could not know, initially, that the leak was from a reactor much farther away, but they were much closer to the truth than were U.S. intelligence officials.

Credibility is one of analysts' most highly prized possessions. Although analysts recognize that they cannot be correct all of the time, they are concerned that they are held accountable to some perhaps impossible standard by policy makers. Their concern over credibility—which is largely faith and trust in the integrity of the intelligence process and in the ability of the analysts whose product is at hand—can lead them to downplay or perhaps mask sudden shifts in analyses or conclusions, out of concern that the shifts will undercut credibility. For example, let us say that intelligence analysis has long shown a production rate of fifteen missiles a year in a hostile state. One year, because of improved collection and new methodologies, the estimated production rate (which is still just an estimate) goes to forty-five missiles per year. Policy makers may view this increase—on the order of 300 percent—with alarm. Rather than put out the new number with an explanation as to how it was derived, an analyst might be tempted to soften the blow. Perhaps a brief memo can be issued suggesting changes in production. Then a second memo, saying that the rate is more likely twenty to twenty-five missiles per year, and so on, until the policy maker sees a more acceptable analytical progression to the new number, rather than a sudden spike upward. Of course, this will take time.

Intelligence products that are written on a recurring basis—such as certain types of national intelligence estimates—may be more susceptible than other products to this type of behavior, since they establish benchmarks that can be reviewed more easily than, say, a memo that is not likely to be remembered, unless the issue is extremely important and the shift is dramatic.

Although policy makers have taken retribution on analysts for sudden shifts in estimates, more often than not the fear in the minds of analysts is greater than the likelihood of a loss of credibility. Much will depend on the prior nature of the analyst/policy maker relationship, the policy maker's appreciation for the nature of the intelligence problem, and the intelligence community's past record. If several revisions have been made in the recent past, then there is reason to suspect a problem. If revision is an isolated phenomenon, then it is less problematical. The nature of the issue, and its importance to the policy maker and to the nation, will also matter. (See box, "Soviet Defense Spending," p. 85.)

Very few intelligence products are written by just one analyst and then sent along to the policy customer. Most have peer reviews and managerial reviews and probably the input of analysts from other offices or other agencies. This is especially true for the intelligence product that several Western agencies call "estimates." The participation of these other analysts and agencies adds a further dimension to the analytical process—bureaucratics, which brings with it various types of behaviors and strategies.

More likely than not, several agencies will have strongly held and diametrically opposed views on key issues within an estimate. How should these be dealt with? The U.S. system in both intelligence and policy making is consensual. No votes are taken; no lone wolves are cast out or beaten to the ground. Everyone must find some way to agree. But if intellectual arguments fail, consensus can be reached in many other ways, few of which have anything to do with analysis:

- Backscratching and logrolling. Although these two behaviors are usually thought of in legislative terms, they also can come into play in intelligence analysis. Basically, they involve a trade-off of concerns: "You accept my view on p. 15 and I'll accept yours on p. 38." Obviously, substance is not a major concern here.

Soviet Defense Spending

The level of Soviet defense spending—usually expressed as a percentage of gross national product (GNP), was a key intelligence issue during the cold war.

At the end of the Ford administration (1974–1977), intelligence estimates of the percentage of Soviet GNP going to defense rose from a range of 6–7 percent to 13–14 percent, largely because of new data, new modeling techniques, and other factors unrelated to Soviet output. This revision was discomforting to the incoming Carter administration. In his inaugural address, President Carter signaled that he did not want to be constantly concerned with the Soviet issue, that he had other foreign policy issues he wanted to pursue. A more heavily armed Soviet Union was not good news.

Carter prided himself on his own analytical capabilities. When faced with the revised estimates, he reportedly chided the intelligence community, noting that they had just admitted to a 100 percent error in their past estimates. That being the case, why should he believe them now?

- False hostages. Agency A is opposed to a position being taken by Agency B but is afraid its own views will not prevail. Agency A can stake out a false position on another issue that it will defend very strongly, not for the sake of the issue itself, but so that it has something to trade in the backscratching and logrolling.
- Lowest common denominator language. One agency believes that the chance of something happening is high; another thinks it is low. Unless these views are strongly held, the agencies may compromise—"a moderate chance"—as a means of resolving the issue. This example is a bit extreme, but it captures the essence of the behavior—an attempt to paper over differences, almost literally, with different words that everyone can accept.
- Footnote wars. Sometimes none of the other techniques will work. In the U.S. estimative process, an agency can always add a footnote in which it expresses its "alternative views." Or more than one agency might add a footnote, or agencies may take sides on an issue. This can lead to vigorous debates about whose view will appear in the main text and whose in the footnote.

All of these behaviors can leave the impression that the estimative process—or any large-group analytical efforts—is false intellectually. That is not so. However, it is also not a purely academic exercise. Other behaviors intrude, and more than just analytical truths are at stake. There will be winners and losers in the estimative process, and careers may rise and fall as a result.

ANALYTICAL ISSUES

In addition to the mindset and behavioral characteristics of analysts noted above, several issues within analysis itself need to be addressed.

DEALING WITH LIMITED INFORMATION.   Analysts rarely have the luxury of knowing everything they wish to know about a topic. In some cases very little may be known. How does an analyst deal with this problem?

One option is to flag the problem so that the policy customer is aware of it. Often, telling policy consumers what you don't know is as important as telling them what you do know. But admitting ignorance may be unattractive, out of concern that it will be interpreted as a failing on the part of the intelligence apparatus. Alternatively, analysts can try to work around the problem, bringing to bear their own experience and skill to fill in the blanks as best they can. This may be more satisfying intellectually and professionally, but it runs the risk of giving the customer a false sense of the basis for the analysis or of being very wrong.

Another option is to arrange for more collection, if time will allow it. Yet another is to widen the circle of analysts working on the problem, in order to get the benefit of their views and experience as well.

CONVEYING UNCERTAINTY.   Just as everything may not be known, so too the likely outcome may not be clear. Conveying uncertainty can be difficult. Analysts shy away from the simple but stark, "We don't know." After all, they are being paid, in part, for making some intellectual leaps beyond what they know. Too often, analysts rely on "weasel words" to convey uncertainty: on the one hand, on the other hand; maybe; perhaps; and so on. These words may convey analytical pusillanimity rather than uncertainty. (Conveying uncertainty seems to be a particular problem in English, which is a Germanic language and makes less use of the subjunctive than do the Romance languages.)

Some years ago a senior analytical manager crafted a system by which potential outcomes would be conveyed by both words and numbers—that is, a 1 in 10 chance, a 7 in 10 chance. Such numerical formulations may be more satisfying than words, but they run the risk of conveying to the policy customer a degree of precision that does not exist. What is the difference between a 6 in 10 chance and a 7 in 10 chance, beyond greater conviction? In reality, the analyst is back to relying on "gut feeling."

INDICATIONS AND WARNING.   I&W, as it is known among intelligence professionals, is one of the most important roles of intelligence— giving policy makers advance warning of important events, usually military ones. The emphasis placed on I&W in the United States reflects the cold war legacy of a long-term military rivalry and the older roots of the U.S. intelligence community in Pearl Harbor, the classic I&W failure.

I&W is, primarily, a military intelligence function, with an emphasis on surprise attack. It relies, to a large extent, on the fact that all militaries operate according to certain regular schedules, forms, and behaviors. These provide a baseline against which to measure activity that may raise I&W concerns. In other words, analysts are looking for anything that is out of the ordinary, any new or unexpected activity that may presage an attack: calling up reserves; putting forces on a higher level of alert; dropping or increasing communications activity; imposing sudden communications silence; sending more naval units than usual to sea. But none of these can be viewed in isolation; they have to be seen within the wider context of overall behavior.

During the cold war, for example, U.S. and NATO analysts worried about how much warning they would receive of a Warsaw Pact attack against Western Europe. Some analysts believed that they could provide policy makers, minimally, several days' warning, as stocks were positioned, additional units were brought forward, and so on. Others believed that the Warsaw Pact had sufficient forces and supplies in place to attack from "a standing start." Fortunately, the issue was never put to the test.

For analysts, I&W can be a trap rather than an opportunity. Their main fear is that of failing to pick up on indicators and to give adequate warning, a fear that in part reflects the harsh view of intelligence when it "misses" an important event. In reaction, analysts may lower the warning threshold and issue warnings about everything, in effect "crying wolf." Although crying wolf may reduce the analyst's exposure to criticism, it has a lulling effect on the policy maker and can cheapen the function of I&W.

Policy makers may want something in addition to warning, for example, "opportunity," as one secretary of state explained to his intelligence officers, by which he meant instances where he could advance his agenda as opposed to reacting to the actions of others. His was an interesting, challenging, and demanding request, and one that depended on the policy maker sharing his goals with his intelligence officers.

ESTIMATES.   As noted, the United States—as well as Britain and Australia—creates and uses analytical products called estimates. These serve two major purposes: to see where a major issue or trend will go over the next several years, and to present the considered view of the entire intelligence community, not just of one agency. In the United States their community-wide origin is signified by the fact that the director of central intelligence signs completed estimates.

It is important to understand the intellectual basis of estimates. Estimates are not predictions of the future. They are considered judgments as to the likely course of events regarding an issue of importance to the nation. Sometimes, more than one outcome may be estimated.

The bureaucratics of estimates are important to their outcome. In the United States, national intelligence officers (NIOs) are responsible for preparing estimates. They circulate the terms of reference (TOR) among colleagues and other agencies at the outset of an estimate. The TOR may be the subject of prolonged discussion and negotiation, as various agencies may believe that the basic questions or lines of analysis are not being framed properly. The NIOs do not do the actual drafting; someone from the NIO's office does, or the NIO recruits a drafter from one of the intelligence agencies. Once drafted, the estimate is coordinated with other agencies, that is, the other agencies read it and give back comments, not all of which will be accepted, since they may be at variance with the drafter's views. Numerous meetings will be held to resolve disputes, but the meetings may end with two or more views on some aspects that cannot be reconciled. A final meeting is chaired by the DCI and attended by senior officials from various agencies. As noted, the DCI signs the estimate once he is satisfied with it. It becomes "his" estimate. DCIs have been known to change the views expressed in estimates with which they disagree. This usually discomforts the drafter but is within the rights of the DCI.

In addition to the bureaucratic game-playing that may be involved in drafting estimates, discussed above, issues of process also influence outcomes. Not every issue is of interest to every intelligence agency. But each agency understands the necessity of taking part in the estimative process, not only for its intrinsic intelligence value but also as a means of keeping watch on the other agencies.

Some people question the utility of estimates. Both producers and consumers of estimates have had concerns about the length of estimates and their sometimes plodding style. Critics also have voiced concerns about timeliness, in that some estimates take more than a year to complete. One of the worst examples of poor timing came in 1979. An estimate on the future political stability of Iran was being written—including the observation that Iran was "not in a prerevolutionary state"—even as the shah's regime unraveled daily. This incongruity led the House Intelligence Committee to observe that estimates "are not worth fighting over."

COMPETITIVE ANALYSIS.   The U.S. intelligence community believes in the concept of competitive analysis—having different agencies with different points of view work on the same issue. Because the United States has several intelligence agencies—including three major all-source analytical agencies (CIA, Defense Intelligence Agency, and State's Bureau of Intelligence and Research)—every relevant actor understands that the agencies will have different analytical strengths and, likely, different points of view on a given issue. By having each of them—and other agencies as well on some issues—analyze an issue, it is believed that the analysis will be stronger and more likely to give policy makers accurate intelligence.

Beyond the day-to-day competition that takes place among the various intelligence publications of each agency, the intelligence community fosters competition in other ways. Intelligence agencies occasionally form "red teams," which take on the role of the analysts of another nation or group as a means of gaining insights into their thinking. A now-famous competitive exercise was the 1976 formation of two teams—Teams A and B—to review intelligence on Soviet strategic forces and doctrine. Team A comprised intelligence community analysts. Team B comprised outside experts, but of a decidedly hawkish viewpoint. The teams disagreed little on the strategic systems the Soviets had built; the key issue was their nuclear doctrine and strategic intentions. Predictably, Team B believed that the intelligence supported a more threatening view of Soviet intentions. But the lack of balance on Team B largely vitiated the exercise, which could have been very useful not only for gaining insight into Soviet intentions but for validating the utility of competitive intelligence exercises.

Dissent channels—bureaucratic mechanisms by which analysts can challenge the views taken by their superiors without risk to their careers—are useful but not widely used. Such channels have long existed for Foreign Service officers in the State Department. Although they are less effective than competitive analysis for articulating alternative viewpoints, they offer a means by which alternative views can survive a bureaucratic process that tends to emphasize mutual consent.

A broader issue is the extent to which competitive intelligence can or should be institutionalized. To some degree, in the U.S. system it already is. But the competition among the three all-source agencies is not often pointed. They often work on the same issue, but with different perspectives that are well understood, thus muting some of the differences that may be seen.

Although the intelligence community believes in competitive analysis, not all policy makers are receptive to the idea. Some of them bridle at the idea that agencies cannot agree on issues, perhaps assuming that there is a single answer to an issue that should be knowable. Indeed, one of the main reasons that President Harry S. Truman created the Central Intelligence Group (CIG) and its successor, the CIA, was his annoyance over receiving intelligence reports that did not agree. He wanted an agency to coordinate the reports so that he could work his way through the contradictory views. Truman was smart enough to realize that agencies might not agree, but he was not comfortable receiving disparate reports without some coordination that attempted to make sense of the areas of disagreement. Other policy makers lack Truman's subtlety and simply cannot abide having agencies disagree, thus vitiating the concept of competitive analysis.

Finally, to those who are not familiar with the idea of competitive analysis, and even to some who are, the planned redundancy may seem more wasteful than intellectually productive.

POLITICIZED INTELLIGENCE.   This issue arises from the line separating policy and intelligence. As noted above, this line is best thought of as a semipermeable membrane—policy makers are free to offer assessments that run counter to intelligence analyses, but intelligence officers are not allowed to make policy recommendations based on their intelligence. For example, in the State Department in the late 1980s, the assistant secretary responsible for the Western Hemisphere, Elliot Abrams, often disagreed with pessimistic INR assessments as to the likelihood that the contras would be victorious in Nicaragua. Abrams would often write more positive assessments on his own that he would forward to Secretary of State George Shultz.

Policy makers and intelligence officers have different institutional and personal investments in the issues on which they work. The policy makers are creating policy and hope to accrue other benefits (career advancement, re-election) from a successful policy. Intelligence officers are not responsible for creating policy or for its success, yet they understand that their own status—both institutional and personal—may be affected by the outcomes.

The issue of politicization arises primarily from concerns that intelligence officers may intentionally alter intelligence from its supposedly objective state to support the preferred options or outcomes held by policy makers. These actions may have a variety of motives: a loss of objectivity over the issue at hand and a preference for specific options or outcomes; an effort to be more supportive; career interests; outright pandering.

Intentionally altering intelligence is a subtle issue because it does not involve the intelligence officer crossing the line from analysis to policy. Rather, the analyst is tampering with his or her own product so that it will be received more favorably. The issue is also made more complex by the

Political Winners and Losers

Although we would prefer to think about intelligence analysis and policy making as largely objective exercises, they inevitably get caught up in partisan politics.

Two cases come to mind. In the late 1940s and early 1950s many of the State Department's experts on China (the "China hands") had their careers sidetracked or were forced from office over allegations that they had "lost" China to the communists. Many scholars and officials customarily interpreted their treatment as a gross injustice. But, as Professor Ernest R. May of Harvard University has pointed out, the U.S. public in the elections of the early 1950s largely repudiated the anti–Chiang Kai-shek views of the China hands by returning the pro-Chiang Republicans to power. So, the China hands not only had ideological foes within the government, they also had no political basis upon which to pursue their preferred policies.

Similarly, the careers of many intelligence officers and Foreign Service officers involved in crafting and promoting the SALT II treaty during the Carter administration also failed to prosper with the advent of the Reagan administration. Reagan appointees were opposed to that treaty and held these career officers responsible. Again, their careers suffered only because of an electoral victory.

One can argue that these punishments were not what the electorate had in mind, but they underscore the fact that the government and the underlying policy processes are essentially political in nature.

fact that at the most senior levels of the intelligence community, the line separating intelligence from policy begins to blur. Senior intelligence officials will be asked by policy makers for their personal views on an issue or policy, which they may give. It is difficult to conceive of a DCI constantly abstaining when asked such a question by the president or the secretary of state.

The size or persistence of the politicization problem is difficult to determine. Some of those who raise accusations about politicized intelligence are "losers" in the bureaucratic battles—intelligence officers whose views have not prevailed or policy makers (in the executive branch or Congress, either loyal to the current administration or in opposition) opposed to current policy directions. Thus, their accusations may be no more objective than the intelligence about which they are concerned. Those unfamiliar with the process are often surprised to hear intelligence practitioners talk about "winners" and "losers." But these debates—with-

---

Potential Politicization: A Recent Example

According to press accounts in November 1998, Vice President Al Gore's staff rejected CIA reports about the personal corruption of Russian premier Viktor Chernomyrdin.

Members of the vice president's staff argued that the administration had to deal with Chernomyrdin, corrupt or not, and that the intelligence was inconclusive. Intelligence analysts countered that the administration set the standard for proof so high that it was unlikely to be met by intelligence. The analysts found that they were censoring their reports so as to avoid further disputes with the White House.

Both policy and intelligence officers denied these allegations.

---

in the policy or the intelligence community—are not abstract academic discussions. Their outcomes have real results that can be significant and even dangerous. And careers can rise and fall as well. Indeed, just as intelligence officers serve policy makers, career officers—both intelligence and policy—serve political appointees, who are less interested in the objectivity of analysis. (*See box, "Political Winners and Losers," p. 91.*)

Politicization by intelligence officers may also be a question of perception. One could probably get common agreement as to what politicized intelligence looked like, but much less agreement as to whether a specific analysis fit the definition.

Thus, politicized intelligence remains a concern—albeit a somewhat vague one. Its vague nature may, in fact, make the issue all the more difficult and important. Many of these issues came out in the hearings surrounding Robert Gates's second nomination as DCI. (Gates asked President Ronald Reagan to withdraw his first nomination during the Iran-contra affair. Gates was subsequently renominated by President George Bush and confirmed in 1991.)

There is a second type of politicized intelligence: that caused by the policy makers. They may react strongly to intelligence, depending on whether it confirms or refutes their own preferences for policy outcomes. (*See box, "Potential Politicization: A Recent Example," this page.*) They may also use intelligence issues for partisan purposes. Two interesting examples of the partisan use of intelligence in the United States are the missile gap (1959–1961) and the "window of vulnerability" (1979–1981). In both cases, the party that was out of power (the Democrats in the first case, the Republicans in the second) argued that the Soviet Union had gained a strategic nuclear advantage over the United States, and that the Soviet advantage was being ignored or not reported. In both cases, the accusing party won the election (not because of their charges) and found the actual intelligence did not support their accusations—which they simply declared to have been resolved!

INTELLIGENCE ANALYSIS: AN ASSESSMENT

Sherman Kent, one of the intellectual founders of the U.S. intelligence community and especially of its estimative process, once wrote that every intelligence analyst had three wishes: to know everything; to be believed; to influence policy for the good (as he understands it). Kent's three wishes offer a yardstick by which to measure analysis. Clearly, an analyst can never know everything in a given field. Indeed, if everything were known, then the need for intelligence would not exist—there would be nothing left to discover. But what Kent is getting at in his first wish is the desire of the analyst to know as much as possible about a given issue before being asked to write about it. The amount of intelligence available will vary from issue to issue and from time to time. So, analysts must be trained to develop some inner, deeper knowledge that will allow them to "read between the lines," to make educated guesses or intuitive choices when the intelligence is insufficient.

Kent's second wish, to be believed, goes to the heart of the relationship between intelligence and policy. Policy makers pay no price for ignoring intelligence—barring highly infrequent strategic disasters such as Joseph Stalin's refusal to accept the signs of an imminent German attack in 1941. Intelligence officers see themselves as honest and objective messengers who add value to the process, who provide not just sources but analysis. Their reward, at the end of the process, is to be listened to, which varies greatly from policy maker to policy maker.

Finally, and derived from his second wish, Kent notes that intelligence officers want to have a positive effect on policy, to help avert disaster and to help produce positive outcomes in terms of the nation's interests. But analysts really want to be more than a Cassandra, constantly warning of doom and disaster. Their wish to have a positive influence also indicates that they want to be kept informed as to what policy makers are doing so as to be able to play a meaningful role.

What, then, constitutes "good intelligence"? This is no small question, and one is reminded of Justice Byron White's response when he was asked to define pornography: "I can't define it," White said, "but I know it when I see it." Good intelligence has something of the same ephemeral quality. At least four qualities come to mind. Good intelligence is:

- Timely. Getting the intelligence to the policy maker on time is more important than waiting for every last shred to come in or for the paper to be pristine, clean, and in the right format. The timeliness criterion runs counter to the first of Kent's three wishes, to know everything. *(See box, "Talleyrand on Timeliness," p. 95.)*

- Tailored. Good intelligence focuses on the specific information needs of the policy maker, to whatever depth and breadth is required, but without extraneous material. This must be done in such a way so as not to lose objectivity or to politicize the intelligence.

- Digestible. Good intelligence has to be in a form and of a length that will allow policy makers to grasp what they need to know as easily as possible. This requirement tends to argue in favor of shorter intelligence products and against longer ones, but it is meant mainly to stress the importance of making sure that the message is clearly presented so that it can be clearly understood. This does not mean that the message cannot be complex, or even incomplete. But whatever the main message is, the policy maker must be able to understand it with a minimum of effort.

- Clear regarding the known and the unknown. Good intelligence must convey to the reader what is known, what is unknown, and what has been filled in by analysis, as well as the degree of confidence in all of the material. The degree of confidence is important because the policy maker must have some sense of the relative firmness of the intelligence. All intelligence involves risk by the very nature of the information being dealt with. The risk should not be assumed by the analysts alone, but should be shared with their customers.

Note that objectivity was not one of the major factors defining good intelligence. Its omission was not an oversight. The need for objectivity is so great and so pervasive that it is taken here as a given. If the intelligence is not objective, then none of the other attributes—timeliness, digestibility, clarity—matters at all.

Also note that accuracy is not a criterion. Accuracy is a more difficult standard for assessing intelligence than might be imagined. Clearly, no one wants to be wrong; but everyone recognizes the impossibility of infallibility. Given these limits, what accuracy standard should we use? One hundred percent is too high and 0 percent is too low. Splitting the difference at 50 percent accuracy is still unsatisfactory. Thus, we are left playing a numbers' game—something more than 50 percent and less than 100 percent accurate.

Talleyrand on Timeliness

Napoleon died on St. Helena in May 1821; news of his death did not reach Paris until July. Charles Maurice de Talleyrand, once Napoleon's foreign minister and later one of his foes, was dining at a friend's when they heard of Napoleon's death. The hostess exclaimed, "What an event!"

Talleyrand corrected her. "It is no longer an event, Madam, it is news."

As unsatisfactory as this standard is, other metrics are not much better. For example, we could construct a batting average over time—for an issue, for an office, for an agency, for a product line. But these, too, are all inadequate. Or, we could assess the quality of intelligence on the number of products produced—estimates, analyses, images exploited. These suggestions are not meant to be as frivolous as they seem. They are meant to give a feel for the difficulty of assessing what is "good intelligence."

This is not to suggest that producing good intelligence is some sort of holy grail that is rarely achieved. Good intelligence is often achieved. But one must distinguish between the steady stream of intelligence that is produced on a daily basis and the small amount within that daily production that stands out for some reason—its timeliness, the quality of its writing, its effect on policy. The view here—and it is one that has been debated with the highest intelligence officials—is that effort is required to produce acceptable, useful intelligence on a daily basis, but that it is much more difficult to produce exceptional intelligence, and that exceptional intelligence is produced less frequently. We face a conflict between the goal of consistency and the desire to be exceptional. An entire intelligence community cannot be exceptional all the time, but it does hope to be consistently helpful to policy. Consistent intelligence and exceptional intelligence are not one and the same. (One is reminded of the cynical observation: "Only the mediocre are at their best all the time.") Consistency is not a bad goal, but it allows analysis to fall into a pattern that lulls both the producer and the consumer. Thus, for all that we know about the distinctive characteristics of good intelligence, it remains somewhat elusive in reality, at least as a widely seen, daily phenomenon.

KEY TERMS

clientism
competitive analysis
current intelligence
estimates
long-term intelligence

lowest-common-denominator
  language
mirror imaging
national intelligence officers (NIOs)
politicized intelligence

FURTHER READINGS

The literature on analysis is rich. These readings discuss both broad general issues and some specific areas of intelligence analysis that have been particularly important. (Readings on U.S. intelligence analysis on the Soviet Union are listed at the end of chapter 11.)

Adams, Sam. "Vietnam Cover-Up: Playing with Numbers; a CIA Conspiracy Against Its Own Numbers." *Harper's Magazine* (May 1975).

Caldwell, George. *Policy Analysis for Intelligence.* Center for the Study of Intelligence, Central Intelligence Agency. Washington, D.C.: CIA, 1992.

Clark, Robert M. *Intelligence Analysis: Estimation and Prediction.* Baltimore, Md.: American Literary Press, 1996.

Davis, Jack. *The Challenge of Opportunity Analysis.* Center for the Study of Intelligence, Central Intelligence Agency. Washington, D.C.: CIA, 1992.

Ford, Harold P. *Estimative Intelligence.* McLean, Va.: Association of Former Intelligence Officers, 1993.

———. *Estimative Intelligence: The Purposes and Problems of National Intelligence Estimating.* Washington, D.C.: Defense Intelligence College, 1989.

Gates, Robert M. "The CIA and American Foreign Policy." *Foreign Affairs* 66 (winter 1987–1988).

Johnson, Loch K. "Analysis for a New Age." *Intelligence and National Security* 11, no. 4 (October 1996): 657–671.

Lowenthal, Mark M. "The Burdensome Concept of Failure." In *Intelligence: Policy and Process,* edited by Alfred C. Maurer, et al. Boulder, Colo.: Westview Press, 1985.

MacEachin, Douglas J. *The Tradecraft of Analysis: Challenge and Change in the CIA.* Washington, D.C.: Consortium for the Study of Intelligence, 1994.

Nye, Joseph S. *Estimating the Future.* Washington, D.C.: Consortium for the Study of Intelligence, 1994.

Pipes, Richard. "Team B: The Reality Behind the Myth." *Commentary* 82 (October 1986).

Price, Victoria. *The DCI's Role in Producing Strategic Intelligence Estimates.* Newport, R.I.: U.S. Naval War College, 1980.

Reich, Robert C. "Re-examining the Team A–Team B Exercise." *International Journal of Intelligence and Counterintelligence* 3 (fall 1989).

Stack, Kevin P. "A Negative View of Comparative Analysis." *International Journal of Intelligence and Counterintelligence* 10 (winter 1998): 456–464.

Steury, Donald P., ed. *Sherman Kent and the Board of National Estimates*. Washington, D.C.: History Staff, Center for the Study of Intelligence, Central Intelligence Agency, 1994.

Turner, Michael A. "Setting Analytical Priorities in U.S. Intelligence." *International Journal of Intelligence and Counterintelligence* 9 (fall 1996): 313–336.

U.S. House Permanent Select Committee on Intelligence. *Intelligence Support to Arms Control*. 100th Congress, 1st session. 1987.

U.S. House Permanent Select Committee on Intelligence. *Iran: Evaluation of U.S. Intelligence Performance Prior to November 1978*. 96th Congress, 1st session. 1979.

U.S. Senate Select Committee on Intelligence. *The National Intelligence Estimates A–B Team Episode Concerning Soviet Strategic Capability and Objectives*. 95th Congress, 2d session. 1978.

U.S. Senate Select Committee on Intelligence. *Nomination of Robert M. Gates*. Hearings. 3 vol. 102d Congress, 1st session. 1991.

U.S. Senate Select Committee on Intelligence. *Nomination of Robert M. Gates to be Director of Central Intelligence*. Report. 102d Congress, 1st session. 1991.

Wirtz, James J. *The Tet Offensive: Intelligence Failure in War*. Ithaca, N.Y.: Cornell University Press, 1991.

CHAPTER 7

The Intelligence Process—
Counterintelligence

Counterintelligence refers to efforts taken to protect one's own intelligence operations from penetration and disruption by hostile nations or their intelligence services. It is both analytical and operational. Counterintelligence (sometimes referred to as CI) is not a separate step in the intelligence process but is an important function throughout the process. CI does not fit neatly with human intelligence, although CI is, in part, a collection issue. Nor does it fit with covert action. CI is one of the most difficult intelligence topics to discuss.

Counterintelligence proceeds from the fact that most nations have intelligence enterprises of some sort. By their very existence these intelligence agencies are extremely valuable intelligence targets for other nations. It is always useful to know what the other side knows, what they do not know, and how they go about their work. It is also extremely useful to know if they are undertaking similar efforts against you.

However, counterintelligence is more than a defensive activity. There are at least three types of CI:

- Collection: gaining information about an opponent's intelligence collection capabilities that may be aimed at you

- Defensive: thwarting efforts by hostile intelligence services to penetrate your service

- Offensive: having identified an opponent's efforts against your system, trying to manipulate these attacks either by "turning" the opponent's agents into double agents or by feeding them false information that they will report home

The world of spy and counterspy is murky at best. Like espionage, counterintelligence is one of the staples of intelligence fiction. But, like all other aspects of intelligence, it is less glamour than it is grinding, painstaking work.

Who Spies on Whom?

Some people assume that "friendly" spy agencies do not spy on one another. But what constitutes "friendly"? The United States and its "English-speaking cousins"—Britain, Australia, and Canada—enjoy a close intelligence partnership and do not spy on one another. Beyond that, all bets are off.

The United States allegedly spied on France for economic intelligence. Israel willingly used Jonathan Pollard, a U.S. Navy intelligence employee who passed sensitive U.S. intelligence that he believed Israel needed to know. Some people were surprised—if not outraged—that post-Soviet Russia would continue using Aldrich Ames to spy against the United States. More recently, a House committee found that China stole nuclear secrets from the United States at a time when the two nations were strategic partners against the Soviet Union.

In the 1970s a "senior U.S. government official" (probably Henry Kissinger) observed, "There is no such thing as 'friendly' intelligence agencies. There are only the intelligence agencies of friendly powers."

INTERNAL SAFEGUARDS

All intelligence agencies establish a series of internal processes and checks, the main purposes of which are to weed out applicants who may be unsuitable and to identify current employees whose loyalty is questionable. The vetting process for applicants includes extensive background checks, interviews with the applicants and close associates, and, in the United States at least, the use of the polygraph. The polygraph, sometimes mistakenly referred to as a lie-detector, is a machine that monitors physical responses (such as pulse, breathing rate) to a series of questions. Changes in these physical signs may indicate falsehoods or deceptions. The use of the polygraph by U.S. intelligence remains controversial. Everyone acknowledges that the polygraph is imperfect and can be deceived. At least two spies, Larry Wu-tai Chin and Aldrich Ames, passed polygraphs when they were involved in espionage against the United States. Advocates of the polygraph are quick to assert that the machine is only a tool that can point to problem areas, some of which may be resolved without prejudice. However, an individual's inability or failure to resolve such issues can lead to termination. In addition to new employees, current employees are re-polygraphed every several years; contractors

Why Spy?

U.S. counterintelligence emphasizes personal financial issues in assessing security risks. Many of the people behind the worst espionage cases suffered by the United States—Aldrich Ames, the Walker spy ring, Ronald Pelton— were motivated largely by greed rather than ideology. Some exceptions to this generalization would be Julius Rosenberg, Alger Hiss, and Larry Wu-tai Chin.

By contrast, many of the people behind the worst espionage cases in Britain—Kim Philby and his associates, or George Blake, for example— spied out of ideological devotion to the Soviet Union.

Although espionage cases of either type (greed or ideology) can arise in either country, some observers have been struck by the difference noted above. Some have attempted to explain the difference, in part, by the fact that Britain has had (and still has) a class system that makes ideology a more likely reason for betrayal, although the most serious British spies have come from the upper class. In the United States, however, the main competition has always been based on economic status rather than social class.

As noted in the discussion of HUMINT, spies may also be motivated by vengeance toward superiors or agencies; by blackmail against themselves or family members; by thrills; or by involvement with a foreign national. Still, most of the spies suffered by the United States have been motivated primarily by money.

are also subject to polygraphs, and these machines are used with defectors as well.

Beyond taking a polygraph (known as "being put on the box"), employees and prospective employees are evaluated for other possible indicators of disloyalty as well. Changes in personal behavior or lifestyle—marital problems, increased use of alcohol, suspected use of drugs, increased personal spending that seems to exceed known resources, running up large debts—*may* be indicators that an individual is spying or susceptible to being recruited to spy. Any of these personal difficulties may befall an individual who will never consider becoming a spy, but past espionage cases indicate some reason for concern. *(See box, "Why Spy?," this page.)* The response of counterintelligence agents to discovery of such problems would depend on the suspect's larger patterns of behavior, how long the problem persisted, and evidence of potentially hostile activity. In the aftermath of the Ames case—where marginal performance, alcohol abuse, and a sudden increase in fairly ostentatious personal

THE INTELLIGENCE PROCESS—COUNTERINTELLIGENCE   101

spending should have been taken as indicators of a problem—U.S. intelligence increased the amount of personal financial information that intelligence personnel must report on a regular basis.

Another internal means of thwarting espionage attacks is the classification system. In U.S. intelligence parlance, the system is "compartmented." In other words, an employee being accorded the privilege of a clearance does not automatically get access to all of the intelligence information that is available. Admission to various compartments is based on a "need to know." Thus, someone working on a new imagery system will likely have different clearances than someone involved in running HUMINT. There are also compartments within compartments. For example, a clearance involving HUMINT may include only specific cases or specific types of HUMINT—for example, proliferation or narcotics.

The clearance system limits access and, thus, limits the damage that can be caused by any one source of leaks. It is not without costs. It may become an obstacle to analysis, either wittingly or inadvertently, by excluding some analysts from a compartment crucial to their work. Administering such a system has direct costs: devising a system, tracking documents, running security checks on employees, and so forth. Indirect costs include safes, couriers, security officers to check officers' clearances, and color-coded or numerically tagged papers, to name a few. This list gives some sense of what is involved in a thorough classification scheme. And, if such a scheme is not thorough, then it is nothing more than annoying and wasteful.

Other safeguards include the certified destruction of discarded material; the use of "secure" phones, which cannot be easily tapped, for classified conversations; and restricted access to buildings or to parts of buildings where sensitive material is used. These are called sensitive compartmented information facilities (SCIFs).

EXTERNAL INDICATORS AND COUNTERESPIONAGE

The discussion thus far has focused on internal measures to prevent or to identify CI problems. Counterintelligence agents also look for external indicators of problems. These may be more obvious, such as the sudden loss of a spy network overseas; a change in military exercise patterns that corresponds to satellite tracks; or a penetration of the other service's apparatus that reveals the possibility of your having been penetrated as well. The indicators may be subtler—the odd botched operation or failed espionage meeting or a negotiation in which the other side seems to be anticipating your bottom line. These are all murkier indicators of a leak or penetration—what some have described as a "wilderness of mirrors."

In 1995 the CIA and NSA published SIGINT intercepts (codenamed VENONA) that had been used to detect Soviet espionage in the United States. From 1943 to 1957 VENONA products helped identify Alger Hiss, Julius Rosenberg, Klaus Fuchs, and others working for Soviet intelligence. As VENONA showed, SIGINT can offer indications of ongoing espionage, although the references to spying may be oblique and are unlikely to identify the spy outright. The VENONA intercepts used code names for the spies but often gave enough additional information to help narrow the search.

The serious problems that flow from being penetrated by a hostile service also highlight the gains to be made by carrying out a successful penetration of your own against the hostile service. Among the intelligence that may be gathered are:

- An opponent's HUMINT capabilities and targets, strengths, and weaknesses
- An opponent's main areas of intelligence interest and current shortfalls
- Possible penetrations of your service or other services
- Possible intelligence "alliances" (for example, the Soviet-era KGB used Polish émigrés in the United States for some defense-industry espionage and Bulgarian operatives for "wet affairs"—assassinations)
- Sudden changes in an opponent's HUMINT operations—new needs, new taskings, changed focuses, a recall of agents from a specific region—each of which can have a host of meanings

Discovering the presence of foreign agents may not lead automatically to their arrest. The agents also present opportunities, since they are conduits back to their own intelligence services. At a minimum, you may try to curtail some of their access without their becoming aware of it and then begin feeding them false information to send home. Alternatively, counterintelligence officers may try a more aggressive approach, attempting to turn them into double agents who, although apparently continuing their activities, are now actually working for your side—providing you with information on their erstwhile employer and knowingly passing back erroneous information. But just as there are double agents, so there are triple agents—agents who have been "turned" once, discovered, and then "turned" again by their own side. The effect, again, is a wilderness of mirrors.

PROBLEMS IN COUNTERINTELLIGENCE

Several problems arise in assessing counterintelligence operations. First, by its very nature, any counterintelligence penetration is going to be covert. Counterintelligence officers are unlikely to come across initially compelling evidence about a successful hostile penetration.

Second, the basic tendency within any intelligence organization (or any organization, for that matter) is to trust your own people, who have been vetted and cleared. They work with one another every day. All of this familiarity can lead to a lowering of your guard or to an unwillingness to believe that your own people may have gone bad. This appears to have been one of the problems in uncovering the espionage of Ames; the CIA was slow to look inward for the cause of severe losses of assets in Moscow.

But the alternative behavior—unwarranted suspicion—can be just as debilitating as having a spy in your midst. James Angleton, who was in charge of CIA's counterintelligence from 1954 to 1974, became convinced that a Soviet mole—a deeply hidden spy—had penetrated the CIA. Some believed that Angleton was reacting to the fact that one of his closest British associates, Kim Philby, had turned out to be a Soviet agent. Angleton was unable to find the mole, and some believe that he tied the CIA in knots by placing virtually anyone under suspicion. Some even suggested that Angleton himself was the mole and that he created a furor to divert attention from himself. Angleton remains a figure of extreme controversy, but his activities give some indication of the intellectual issues that can be involved in spying and counterintelligence.

For many years counterintelligence was a major source of friction between the CIA and the FBI. Some of the friction was a legacy of the resentment of longtime FBI director J. Edgar Hoover toward the CIA and the CIA's reciprocation of Hoover's feelings. The friction also stemmed from differing views of the problem. As noted, a discovered spy is a problem as well as a counterespionage opportunity that the CIA may wish to exploit. However, for the FBI, spying is a prelude to prosecution. As late as the Ames case of the early 1990s, the CIA and FBI were not coordinating their counterintelligence efforts, which probably prolonged Ames's activities. As a result of Ames's arrest and the subsequent investigation, the CIA and FBI created a jointly staffed counterintelligence office, to correct the mistakes of the past.

In 1999, as part of a government-wide response to revelations about Chinese espionage, the FBI proposed dividing its National Security division into two separate divisions, one to deal with counterespionage and one to deal with terrorism. It also proposed broadening the National Security Threat List, on which it assesses counterespionage threats, to include corporations and international criminal organizations as well as foreign governments.

In addition to the FBI, which has the primary CI responsibility in the United States, and the CIA, the Defense Investigative Service and the counterintelligence units of virtually all intelligence agencies or offices share some CI responsibility. The diffusion of the CI effort reflects the organization of the community and also highlights why coordination on CI cases has been problematic.

Double agents raise a host of concerns about loyalty. Have they really been turned, or are they playing a role while remaining loyal to their own service? Investigations of U.S. citizens suspected of spying raise legal issues because of constitutional safeguards of civil liberties. Domestic phones can be tapped, but only after intelligence agents have obtained a warrant from a special federal court (the Foreign Intelligence Surveillance Court) set up by the Foreign Intelligence Surveillance Act of 1978 (FISA, pronounced "fy-za") to review such applications. Agents also use other intrusive techniques, such as listening devices or going through garbage.

Prosecuting intelligence officers for spying was a major source of concern for the intelligence agencies, which feared that accused spies would threaten to reveal classified information in open court as a means of avoiding prosecution. This was known as "graymail" (as opposed to blackmail). To preclude this possibility, Congress in 1980 passed the Classified Intelligence Procedures Act (also known as the Graymail Law), which allows judges to review classified material in secret, so that the prosecution can proceed without fear of publicly disclosing sensitive intelligence.

As VENONA confirms, the espionage threat during the cold war was pointed and obvious, even though some cases of Soviet espionage—such as those of Rosenberg and Hiss—still remain controversial to a few. But, as the Ames case showed, Russian espionage did not end with the cold war. Indeed, neither did U.S. activities against Russia, given the various Russians arrested by dint of Ames's spying. In 1999 the Cox Committee, created by the House of Representatives, found that China had stolen U.S. nuclear weapons designs, apparently during the 1980s, when the two states were tacit allies against the Soviet Union. Assessing the nature and scope of the espionage threat to the United States may be more difficult in the post-cold war world than it had been before the demise of the Soviet Union, not only because the ideological conflict is over but because the sources and goals of penetrations may have changed. But it would be naïve to believe that the need for rigorous counterintelligence and counterespionage ended with the end of the cold war.

KEY TERMS

CI
compartmented
counterespionage
counterintelligence
double agents

graymail
mole
need to know
polygraph

FURTHER READINGS

Reliable and comprehensible discussions of counterintelligence—apart from mere "spy stories"—are rare.

Benson, Robert Louis, and Michael Warner, eds. *VENONA: Soviet Espionage and the American Response, 1939–1957.* Washington, D.C.: National Security Agency and Central Intelligence Agency, 1996.

Godson, Roy S. *Dirty Tricks or Trump Cards: U.S. Covert Action and Counterintelligence.* Washington, D.C.: Brasseys, 1995.

Hood, William, James Nolan, and Samuel Halpern. "Myths Surrounding James Angleton: Lessons for American Counterintelligence." Washington, D.C.: Working Group on Intelligence Reform, Consortium for the Study of Intelligence, 1994.

Johnson, William R. *Thwarting Enemies At Home and Abroad: How To Be a Counterintelligence Officer.* Bethesda, Md.: Stone Trail Press, 1987.

Perkins, David D. "Counterintelligence and Human Intelligence Operations." *American Intelligence Journal* 18, nos. 1 and 2 (1988).

Shulsky, Abram N., and Gary J. Schmitt. *Silent Warfare: Understanding the World of Intelligence.* 2d rev. ed. Washington, D.C.: Brasseys, 1983.

U.S. House Permanent Select Committee on Intelligence. *Report of Investigation: The Aldrich Ames Espionage Case.* Report, 103d Congress, 2d session. 1994.

U.S. House Permanent Select Committee on Intelligence. *United States Counterintelligence and Security Concerns—1986.* Report, 100th Congress, 1st session. 1987.

U.S. House Select Committee on U.S. National Security and Military/Commercial Concerns with the People's Republic of China (Cox Committee). Report, 106th Congress, 1st session. 1999.

Zuehlke, Arthur A. "What is Counterintelligence?" In *Intelligence Requirements for the 1980s: Counterintelligence,* edited by Roy S. Godson. Washington, D.C.: National Strategy Information Center, 1980.

CHAPTER 8

The Intelligence Process—
Covert Action

Covert action is, along with spying, a mainstay of popular conceptions of intelligence. Like spying, covert action is fraught with myths and misconceptions. Covert action, even when understood, remains one of the most controversial of intelligence topics.

Covert action is defined in the National Security Act, Sec. 503 (e), as "An activity or activities of the United States Government to influence political, economic or military conditions abroad, where it is intended that the role of the United States Government will not be apparent or acknowledged publicly."

Some intelligence specialists have objected to the phrase "covert action," believing that the word "covert" emphasizes secrecy over policy. (The British had earlier referred to this activity as "special political action"—SPA.) This is an important distinction, because even though these activities are, indeed, secret, the most important point is that they are undertaken as one means to advance policy goals. This cannot be stressed enough. Proper covert actions are undertaken because policy makers have determined that these are the best way to achieve a desired end. These operations are not—or should not be—undertaken on the initiative of the intelligence agencies.

During the Carter administration (1977–1981)—which exhibited some qualms about force as a foreign policy tool—the innocuous and somewhat comical phrase "special activity" was crafted to replace covert action. The administration replaced a euphemism with a euphemism. But when the Reagan administration came into office, with very different views on intelligence policy, it continued to use the phrase "special activity" in its executive order governing intelligence.

Ultimately, what these activities are called should not matter that much. The fact that the United States has gone through these various changes in appellation are interesting in that they reveal a degree of official discomfort with the tool.

The classic rationale behind covert action is that policy makers need a "third option" (yet another euphemism) between doing nothing (the first option) in a situation where vital interests may be threatened and sending in military force (the second option), which raises a host of difficult political issues. Not everyone would agree with this rationale, including those who would properly note that diplomatic activity is more than "doing nothing" without resorting to force.

As with counterintelligence, it is pertinent to ask whether covert action was a product of the cold war and whether it remains relevant today. As noted in chapter 2, covert action became—under the leadership of DCI Allen Dulles during the Eisenhower administration (1953–1961)—an increasingly attractive option. It had both successes and failures, but it was seen as a useful tool in a broad-based struggle with the Soviet Union. In the post-cold war period one could conceive of situations—against terrorists or narcotics traffickers—where some sort of covert action might be the preferred means of action.

THE COVERT ACTION DECISION-MAKING PROCESS

To repeat, covert action makes sense—and should be undertaken—only when tasked by duly authorized policy makers in pursuit of specific policy goals that cannot be achieved by any other means. Covert action cannot substitute or compensate for a poorly conceived policy. The structure that follows, therefore, presumes that policy makers have formulated legitimate policy goals and that covert action is a viable means of achieving them. The planning process for covert action must begin with policy makers justifying the policy and defining clearly the national security interests and goals that are at stake.

Maintaining a covert action capability entails expenses, not only for an operation itself but also for the infrastructure involved in mounting a covert action. Even though covert actions are not planned and executed overnight, a certain level of preparedness—such as equipment, transportation, false documents, and trained personnel, including foreign assets—must be kept on hand at all times. Forming and maintaining this stand-by capability takes time and costs money. But the key question at this point in the decision-making process is whether the cost of carrying out a covert action is justified. Cost becomes especially important when looking at covert actions that may run for months or longer.

Alternatives to covert action are a key issue. If overt means of producing a similar outcome are available, then these alternatives will almost certainly be preferable to a covert action. Using them does not preclude the use of covert action later if the overt means fail, or in conjunction with overt means, but the overt means should be tried first.

Policy makers and intelligence officials examine at least two levels of risk before approving a covert action. The first is the risk of exposure. Former DCI William Colby—perhaps reflecting the large-scale investigations of intelligence that dominated his tenure as DCI (1973–1976)—said a director should always assume that an operation will become known at some point. Clearly, there is a difference between an operation that is exposed while under way or shortly after its conclusion and an operation that is revealed years later. Nonetheless, even a much postponed exposure may prove to be embarrassing or worse.

The second risk to be weighed is the risk of failure. Failure may be costly at several levels: in human lives and as a political crisis both for the nation carrying out the operation and for those it may be trying to help as well. Decision makers must weigh the relative level of risk against the interests that are at stake. A highly risky operation may still be worth undertaking if the stakes are high enough and there are no alternatives. In other words, the ends may justify the means, or at least the risks. For example, in the 1980s the United States was looking for ways to aid the Mujaheddin rebels in Afghanistan fighting Soviet invaders. One option was to arm the rebels with Stinger antiaircraft missiles, which would counter the successful Soviet use of helicopters. But policy makers were concerned that some Stingers would fall into the wrong hands, even be captured by the Soviets. Ultimately, the Reagan administration decided to send the Stingers, which helped turn the course of the war. It also left Stingers in the hands of the Mujaheddin after their victory, but policy makers deemed that a smaller risk than Soviet victory in Afghanistan.

Even though intelligence analysis and operations exist only to serve policy, intelligence officers may be eager to demonstrate their covert action capabilities. Several factors may drive officers to do so: a belief that they can deliver the desired outcome; a bureaucratic imperative to prove their value; their professional pride in doing this type of work. However, unless the operation is closely tied to agreed-upon policy goals and supported as a viable option by the policy community, it starts off severely hampered. Thus, covert action planners must closely coordinate their plans and actions with policy offices.

Covert actions are extraordinary steps, something between the states of peace and war. That alone is enough to raise broad ethical questions, although their willingness to maintain a covert action capability indicates some agreement among policy makers over the propriety of its use. The specific details of an operation are likely to raise ethical issues as well. Should a democratically elected government that is procommunist be subverted and overthrown (Guatemala, 1954)? Should a nation's economy be disrupted—with attendant suffering for the populace—to over-throw the government (Cuba, 1960s)? Should a group opposed to a hostile government be armed, with a view toward fomenting an insurgency (Nicaragua, 1980s)? These issues are important not only intrinsically, but also because of the risk of exposure. How do these actions fit with the causes, standards, and morals that the United States supports?

In evaluating proposed covert actions, policy makers should examine analogous past actions. Have other operations been tried in this same nation or region? What were the results? Are the risk factors different? Has this type of operation been tried elsewhere? Again, with what results? As common sense as these questions seem to be, they run up against a fascinating governmental phenomenon: the inability to use historical examples. Decision makers are so used to concentrating on near-term issues that they tend not to remember accurately past analogous situations in which they have been involved. They move from issue to issue in rapid succession, with little respite and even less reflection. Or, as Ernest R. May and Richard Neustadt pointed out in *Thinking in Time: The Uses of History for Decision Makers* (1988), decision makers "learn" somewhat false lessons from the past, which they misapply to new circumstances.

Congressional reaction to covert actions is more an issue for the United States than for other democracies. The congressional committees that oversee the intelligence community are an integral part of the process, not only for funding but as decision makers who need to be apprised of a planned operation and whose support is important although not mandatory.

Having laid out the factors that must be considered in evaluating a proposed covert action, it is worth describing the process by which covert actions are ordered in the United States. To repeat, covert actions should be closely tied to agreed policy goals, and they usually are not planned overnight. The long lead times required for covert actions also mean they can be put into the budget process in advance, so that funds can be allocated for them.

Assuming that all of the questions raised above have been successfully answered, the action still requires formal approval. The president must sign an order approving the operation based on his finding that the operation is "necessary to support identifiable foreign policy objectives of the United States, and is important to the national security of the United States." In intelligence parlance, this document is called a "presidential finding." Congress and the American public did not know that the president signed off on each operation until Secretary of State Henry Kissinger was forced to reveal as much before a congressional committee in the mid-1970s. Presidential findings are now required by law and must be in writing (with exceptions for emergencies, in which cases a written record must be kept and a finding produced within forty-eight hours).

The finding is transmitted not only to those responsible for the operation but to Congress (the House and Senate Intelligence Committees, or a more limited congressional leadership group) as well. Often, because of the long timelines involved, the congressional committees will already have learned about the operation via the budget process, which includes a review of the year's covert action plan. Congress may wish to be briefed on the specifics of the finding and the operation as well. These briefings are advisory in nature. Other than denying funding during the budget process, Congress has no basis for approving or disapproving an operation, unless specific laws or executive orders ban them—such as the various acts passed by Congress in the 1980s limiting aid to the contras, or the executive order banning assassination.

However, should committee members or the staffs raise serious questions, a prudent covert action briefing team will report that fact to the executive. This should be enough to cause the operation to be reviewed. The executive branch may still decide to go ahead, or it may make changes in the operation to respond to congressional concerns.

The covert action policy system, for all of its rules, remains fragile by the fact of it being covert. The Iran-contra scandal underscored some of its weaknesses. The main points of the scandal are as follows: Congress, opposed to support for the contras in Nicaragua, cut off funding. President Reagan, in his usual broad manner, urged his NSC staff to help the contras "keep body and soul together." NSC staffer Lt. Col. Oliver North did this by soliciting donations from private individuals and foreign governments. North alleged that DCI Casey, who died just as the scandal broke, approved these activities. North also argued that Congress's restrictions applied to Defense Department and intelligence agencies, and not to the NSC staff. In parallel, the NSC staff pursued clandestine efforts to improve ties to Iran and to free hostages in the Middle East, despite earlier objections to this policy by the secretaries of state (George Shultz) and defense (Caspar Weinberger). Israel shipped antitank missiles to Iran at the behest of the NSC staff, with the U.S. replacing them. North became involved in the Iranian initiative as well and suggested diverting the money paid by Iran to the contras.

Iran-contra pointed up several problems in the covert action process:

- there were questionable delegations of authority to order and manage covert actions (the actions of North on the NSC staff);
- presidential findings were postdated and signed ex post facto (the finding authorizing the sale of missiles to Iran);

- disparate operations were merged (using the Iranian money to fund the contras); and
- the executive branch failed to keep Congress properly informed (disregarding the laws restricting aid to the contras and not briefing on the finding to sell missiles to Iran).

Debates on the worthiness of the respective policies involved in Iran-contra notwithstanding, NSC staff and other executive branch officials violated a host of accepted norms and rules in managing the operations.

THE RANGE OF COVERT ACTIONS

Covert actions cover many types of activities. Several of the main types will be discussed here, going from the least to the most violent.

Propaganda is the very old political technique of disseminating information that has been created with a specific political outcome in mind. Propaganda can be used to support individuals or groups friendly to you or to undermine your opponents. Propaganda can be used to create false rumors of political unrest, economic shortages, or direct attacks on individuals, to name a few techniques. Propaganda is usually carried out in mass media outlets.

Political activity is a step above propaganda, although the two may be used together. But political activity tends to be more pointed; through political activity, an intelligence operation intervenes more directly in the political process of the targeted nation. As with propaganda, political activity can be used to help friends or to impede foes. For example, in the late 1940s the United States supplied scarce newsprint to centrist, anti-communist political parties in Italy and France during closely contested elections. The United States has also funneled money to political parties overseas to help during elections. Or, a state can use political activity more directly against its foes—disrupting rallies, interfering with their publications, and so on.

The United States has tended to use economic activity against governments deemed to be hostile. Every political leadership—democratic or totalitarian—worries about the state of its economy. The economy has the greatest daily effect on the population: the availability of needed food and commodities, the stability of prices, the relative ease or difficulty with which basic daily needs can be met. Economic unrest often leads to political unrest. Again, other techniques may be used in conjunction with economic activity, such as propaganda to create false fears about shortages. Or the economic techniques may be more direct, such as attempts to destroy vital crops or to flood a state with counterfeit currency so as to

FIGURE 8-1   The Covert Action "Ladder"

destroy faith in the monetary system. For years, the United States attacked Cuba's economy directly as well as indirectly via a trade embargo. Economic unrest was also a key factor in U.S. efforts to undermine the government of Salvador Allende in Chile in the early 1970s.

Coups, the actual overthrow of a government, either directly or through surrogates, are another step up on the covert action ladder. Again, a coup may be the culmination of many of the other techniques—propaganda, political activity, economic unrest. The United States used coups successfully in Iran in 1953 and in Guatemala in 1954. The United States was involved in undermining the Allende government, but the coup that brought down his government was indigenous.

Paramilitary operations represent the largest, most violent, and most dangerous covert actions. They involve equipping and training large armed groups with a view toward a direct assault on your enemies. They do not involve the use of a state's own military personnel in combatant units, which technically would be an act of war. The United States was successful in this type of operation in Afghanistan in the 1980s but failed abysmally at the Bay of Pigs in 1961. The contra war against the Sandinistas in Nicaragua was neither won nor lost, but the Sandinistas were defeated at the polls when they held a free election amid a deteriorating economy.

Some nations have also practiced a "higher" level of covert military activity—secret participation in combat. For example, Soviet pilots flew combat missions during the Korean War against U.N. (primarily U.S.) aircraft. This type of activity raises several issues: military action without an act of war and possible retaliation; and the rights of combatants if captured. The United States has largely eschewed this practice because of these complications, preferring to allow intelligence officers to take part in paramilitary activities.

ISSUES IN COVERT ACTION

Covert action, both in concept and practice, raises a host of issues. This section will pose questions more than provide answers.

The most fundamental issue is whether such a policy option is "legitimate." As with most questions of this sort, there is no "correct" answer. One can divide the prevailing opinions into two schools—idealists and pragmatists. Idealists argue that covert intervention by one state in the internal affairs of another violates acceptable norms of international behavior. They argue that the very concept of a third option is illegitimate. Pragmatists may accept the arguments of the idealists but argue that the self-interest of a state occasionally makes covert action necessary and legitimate. Historical practice over several centuries would tend to favor the pragmatists. Idealists would respond that the historical record still does not justify covert intervention. (This debate took a curious turn with passage of the 1998 Iraq Liberation Act, in which Congress and the president agreed to spend $97 million to replace the regime of Saddam Hussein—an overt commitment to interfere in Iraq's internal affairs.)

We can move from this abstract argument on propriety and legitimacy to a more specific discussion about the U.S. use of covert action during the cold war. In several instances during the nineteenth and twentieth centuries the United States intervened in other nations, primarily in the Western Hemisphere. But those interventions were largely overt and usually military in nature. The United States began to use covert action in the context of the cold war. Did the nature of the Soviet threat make covert action legitimate? Did the use of this option—not only directly against the Soviet Union but in Third World nations that were often the battlegrounds of the cold war—lessen the moral differences between the United States and the Soviet Union? Again, there are broad differences of opinion. To the U.S. policy makers during the administrations of Harry S. Truman (1945–1953) and Dwight D. Eisenhower (1953–1961) the Soviet threat was so large and multifaceted that the question of the legitimacy of covert action never really arose. Indeed, they preferred covert action to the possibility of a general war in Europe. On the other hand, some people believe that the use of this option blurred distinctions between the two nations that should have been important.

Assuming that, in broad terms, covert action is an acceptable option, is it circumscribed by the nature of the state against which it is being carried out? Or does this question become irrelevant if one accepts the legitimacy of covert action? For example, the United States used covert economic destabilization against Castro's Cuba and Allende's Chile. Both were communists, but Castro had seized power after a guerrilla war; Allende never commanded an electoral majority, but he had been elected according to the Chilean constitution. Castro turned Cuba into a hostile Soviet base. Allende showed only disturbing signs of friendliness to Castro and to other Soviet allies. Rather than have a second Soviet satellite in the Western Hemisphere, the United States opted to destabilize Allende in the hopes of fomenting a coup against him. Should the fact that Allende had been elected according to Chilean law have been sufficient to preclude covert action by the United States? Or were U.S. national security concerns of sufficient primacy to make the covert option legitimate? This was not the first time the United States had intervened in democratic processes. As noted, the U.S. gave covert assistance in a variety of forms to centrist parties in Europe in the late 1940s to preclude communist victories.

Central to the U.S. concept of covert action has been the concept of "plausible deniability": that U.S. denials of a role in the events stemming from a covert action would appear plausible. The need to mask the role of the United States stems directly from the idea that the action has to be covert. If the situation could be addressed overtly, then the role of the United States would not be an issue.

Plausible deniability depends almost entirely on the origin of the action remaining covert. Once that is lost, deniability is barely plausible. Deniability may have been sustainable during the 1950s and 1960s, but it has become more difficult to sustain since the revelation that the president signs each finding to order a covert action.

The scale of the activity also matters. For example, in the aftermath of the Bay of Pigs debacle, President John F. Kennedy sought counsel from his predecessor, President Eisenhower. Kennedy defended his decision not to commit U.S. air power to assist the invasion on the grounds of maintaining deniability of a U.S. role. Eisenhower scoffed, asking how— given the scale and nature of the operation—the U.S. could plausibly deny a role.

Plausible deniability raises concerns about accountability as well. If one of the premises of covert action policy is the ability to deny a U.S. role, does this also allow U.S. officials to avoid responsibility for an operation that is controversial or perhaps even a failure? Or does the fact that the president must sign a finding put the responsibility on him?

The main controversy raised by propaganda activities is that of "blowback." The CIA is precluded from undertaking any intelligence activities within the United States. It is possible, however, for a story that is planted in a media outlet overseas to be reported back in the United States. That is blowback. This risk is probably higher today with global twenty-four-hour news agencies than it was during the early days of the cold war. Thus, inadvertently, a CIA-planted story that is false can be reported in a U.S. media outlet. In such a case, does the CIA have a responsibility to inform the U.S. media outlet of the true nature of the story? Would doing so compromise the original operation? If such notification should not be given at the time, should it be given afterward?

Not all covert actions remain covert. One of the key determinants seems to be the scale of the operation. The smaller and more discreet the operation, the easier it is to keep secret. But as operations become larger, especially paramilitary operations, the ability to keep them covert declines rapidly. Two operations undertaken during the Reagan administration—aid to the contras in Nicaragua and to the Mujaheddin in Afghanistan—illustrate the problem. Should the possibility of public disclosure affect decision makers when they are considering paramilitary operations? Or should disclosure be accepted as one of the costs of undertaking this type of effort, with the understanding that it is likely to be something less than covert and not plausibly deniable?

Despite the desired separation between intelligence and policy, covert action blurs the distinction in ways that analysis does not. Instead of providing intelligence to assist in the making of decisions, through covert action the intelligence community is being asked to help execute policy. Of necessity, the intelligence community will have a role in determining the scale and scope of an operation, about which it has the greatest knowledge. The intelligence community will also have a day-to-day role in managing an operation.

The distinction blurs further because the intelligence community has a vested interest in the outcome of a covert action in ways that are vastly different from its interest in the outcome of a policy for which it has provided analysis. Covert action is not just an alternative means of achieving a policy end; it is also a means for the intelligence community to demonstrate its capabilities and its value.

Thus, covert action makes the policy and intelligence community closer collaborators, as the separation between them diminishes. Conversely, the intelligence community takes on additional responsibilities in the eyes of the policy community. The intelligence community will bear a greater burden for a less-than-successful covert action than it will for less-than-perfect intelligence analysis.

Paramilitary operations raise numerous questions, some of which have already been addressed above. In addition to the problem of keeping them covert and the strains they put on plausible deniability, paramilitary operations raise serious questions about the amount of time available to achieve their stated goals. Unless these operations appear to have a reasonable chance of success in a well-defined period of time, policy makers find their ensuing options rather limited. On the one hand, they can decide to continue the operation even if the chances of success—usually defined as some sort of military victory—appear slim. It may be that the paramilitary force is unlikely to be defeated but unlikely to win, offering the prospect of an open-ended operation. Alternatively, policy makers can decide to terminate the operation. The abandonment of the Kurds by the United States in the 1970s is a case in point. Briefly, the United States had been supporting the Kurds in their struggle against Iraq to create an independent homeland. The United States provided covert aid to the Kurds via Iran, which also had an interest in weakening its neighbor. The Kurdish effort remained inconclusive. In the mid-1970s, however, the shah decided to resolve his differences with Iraq and ordered the operation to cease. The United States complied, abruptly leaving the Kurds to fend for themselves. But when an operation such as the Kurdish one is shut down, it may not be possible to extricate all of the combatants. In such a case, what is the obligation of the power backing the operation to the combatants? Do the combatants understand the risks they have undertaken, or are they really assets of the power that is backing the covert action?

Within the United States debate continues about which agency should be responsible for paramilitary operations: the CIA or the Defense Department. The CIA has traditionally run paramilitary operations because, initially, the Defense Department wanted no involvement in them. Second, if covert action is an alternative to military operations, the Defense Department might find it difficult to keep the two options separate. International law poses a third difficulty. Although there is no international sanction for covert action, the target may consider the use of military personnel (in uniform) in such an activity to be an act of war. Finally, the involvement of the Defense Department may undercut the effort to achieve plausible deniability.

On the other hand, the Defense Department has greater expertise in the conduct of military operations and has a greater infrastructure to carry them out, which might save some money. Removing paramilitary operations from the CIA might also save the intelligence community from some of the internal strains caused by having responsibility for both analysis and operations (see below). Of course, new strains might subsequently appear in the Defense Department.

One concern raised by the conduct of covert actions is their possible effect on intelligence analysis, which is carried out, in part, by the same agency conducting the operation. If the CIA is conducting an operation—particularly a paramilitary operation—is it reasonable to expect the analytical part of the CIA to produce objective reports on the situation in that country and the progress of the paramilitary operation? Or will there be a certain impetus, perhaps unstated, to be supportive of the operation? DCI Allen Dulles kept the Directorate of Intelligence—the CIA's analytical arm—ignorant of operations in Indonesia (1957–1958) and at the Bay

Assassination: The Hitler Argument

Adolf Hitler is often cited as a good argument in favor of assassination as an occasional but highly exceptional policy option. The arguments in favor of assassinating Hitler are fairly obvious, but when would a policy maker have made that decision? Hitler assumed power legally in 1933. Throughout the 1930s he was not the only dictator in Europe who repressed civil liberties or arrested and even killed large numbers of his own population. Indeed, Joseph Stalin probably killed more Soviet citizens during collectivization and the great purges than the Nazis sent to death camps. Deciding to kill Hitler prior to his attacks on the Jews or the onset of World War II would have required a fair amount of foresight as to his ultimate purposes. Indeed, very little about Hitler was extraordinary until he invaded Poland in 1939 and approved the "final solution" against the Jews in 1942.

Interestingly, Britain revealed in 1998 that British intelligence considered assassinating Hitler during the war, even as late as 1945. The British abandoned the plan not because of moral qualms or concerns about success but because they decided that Hitler was so erratic as a military commander that he was actually an asset for the Allies!

of Pigs (1961) so as not to "contaminate" them with knowledge of these operations.

In seventeenth- and (to a lesser extent) eighteenth-century Europe, statesmen occasionally used assassination as a foreign policy tool. Heads of state, who were royalty, were exempt from this occasional use of officially sanctioned assassination, but their ministers and generals were not. Soviet intelligence occasionally undertook "wet affairs," as it referred to assassinations. Israeli intelligence has allegedly killed individuals outside of Israel on several occasions. The Church Committee, a Senate select panel formed in 1975 to investigate allegations that the CIA had exceeded its charter, found in 1976 that the United States was involved in several assassination plots in the 1960s and 1970s—the most famous being that against Fidel Castro—although none succeeded.

Since 1976 the United States has formally banned the use of assassination, either directly by the United States or through a third party. This ban has been written into three successive executive orders, the most recent signed by President Reagan in 1981.

Still, the policy remains controversial. Although support for the ban was fairly widespread when instituted by President Gerald R. Ford, debate over the policy has been growing. Opponents continue to hold that it is

---

The Assassination Ban:
A Modern Interpretation

In August 1998 the United States launched a cruise missile attack against targets in Afghanistan associated with Osama bin Laden. The United States believed that bin Laden was behind the terrorist attacks earlier that month against two U.S. embassies in East Africa.

The Clinton administration later stated that one goal of the raid was to kill bin Laden and his lieutenants. Administration officials also argued that their targeting of bin Laden did not violate the longstanding ban on assassinations. Their view was based on an opinion written by National Security Council lawyers that the United States could legally target terrorist infrastructures and that bin Laden's main infrastructure was "human."

---

morally wrong for a state to target specific individuals. But some have argued that assassination might be the best option in some instances and might be morally acceptable, depending on the nature of the target. Drawing up such guidelines still appears to be so difficult as to preclude a return to the previous policy. (See chapter 13 for a more detailed discussion of the ethical and moral issues raised by assassination.)

ASSESSING COVERT ACTION

As with analysis, assessing covert action raises several issues. When assessing a covert action, what constitutes success? Is it just achieving the aims of the operation? Or should human costs, if any, be factored into the equation? Is the operation still a success if its origin has been exposed?

Some also question the degree to which covert actions produce useful outcomes. Critics point, for example, to the 1953 coup against Mohammad Mossadegh in Iran and argue that it helped lead to the Khomeini regime in 1979. On the other hand, proponents can argue that an operation that put in place a regime friendly to the United States for twenty-six years, in a region as volatile as the Middle East, was very successful.

As with all other policies, the record of covert action is mixed, and there are no hard-and-fast rules for assessing them. Assistance to anticommunist parties in western Europe in the 1940s was very successful; the Bay of Pigs was a fiasco. The view here is that the Mossadegh coup was a success, for the reasons noted above. But covert action is also subject to the law of unintended consequences. Abetting the fall of Allende helped lead to the regime of Gen. Augusto Pinochet. The average Chilean was probably better off, but many people suffered repression and a period of internal terror. Aid to the Mujaheddin in Afghanistan was highly successful and played an important role in the collapse of the Soviet Union. At the same time, Afghanistan remained mired in a civil war ten years after the last Soviet troops withdrew and is not friendly toward the United States.

To repeat the two key points: covert action tends to be successful the more closely it is tied to very specific policy goals and the more carefully defined the operation is.

KEY TERMS

blowback
covert action
paramilitary operations
plausible deniability

presidential finding
propaganda
third option

FURTHER READINGS

The works selected here do not go into the details of specific operations. Rather, they focus on the major policy issues discussed in this chapter.

Barry, James A. "Covert Action Can Be Just." *Orbis* 37 (summer 1993): 375–390.
Berkowitz, Bruce D., and Allan E. Goodman. "The Logic of Covert Action." *National Interest* 51 (spring 1998): 38–46.
Chomeau, John B. "Covert Action's Proper Role in U.S. Policy." *International Journal of Intelligence and Counterintelligence* 2 (fall 1988): 407–413.
Godson, Roy S. *Dirty Tricks or Trump Cards: U.S. Covert Action and Counterintelligence.* Washington, D.C.: Brasseys, 1996.
Johnson, Loch K. "Covert Action and Accountability: Decision-Making for America's Secret Foreign Policy." *International Studies Quarterly* 33 (March 1989): 81–109.
Knott, Stephen F. *Secret and Sanctioned: Covert Operations and the American Presidency.* New York: Oxford University Press, 1996.
Prados, John. *Presidents' Secret Wars: CIA and Pentagon Covert Operations Since World War II.* New York: William Morrow, 1986.
Reisman, W. Michael, and James E. Baker. *Regulating Covert Action: Practices, Contexts, and Policies of Covert Coercion Abroad in International and American Law.* New Haven, Conn.: Yale University Press, 1992.
Rositzke, Harry. *The CIA's Secret Operations: Espionage, Counterespionage and Covert Action.* New York: Reader's Digest Press, 1977.
Shulsky, Abram N., and Gary J. Schmitt. *Silent Warfare: Understanding the World of Intelligence.* 2d rev. ed. Washington, D.C.: Brasseys, 1993.
Treverton, Gregory F. *Covert Action: The Limits of Intervention in the Postwar World.* New York: Basic Books, 1987.

CHAPTER 9

The Intelligence Process—
The Role of the Policy Maker

The policy maker is not considered by most authors or experts to be part of the intelligence process. They believe that once the intelligence has been given over to the policy customers, the intelligence process is complete. As was stated in chapter 1, the view in this book is that the policy makers are so central at all stages of the intelligence process that to omit them is a mistake. Policy makers do more than receive intelligence; they shape it throughout the intelligence process. Indeed, without a constant reference to policy, intelligence is rendered meaningless. Moreover, as will be discussed in this chapter, policy makers can play a determining role at every phase of the intelligence process.

THE NATURE OF THE NATIONAL SECURITY POLICY PROCESS IN THE U.S. GOVERNMENT

Although much of this book is intended to be a generic discussion of intelligence, the main reference point is the U.S. government. Therefore, a brief discussion of how national security policy is formed in the United States is appropriate.

STRUCTURE AND INTERESTS.   The five main loci of the policy process are:

1. The president, as an individual
2. The departments, particularly the State Department and the Defense Department, which has two major components: the civilian (the Office of the Secretary of Defense) and the military (the Joint Chiefs of Staff and the Joint Staff). On certain issues, other departments may also be involved, including Justice, Commerce, Treasury, Agriculture

3. The National Security Council staff, which is the hub of the system

4. The intelligence community

5. Congress, which controls all expenditures, makes policy in its own right, and performs oversight

The main national security structure has been remarkably stable since its creation in the National Security Act of 1947.

These five groups have somewhat varying interests. The president is a transient, mainly concerned about broad policy initiatives and, eventually, his place in history. Richard Nixon, who was intensely suspicious of the permanent bureaucracy, argued—correctly—that a gulf exists between the president's interests and those of the permanent bureaucracy. Sometimes they will work together; at other times they will be at odds. The bureaucracy tends to be more jaded and, on occasion, to take the view that it can outlast the president, his appointees, and their preferred policies.

The main interest of the State Department is maintaining diplomatic relations as a means of furthering U.S. policy interests. Critics of the State Department argue that Foreign Service officers sometimes forget which nation they represent, becoming advocates for the nations on which they are expert rather than for the United States.

The Defense Department is primarily concerned about having a military capability sufficient to deter hostile nations from using force or to defeat any threats as quickly as possible. Critics of the Defense Department hold that the department overestimates its needs and threats and requires too large a margin against any potential foe. In the aftermath of Vietnam, the unofficial but very influential rules for the use of force promulgated by Secretary of Defense Caspar Weinberger and JCS Chairman Gen. Colin Powell set very high requirements for domestic political support and force preponderance by the United States before any troops should be committed.

Discussing the National Security Council requires a brief definition of terms. The NSC itself is defined in law. It consists of the president, the vice president, and the secretaries of state and defense. The chairman of the Joint Chiefs of Staff serves as the military adviser; the director of central intelligence is subordinate to the NSC and serves as the intelligence adviser. As a corporate group, the NSC meets irregularly. (A Deputies Committee, below the NSC, meets more often.) The NSC staff consists of career civil servants and political appointees who have day-to-day responsibility for conveying the wishes of the president to the policy and intelligence communities and for coordinating among the various departments and agencies. The NSC staff is primarily interested in the execution of policy as defined by the president and senior presidential appointees.

The intelligence community has no policy interests per se, although it has strong interests in staying informed about the course of policy so that it can make a contribution to it.

POLICY DYNAMICS—"THE INTERAGENCY."   Policy makers often refer to the "interagency process" or to "the interagency." The term reflects the involvement of any and all necessary agencies and players in the process. The ultimate goal of the U.S. policy process is to arrive at a consensus that all parties can support. But consensus means agreement down to the very last detail of any paper being considered.

The process has no "override mechanism," that is, no way of forcing agreement, of isolating an agency that refuses to go along. The reason for this is to safeguard the rights and interests of all agencies, because the agency that is isolated on an issue today may not be the one that is isolated tomorrow. To ensure that an agency is not coerced, the interagency process emphasizes bargaining and negotiation rather than majority rule. Bargaining has three immediate effects. First, it can require a great deal of time to arrive at positions that everyone can accept. Second, this system gives tremendous leverage to any agency that refuses to reach an agreement. In the absence of any override process, the agency that "just says 'no' " can wield enormous power. Third, the necessity of reaching agreement generates a great deal of pressure in favor of lowest-common-denominator decisions.

On controversial issues, the system can suffer inertia, as agencies constantly redraft papers that never achieve consensus or that one agency refuses to support, effectively bringing the system to a halt. The only way to break such logjams is for the NSC staff or someone higher, meaning the president and his senior appointees, to apply pressure from above. Without their intervention, the system will spin endlessly if the holdout agency continues to hold out. Senior pressure renews the impetus to reach a conclusion or raises the prospect that officials in the holdout agency will be told to support what the president wants or to resign. But without pressure from above, holdouts suffer no penalty.

Neither the policy community nor the intelligence community is a monolith. Each has multiple players with multiple interests, which do not always coincide with one another.

THE ROLE OF THE INTELLIGENCE COMMUNITY IN THE SYSTEM.   Policy makers accept the intelligence community as an important part of the system. But the role of intelligence varies with each administration and sometimes with each issue within an administration. The way in which an administration treats intelligence is the key determinant of the role that it plays.

Everyone accepts the utility of intelligence as part of the basis upon which decisions will be made. Again, translating this generality into practice is the important issue. Policy makers have many reasons to quibble with, carp on, or even ignore intelligence. As will be discussed below, policy makers do not necessarily view intelligence in the same way as those who are producing it.

Policy makers also accept that the intelligence community can be called upon to carry out certain types of operations. Again, the willingness to use this capacity and the specific types of operations that are deemed acceptable vary with the political leadership. The political leaders are the ones who must make the final decisions on operations and who will be held accountable, in a political sense, if the operations fail. To be sure, intelligence officers can and do get their share of the blame, but policy makers perceive that their own costs are much greater.

WHO WANTS WHAT?

The fact that the government is not a unitary, monolithic organization helps explain why policy makers and intelligence officers hold differing interests. At a very high macro level, everyone "wants the same thing"— successful national security policy. But this is so general a statement as to be misleading. Success can mean quite different things to policy makers and intelligence officials.

Policy makers (by which we mean the administration's senior political appointees and the president) define success as the advancement of their agenda. Even though there is broad continuity in U.S. foreign policy, each administration interprets goals individually and fosters initiatives that are uniquely its own. The success of an administration's agenda must be demonstrable in ways that are easily comprehended, because its successes are expected to have a political dividend. This is not as crass as it sounds. It is important to remember that national security policy is created within a political system and process, the ultimate rewards of which are election and re-election to national power. Finally, policy makers expect support for their policies from the permanent bureaucracy.

The intelligence community defines its goals differently. As noted in chapter 6, Sherman Kent said that intelligence officers had three wishes: to know everything; to be listened to; and to influence policy for the good, as they understand it. The intelligence community also wants to maintain its objectivity regarding policy. Intelligence officials do not want to become, or even to be seen as becoming, advocates for policies other than those that directly affect their activities. Only by maintaining their distance from policy can they hope to produce intelligence that is objective. But objectivity is not always easily achieved. To cite a recent example, Director of Central Intelligence George Tenet (1997–) was intimately involved in the Israeli-Palestinian negotiations in October 1998. The CIA took responsibility for creating a security relationship between the two sides. Thus, the CIA now has a vested interest in the outcome of the agreement, not because of any intelligence it has produced but because it has become a participant. In this sort of case, legitimate questions can be raised about the potential effect on subsequent analyses of the implementation of the agreement. Will analysts feel free to report that security arrangements are failing, if that is the case, knowing that their own agency is charged with implementing these same arrangements? The answer may be "yes," but it is subject to serious question.

The intelligence community also wants to be kept informed about policy directions and preferences. Although this would seem obligatory if the intelligence community is to be expected to provide relevant analysis, it does not always happen. All too often, policy makers do not inform intelligence, either by design or oversight. Behavior of this sort not only makes the role of intelligence more difficult but can lead to resentment that may be played out in other ways.

Finally, the policy makers' expectation of support from the permanent bureaucracy extends to the intelligence community. But their expectation may be for intelligence that supports known policy preferences, thus running the risk of politicization. Politicization can also work in the other direction. The intelligence officer's desire to be listened to (Kent's second wish) may lead to analysis that is meant to please the policy makers, either consciously or unwittingly. In either case, the desire for a good working relationship can directly undermine the desired objectivity of intelligence.

THE INTELLIGENCE PROCESS: POLICY AND INTELLIGENCE

The differences between the policy and intelligence communities—and the potential for tension—appear at each stage of the intelligence process.

REQUIREMENTS.   Requirements are not abstract concepts. Requirements, in reality, are the policy makers' agenda. All policy makers will have areas on which they must concentrate as well as those on which they wish to concentrate. There will also be areas on which they have no interest at all, but to which they must, on occasion, pay attention. This mixture of preferences will be very important in forming the agenda and thus the requirements. For example, Secretary of State James Baker was very clear, upon taking office in 1989, that he was not going to spend a lot of time on the Middle East. His preference was based not on a view that the region was unimportant, but rather on a view that he was unlikely to achieve much in the Middle East and that his own time was better spent elsewhere. Senior subordinates could handle the Middle East. Iraq's invasion of Kuwait undermined his choice. Ironically, it also helped lead to the Madrid conference—presided over by Secretary Baker—at which Israel and its Arab foes met as a group for the first time.

The intelligence community wants guidance as to the priorities of the agenda so that its collection and reporting can be as helpful as possible. At the same time, the intelligence community tends to understand that it rarely has the luxury of ignoring a region or issue entirely, even if it is not high on the agenda. Sooner or later, one of them is likely to blow up. That said, the intelligence community regularly makes resource choices that lead to some regions or issues receiving very little attention.

This difference in the approaches of policy makers and intelligence officials to requirements is not played out in formulating the requirements themselves, but in the ensuing parts of the intelligence process.

COLLECTION.   Policy makers tend not to be involved in the details of collection unless they involve political sensitivities. In those cases, policy makers can have direct and dramatic effects. *(See box, "Policy Makers and Intelligence Collection," p. 126.)* Their practical concerns lie, first, in the budget, as collection is one of the major costs, particularly in technical intelligence. But policy makers also tend to assume, incorrectly, that "everything" is being covered, at least at some minimal level. Thus, when one of the low priority issues explodes, policy makers expect that a certain low level of collection and on-the-shelf intelligence already exists, and that collection can be quickly increased. Both assumptions may be strikingly false.

The intelligence community would rather collect more than less, although officials recognize that they cannot cover everything and hope to get policy makers to concur in the areas they leave uncovered. Still, collection is the bedrock of intelligence. However, when policy makers place limits on collection, the intelligence community obeys, even if its preference is to collect. Like the policy makers, intelligence officials are aware of the costs of collection. But the intelligence community cannot spend more on collection than the policy community is willing to allocate in the first place. The customary practice is for the policy community to set limits on collection resources that are lower than the intelligence community would like.

Policy Makers and Intelligence Collection

In several instances, policy makers have intervened in intelligence collection for political reasons.

In Cuba, at the onset of the missile crisis in 1962, Secretary of State Dean Rusk opposed sending U-2s over the island because a Chinese Nationalist U-2 had recently been shot down over China and an Air Force U-2 had accidentally violated Soviet air space in Siberia. The need for imagery of possible Soviet missile sites in Cuba was great, but Rusk had other—also legitimate—concerns.

In Iran, several successive U.S. administrations imposed limits on intelligence collection. Basically, intelligence officers were not allowed to have contact with the opposition to the shah in the *souks* (the markets and bazaars), since this would offend the shah's regime. Instead, U.S. intelligence had to rely on the shah's secret police, Savak, which had an institutional interest in denying that any opposition existed. Thus, as the shah's regime unraveled in 1978–1979, policy makers denied U.S. intelligence the sources and contacts it needed to better analyze the situation or to influence the opposition.

Again, in Cuba, President Jimmy Carter unilaterally suspended U-2 flights as a gesture to improve bilateral relations. Carter came to regret his decision in 1980, when he faced the possibility that a Soviet combat brigade was in Cuba and he required better intelligence on the issue.

In each case, responsible political leaders made decisions that directly affected intelligence collection.

Finally, the intelligence community has a greater understanding, as would be expected, of the limits of collection at any given time. Intelligence officials know that they are not collecting everything. Indeed, they make decisions on a regular basis to exclude certain regions or issues from collection. The intelligence community sees no reasons to convey this fact to the policy makers. At one level, doing so is unnecessary. An uncovered region may stay quiet—which is the bet that the intelligence managers are making. At another level, it may undermine their relationship with policy makers. Why arouse concerns about collection coverage over an issue that is expected not to be of any significant priority? Obviously, their choices can lead to even worse relations should one of the regions suddenly become of concern and collection be found wanting.

Intelligence Uncertainties and Policy

In 1987 U.S.-Soviet negotiations were drawing to a close on the Intermediate Nuclear Forces (INF) Treaty. The U.S. intelligence community had three different methods for estimating the number of Soviet INF missiles that had been produced—all of which had to be accounted for and destroyed. Any final number given by the Soviet Union would be suspect.

Each of the three major intelligence agencies advocated its methodology and its number as the one that should go forward. But the senior intelligence officer responsible for the issue decided, correctly, that all three numbers had to go to President Reagan. Some agency representatives argued that this was simply pusillanimous hedging. But the intelligence officer argued that the president had to be aware of the intelligence uncertainties and the possible range of missile numbers before he signed the treaty. That was the right answer, rather than choosing, perhaps arbitrarily, among the methodologies.

ANALYSIS. Policy makers want information that will enable them to make an informed decision. But they do not come to this part of the process as blank slates or wholly objective observers. Policy makers already have preferred policies and outcomes, and they would like to see intelligence that supports their preferences. Again, this is not necessarily as crass as it sounds. It is only natural for policy makers to prefer intelligence that will enable them to go where they want. This attitude becomes problematic only when policy makers ignore intelligence that is compelling but contrary to their preferences.

Some policy makers also prefer to keep their options open for as long as possible. Indeed, they may resist making important decisions. (President Franklin Roosevelt often exhibited this behavior.) Intelligence can occasionally serve to limit options by indicating that certain options are either insupportable or may have dangerous effects or outcomes. This may serve as yet another area of friction.

Intelligence often deals in ambiguities and uncertainties. If a situation were known with certainty, there would be no need for intelligence. Honestly reported intelligence highlights uncertainties and ambiguities. (*See box, "Intelligence Uncertainties and Policy," this page.*) However, these may prove to be discomforting to policy makers, for several reasons. First, if their goal is intelligence that will help them make decisions, intelligence that is uncertain and ambiguous is going to be less helpful or perhaps even unhelpful. Second, some policy makers cannot appreciate why the multibillion-dollar intelligence community cannot resolve issues. Many policy makers assume that important issues are ultimately "knowable," when in fact many are not.

Policy makers may also be suspicious of intelligence that supports their rivals in the interagency policy process. They may suspect that rivals have consorted with the intelligence community to produce intelligence that undercuts their position. Finally, policy makers are free to ignore, disagree with, or even rebut intelligence and offer analyses of their own. This is inherent in a system that is dominated by the policy makers.

All of the behaviors noted above undermine Kent's second and third wishes (for the intelligence community to be listened to and to influence policy for the good). The intelligence community also tries to maintain its objectivity. The questions raised by some policy makers can undermine the ability of the intelligence community to fulfill Kent's two wishes and to be objective. Some of the conflicts or disconnects noted above can be avoided or ameliorated if the intelligence community makes an initial effort to convey to policy makers as early as possible the limits of intelligence analysis. The goal should be to establish realistic expectations and rules of engagement early on. (See box, "Setting the Right Expectations," p. 129.)

COVERT ACTION.   Covert action can be attractive to policy makers because it increases available options and theoretically decreases direct political costs. Policy makers may assume that an extensive "on-the-shelf" operational capability exists and that the intelligence community can mount an operation on fairly short notice. These assumptions are, in effect, the operational counterpart to the assumption that all areas of the world are receiving some minimal level of collection coverage.

Obviously, policy makers want covert actions that will be successful. As has been seen, success is easier to define for short-term operations. But as one gets into longer-term operations, success may be elusive. This can be a source of tension between the two communities, since the most senior policy makers tend to think in blocks of time no longer than four years—the tenure of a single administration. The intelligence community, as part of the permanent bureaucracy, can afford to think in longer periods of time. It does not face the deadline imposed by elections on the administration.

The intelligence community harbors a certain ambivalence about covert action. A covert action provides the intelligence community with an opportunity to display its capabilities in an area that is of extreme importance to policy makers. Covert action is also an area where the intelligence community's skills are unique and are less subject to rebuttal or

Setting the Right Expectations

During the briefings that each new administration receives, an incoming under secretary of state was meeting with one of his senior intelligence officers on the issue of narcotics. The intelligence officer laid out in detail all the intelligence that could be known about narcotics: amounts grown, shipping routes, street prices, and so forth. "That said," the intelligence officer concluded, "there is very little you will be able to do with this intelligence."

The under secretary asked why the briefing had ended in that manner.

"Because," the intelligence officer replied, "this is an issue where the intelligence outruns policy's ability to come up with solutions. You are likely to grow frustrated by all of this intelligence while you have no policy levers with which to react. I want to prepare you for this at the outset of our relationship so as to avoid problems later on."

The under secretary understood.

alternatives than is the community's analysis. However, the possibility of disagreement over covert action is high if policy makers request an operation that intelligence officials believe to be unlikely to succeed or inappropriate. Once the intelligence community is committed to an operation, it does not want to be left in the lurch by the policy makers. For example, in paramilitary operations, the intelligence community will likely feel more of an obligation to the forces it has enlisted, trained, and armed than will the policy makers. A decision to end the operation will not be viewed in similar ways by the two communities.

POLICY MAKER BEHAVIORS.   Just as certain analyst behaviors matter, so too certain policy maker behaviors matter. Not every policy maker consumes intelligence in the same way: some like to read, others like to be briefed. Policy makers are better served if they convey their preferences early on, rather than leave them to guesswork.

Policy makers do not always appreciate the limits of what can be collected and what can be known with certainty; the reasons behind ambiguity; and, occasionally, the propriety of intelligence. They will sometimes confuse the lack of a firm estimate with pusillanimity, when that may not be the case.

Given the range of issues on which they must work, senior policy makers will probably not be fully conversant with every issue. The best policy makers will know what they do not know and will take steps to learn more. Some will not be so self-aware and will either learn as they go or fake it.

The most dreaded reaction to bad news is "killing the messenger," referring to the practice of kings who would kill the herald who brought bad news. Of course, messengers—including intelligence officers—are no longer killed for bringing bad news. But bureaucratic deaths do occur. An intelligence official can lose access to a policy maker or be cut out of important meetings. Both consequences befell DCI John McCone (1961–1965) as he took issue with President Lyndon Johnson's strategy for the Vietnam War. Policy makers have also been known to bad-mouth intelligence officers behind their backs.

OTHER ISSUES.   Ideally, the relationship between policy makers and the intelligence community should be symbiotic: policy makers should rely upon the intelligence community for advice, which is a major rationale for the existence of the intelligence community. In order for the community to produce good advice, policy makers should keep intelligence officers informed as to the major directions of policy and their specific areas of interest and priority. That said, the relationship is not one of equals. Policy makers can exist and function without the intelligence community; the opposite is not true. Intelligence is dependent on policy for its existence; policy can exist without the support of intelligence.

The line that divides policy and intelligence—and the fact that policy makers can cross it but intelligence officers cannot—also affects the relationship. Policy makers tend to be vigilant in seeing that intelligence does not come too close to the line. However, policy makers may ask intelligence officers for advice in choosing among policy options—or for some action—that would take intelligence over the line. If intelligence officers decline, as they should to preserve their objectivity regardless of the outcome, they may create resentment on the part of policy makers. It is also important to remember that at the very highest levels of the intelligence community the line blurs and the DCI may be asked for advice that is, in reality, policy.

In the United States, partisan politics has also become a factor in the policy–intelligence relationship. Although there were differences in emphasis from administration to administration (such as the greater emphasis on political covert action in the Eisenhower administration), there was general continuity in intelligence policy. Moreover, until 1976 intelligence was not seen as part of the "spoils" of an election victory. DCIs were not automatically replaced with each new administration, as were the heads of virtually all other agencies and departments. President Richard Nixon (1969–1974) tried to use the CIA for political ends, in an attempt to curtail the investigations into Watergate. But it was the Carter administration (1977–1981) that ended the political "separateness" of the intelligence community. Jimmy Carter, in his 1976 campaign, lumped together Vietnam, Watergate, and the recent investigations of U.S. intelligence. When Carter won, DCI George Bush (1976–1977) offered to stay on and eschew all partisan politics, saying that the CIA needed some continuity after the investigations and four DCIs in as many years. President-elect Carter said he wanted a DCI of his own choosing. This was the first time a serving DCI had been asked to step down by a new administration. Similarly, Ronald Reagan made "strengthening the CIA" part of his 1980 campaign and also brought in a new DCI, William Casey (1981–1987). In a presidential transition within the same party, President Bush kept on DCI William Webster (1987–1991) for most of his term, but Bill Clinton replaced DCI Robert Gates (1991–1993) with James Woolsey (1993–1995). Thus, a partisan change in the White House now tends to mean a change in DCIs as well.

The argument made in favor of changing DCIs with a new administration is that the presidents must have a DCI with whom they are comfortable. But in the days of a nonpartisan DCI, many people in Washington emphasized the professional nature of the DCI (even those DCIs who were not career intelligence officers) and had the sense that intelligence was in some way "different" from the rest of the structure that each president inherited and filled with his own appointees. An objective intelligence community was not to be part of the partisan spoils of elections. The shift since 1977 has affected the policy–intelligence relationship by tagging DCIs with a partisan coloration that they did not have in the past. The shift has also meant a movement away from professional intelligence officers as DCIs. Although professionals were not the only people selected in the past, their selection is less likely in the future.

Finally, one must note the potential effect of external intrusions on the relationship, particularly that of the electronic news media. Contrary to popular belief, television news does not foster major changes in policy. It does serve as a means for states and their leaders to communicate, and it acts as a competitor to the intelligence community as an alternative source of information. The media do occasionally "scoop" the intelligence community. This is not a case of the media knowing things that the intelligence community does not. Rather, the electronic media—especially the twenty-four-hour operations such as CNN—put a premium on speed and have the capacity and willingness to make updates and corrections as necessary. The intelligence community does not have the same luxury and tends to take more time in preparing its initial report. Being scooped by the media can lead policy makers to believe mistakenly that the media offer much the same coverage—at greater speed and less cost—as the intelligence community.

This chapter has emphasized those issues on which the policy makers and the intelligence community are likely to come into conflict. It would be incorrect to suggest that conflict is the mainstay of the policy–intelligence relationship. Close and trusting working relationships prevail between policy makers and intelligence officers at all levels. But a good working relationship is not a "given," and it cannot be fully appreciated without understanding all of the potential sources of friction as well.

FURTHER READINGS

Despite its centrality to the intelligence process, the policy maker–intelligence relationship has not received as much attention as other parts of the process.

Betts, Richard K. "Policy Makers and Intelligence Analysts: Love, Hate or Indifference?" *Intelligence and National Security* 3, no. 1 (January 1988): 184–189.

Heymann, Hans. "Intelligence/Policy Relationships." In *Intelligence: Policy and Process,* edited by Alfred C. Maurer et al. Boulder, Colo.: Westview Press, 1985.

Hulnick, Arthur S. "The Intelligence Producer–Policy Consumer Linkage: A Theoretical Approach." *Intelligence and National Security* 1, no. 2 (May 1986): 212–233.

Kovacs, Amos. "Using Intelligence." *Intelligence and National Security* 12, no. 4 (October 1997): 145–164.

Lowenthal, Mark M. "Tribal Tongues: Intelligence Consumers and Intelligence Producers." *Washington Quarterly* 15 (winter 1992): 157–168.

Thomas, Stafford T. "Intelligence Production and Consumption: A Framework of Analysis." In *Intelligence: Policy and Process,* edited by Alfred C. Maurer et al. Boulder, Colo.: Westview Press, 1985.

CHAPTER 10

The Intelligence Process—
Oversight and Accountability

"Sed quis custodiet ipso custodes?" (But who will guard the guards?), the Roman poet and satirist Juvenal asked. The oversight of intelligence has always been a problem. The ability to control information is an important power in any state, whether democratic or despotic. Information that is not available by any other means and whose dissemination is often restricted is the mainstay of intelligence. By controlling an important body of information; by having expertise in surveillance, eavesdropping, and other operations; and by operating behind a cloak of secrecy, an intelligence apparatus always has the potential to threaten heads of government. Thus, government leaders' ability to oversee intelligence effectively is important.

In democracies, oversight tends to be a shared responsibility of the executive and legislative powers. The oversight issues are somewhat generic: budget, responsiveness to policy needs, control of operations, propriety of activities. Like the other chapters, this chapter will concentrate on the United States, which is unique in the large oversight responsibilities and powers that reside in the legislative branch. Other parliaments have committees devoted to intelligence oversight, but none have the same broad oversight powers.

EXECUTIVE OVERSIGHT ISSUES

Many of the oversight issues with which the executive deals have been discussed in earlier chapters. The core oversight question is whether the intelligence community is properly carrying out its functions, that is, whether the community is asking the right questions, is responding to policy makers' needs, is being rigorous in its analysis, and has the right operational capabilities (collection and covert action) on hand. Policy makers cannot trust the intelligence community to answer these ques-

A Linguistic Aside:
The Two Meanings of Oversight

Oversight has two definitions that are distinct, if not opposites:
- supervision; watchful care (as in "We have oversight of that activity.")
- failure to notice or consider (as in "We missed that. It was an oversight.")

In overseeing intelligence, Congress and the executive try to carry out the first definition and to avoid the second.

tions alone. At the same time, senior officials outside the intelligence community (the national security adviser, the secretaries of state or defense, the president) cannot maintain a constant vigil over such questions. Outside of the intelligence community itself, the NSC Office of Intelligence Programs is the highest level organization within the executive branch that provides day-to-day oversight and policy direction of intelligence.

Since the administration of Dwight D. Eisenhower (with two brief lapses), presidents have relied on the President's Foreign Intelligence Advisory Board (PFIAB) to carry out high-level and more objective oversight than the NSC Office of Intelligence Programs. PFIAB members are appointed by the president and usually include former senior intelligence and policy officials and individuals with relevant commercial backgrounds. (Since the 1990s, some appointees have been put on PFIAB largely as political favors.) PFIAB can respond to problems (such as the investigation of alleged Chinese spying at Los Alamos National Laboratory) or can initiate activities (such as the Team A–Team B competitive analysis on Soviet strategic capabilities and intentions).

The executive branch tends to focus its oversight on issues related to espionage and covert action. Espionage oversight tends to focus on lapses—such as the Ames case or allegations of Chinese espionage. For example, in 1999 PFIAB issued a scathing report on Department of Energy security practices related to the Chinese espionage. As with all other activities, executive branch organizations divide responsibility for overseeing covert action. The president is responsible for approving all covert actions, but the day-to-day responsibility for managing them resides with the DCI and the Directorate of Operations.

One oversight issue relating to covert action centers on the operating concept of "plausible deniability." In the case of large-scale paramilitary operations—such as the Bay of Pigs or the contras—deniability is somewhat implausible. But many covert actions are of a much smaller scale, where it is possible to deny plausibly any U.S. role. Some critics of covert action argue that plausible deniability undermines accountability by giving operators an increased sense of license. Since the president will deny any connection to their activities, they operate under less constraint. The critics raise an interesting point but overlook the professionalism of most officers.

Another covert action oversight issue has to do with broad presidential findings, sometimes called global findings, versus narrow ones. The broader the finding, and thus the less specificity it contains, the greater is the scope for the intelligence community to define the operations involved. This is not to suggest that the president should precisely define covert actions, but a broad finding does run a greater risk of disconnecting policy preferences from operations.

Policy makers must also be concerned about the objectivity of the intelligence community when it is asked to assess or to draw up a covert action. Once again, intelligence officers who feel a need to demonstrate their capabilities may not be able to assess in a cold-eyed manner the feasibility or utility of a proposed action.

Similar concerns may arise when assessing the relative success of an ongoing covert action. Have policy makers and intelligence officials agreed on the signs of success? Are these signs being seen? If not, what are the accepted timelines for terminating the action? What are the plans for terminating it?

Finally, can intelligence analysts offer objective assessments of the situation in a country where their colleagues are carrying out a major covert action—particularly a paramilitary one? This issue may be of heightened concern in view of the new and closer "partnership" between the Directorate of Operations and Directorate of Intelligence.

The propriety of intelligence activities also figures into oversight. Are the actions being conducted in accordance with law and with executive orders? All intelligence agencies have inspectors general and general counsels. In addition, the President's Intelligence Oversight Board (PIOB), a subset of PFIAB, can investigate in this area. However, the PIOB is a reactive body. It has no power to initiate investigations or to subpoena. It is dependent on executive branch officials referring issues to it. Nonetheless, the PIOB has carried out some useful classified investigations.

THE BASIS OF CONGRESSIONAL OVERSIGHT

Congress comes at intelligence oversight—and at all oversight issues, whether national security or domestic—from a different but equally legitimate perspective from that of the executive.

The concept of congressional oversight is established in the Constitution. Article I, section 8, paragraph 18 states: "Congress shall have the power . . . To make all Laws which shall be necessary and proper for carrying into Execution the foregoing Powers, and all other Powers vested by this Constitution in the Government of the United States, or in any Department or Officer thereof." Courts have found that this legislative power includes the power to require reports from the executive on the various issues subject to legislation. The ability to gain access to information, usually held by the executive, that is relevant to the functioning of the government is the essence of congressional oversight.

Apart from its constitutional mandate, a major factor driving Congress in all oversight is the desire to be treated by the executive as an equal branch of government. This is not always easy to achieve, since the executive branch ultimately speaks with one voice, that of the president, while Congress has 535 members. Indeed, this significant difference leads some to question whether Congress's constitutional authority works in reality.

Moreover, in the area of national security, Congress has often given presidents a fair amount of leeway to carry out their responsibilities as commander in chief. This is not to suggest that partisan debates do not arise over national security or even intelligence issues—such as the missile gap or the window of vulnerability. To the contrary, debate over national security has become more partisan in the post-cold war period, when the threats to U.S. national security have greatly decreased.

THE LEVERS OF CONGRESSIONAL OVERSIGHT

Congress has several levers by which it carries out its oversight functions.

BUDGET.   Control over the budget of the entire federal government is the most fundamental lever of congressional oversight. Article I, section 9, paragraph 7 of the Constitution states: "No money shall be drawn from the Treasury, but in consequence of appropriations made by law; and a regular statement and account of the receipts and expenditures of all public money shall be published from time to time."

The congressional budget process is complex and duplicative. It comprises two major activities: authorization and appropriation. Authorization consists of approving ("authorizing") specific programs and activities that will be funded. During the authorization process, authorizing committees suggest dollar amounts for the various programs. The House Permanent Select Committee on Intelligence and the Senate Select Committee on Intelligence are the primary authorizers of the intelligence budget. Some defense-related intelligence programs are authorized by the House and Senate Armed Services Committees. Appropriation consists of allocating specific dollar amounts to authorized programs. The defense subcommittees of the House and Senate Appropriations Committees perform this function for intelligence.

Technically speaking, Congress may not appropriate money for a program that it has not first authorized. If authorizing legislation does not pass before a congressional session ends (this has not happened to date for intelligence), the appropriations bills contain language stating that they will also serve as authorizing legislation until such legislation is passed. (President Bush once vetoed an intelligence authorization bill because Congress had written into it a requirement that the president give Congress forty-eight hours' prior notice of covert actions, but Congress ultimately passed a new authorization bill omitting that language.)

There is usually some tension between the authorizers and the appropriators. Authorization and appropriations bills sometimes vary widely. For example authorizers may approve a program to which the appropriators do not give significant money. This is called "hollow budget authority." Or, appropriators may vote money for programs or activities that have not been authorized. These funds are called "appropriated but not authorized" (or "A not A"). In both of these cases, the appropriators are calling the tune and taking action that disregards the authorizers. (*See box, "Congressional Humor: Authorizers versus Appropriators," p. 138.*)

When funds are appropriated but not authorized, the agency receives the money but may not spend it. Congress still has to pass a bill to authorize spending. Sometimes, however, an agency will submit a reprogramming request to Congress, asking permission to spend the money. Congress can agree informally to such a request. If Congress neither passes a new authorization bill nor approves a reprogramming request, then the money reverts to the Treasury at the end of the fiscal year.

The centrality of the budget to oversight should be obvious. In reviewing the president's budget submission and crafting alternatives or variations, Congress gets to examine the size and shape of each agency, the details of each program, and the plans for spending money over the next year. No other activity offers the same degree of access or insight. Moreover, given the constitutional requirement for congressional approval of all expenditures, in no other place does Congress have as much leverage as in the budget process.

Congressional Humor:
Authorizers versus Appropriators

The tension between those who sit on authorizing committees and those who sit on appropriations committees is pithily characterized by the following joke often heard on Capitol Hill:

"Authorizers think they are gods; appropriators know they are gods."

Critics of the annual budget process argue that it not only gives Congress insights and power but also subjects the executive to frequent perturbations in funding levels, since they can vary from year to year. Every executive agency dreams of having multiyear appropriations or "no year" appropriations, that is, money that does not have to be spent by the end of the fiscal year. Although some funds are allocated in each of these ways, Congress is resistant to doing so on a large scale, since this would fundamentally undercut its power of the purse.

The budget gives Congress power over intelligence. In the 1980s, for example, Congress used the intelligence budget to restrict Reagan administration policy in Nicaragua, passing a series of amendments sponsored by the chairman of the House Permanent Select Committee on Intelligence, Edward Boland (D, Mass.), that denied combat-support funds for the contras. Efforts to get around these restrictions led to the Iran-contra scandal.

HEARINGS.   Hearings are also essential to the oversight process, as a means of requesting information from responsible officials and of hearing alternative views from outside experts. Hearings can be open to the public or closed, depending on the subject under discussion. Given the nature of intelligence, a majority of the hearings of the two intelligence committees are closed.

Hearings are not necessarily hostile, but they are adversarial. Hearings are not objective discussions of policy. Each administration uses hearings as a forum for advancing its specific policy choices and as opportunities to "sell" policy to Congress and to interested segments of the public. Congress understands this and is a skeptical recipient of executive-branch information, regardless of party affiliation. Intelligence officials are somewhat exempt from "selling" policy, in that they often give Congress the views of the intelligence community on an issue without supporting or attacking a given policy. They gain some protection against congressional recriminations from the line separating policy and intelligence. (Executive branch policy makers may see the intelligence community's congressional testimony as unsupportive or as undermining policy—even if that was not the intelligence community's intent.) However, when intelligence officials testify about intelligence policies—capabilities, budgets, programs, intelligence-related controversies—then they are also in a "sales" mode vis-à-vis Congress.

NOMINATIONS.   The power to confirm or reject nominations is an extremely important political power, which resides in the Senate. Nominations for the DCI were not controversial until 1977, when President Jimmy Carter's nominee, Theodore Sorensen, withdrew his nomination after appearing before the Senate Select Committee on Intelligence and responding to a number of issues that had been raised publicly about him. The issues included Sorensen's wartime status as a conscientious objector, which raised questions about his willingness to use covert action; and the possible misuse of classified documents in his memoirs and in his defense of Daniel Ellsberg, the man who leaked the so-called Pentagon Papers (a Defense Department study of the Vietnam War), both of which raised concerns about his ability to protect intelligence sources and methods.

Since 1977 the Senate has held several other controversial DCI-nominee hearings. Robert Gates withdrew his first nomination in 1987 as the Iran-contra scandal unfolded. His second nomination, in 1991, featured a detailed investigation of charges that Gates had politicized intelligence in order to please policy makers. In 1997 Anthony Lake withdrew his nomination at the onset of what promised to be a grueling and perhaps unsuccessful series of hearings.

Critics of the nomination process—not just for intelligence positions but across the board—charge that the process has gotten increasingly political and increasingly personal, delving into issues that are not germane to the fitness of a nominee for office. Defenders of the process respond that it is a political process, that the Senate is not supposed to be a rubber stamp, and that careful scrutiny of a nominee may preclude embarrassments later on. Regardless of which view is correct, it is fair to say that the nomination process has become, in the late 1990s, so formidable as to convince some potential nominees to decline office.

TREATIES.   Advising and consenting to an act of treaty ratification is also a power of the Senate. Unlike nominations, which require a majority vote of the senators present, treaties require a two-thirds vote of those present. Intelligence became a significant issue in treaties during the era of U.S.-Soviet arms control in the 1970s. The ability to monitor adherence to treaty provisions was and is an intelligence function. U.S. policy makers also called upon the intelligence community to give "monitoring judgments" on various treaty provisions—that is, to adjudge the likelihood that "significant" cheating would be detected. The Senate Select Committee on Intelligence, created in 1976, was later given responsibility for evaluating the ability of the intelligence community to monitor arms control treaties. This committee gave the Senate another lever with which to influence intelligence policy. In 1988, for example, the Senate Select Committee on Intelligence, upon evaluating the Intermediate Nuclear Forces (INF) Treaty, and concerned about the upcoming Strategic Arms Reduction Treaty (START), demanded the purchase of additional imagery satellites. The Reagan administration, which had not been averse to spending money on intelligence, argued that the additional satellites were not necessary. However, the chairman of the Senate committee, David Boren (D, Okla.), made it clear that purchase of the satellites was the price of Senate consent to the treaties.

REPORTING REQUIREMENTS.   The separation of powers between the executive branch and Congress puts a premium on information. The executive tends to forward information that is supportive of its policies; Congress tends to seek fuller information so as to make decisions on more than just the views that the executive volunteers. One of the ways in which Congress has sought to institutionalize its broad access to information is to levy reporting requirements on the executive branch. Congress often mandates that the executive report on a regular basis (often annually) on specific issues, such as human rights practices in foreign nations, the arms control impact of new weapons systems, or, during the cold war, Soviet compliance with arms control and other treaties.

Reporting requirements, which grew dramatically in the aftermath of the Vietnam War, raise several issues. Does Congress require so many reports that it cannot make effective use of them? Do the reports place an unnecessary burden on the executive branch? Would the executive branch forward the same information if there were no reporting requirements?

INVESTIGATIONS AND REPORTS.   One of Congress's functions is to investigate, and it may investigate virtually any issue it desires. The modern intelligence oversight system arose from the congressional investigations of intelligence in the 1970s. Investigations tend to result in reports that summarize findings and offer recommendations for change. Investigations are effective tools in exposing shortcomings or abuses and in helping craft new policy directions. Every year the two intelligence committees report publicly on issues that have come before them. These reports may be brief because of security concerns, but they assure the rest of Congress and the public that effective oversight is being carried out and they create policy documents that the executive must consider.

HOSTAGES.   If Congress cannot get agreement from the executive branch on some issue, it may seek means of forcing the executive branch to agree. One way is to "take hostages"—that is, to withhold action on issues that are important to the executive until the desired action is taken. This type of behavior is not unique to Congress; it was noted as a bargaining tactic used by intelligence agencies in formulating NIEs and other interagency products.

The demands of the Senate Select Committee on Intelligence for new imagery satellites during the debate on the INF Treaty was one case of hostage taking. In 1993 Congress threatened to withhold action on the intelligence authorization bill until the CIA provided information on one of the Clinton administration's Defense Department nominees, Morton Halperin. Halperin eventually withdrew his nomination. Critics argue that hostage taking is a blunt and unwieldy tool; supporters of Congress argue that it is used only when other means of reaching agreement with the executive have failed.

PRIOR NOTICE OF COVERT ACTION.   One of Congress's main concerns is that it not be surprised by presidential actions, that it receive prior notice of them. Most members understand that prior notice is not the same as prior congressional approval, which is required for very few executive decisions. One of the areas where prior notice has been fought out is covert action. As a rule, Congress receives advance notice of covert action in a process that has been largely institutionalized, but successive administrations have refused to make prior notice a legal requirement. A congressional demand for at least forty-eight hours' notice of covert actions led to the first veto of an intelligence authorization bill, by President Bush in 1990.

ISSUES IN CONGRESSIONAL OVERSIGHT

Oversight of intelligence raises a number of issues that are part of the "invitation to struggle," as the separation of powers has often been called.

HOW MUCH OVERSIGHT IS ENOUGH?   From 1947 to 1975—the first twenty-eight years of the modern intelligence community's existence—the atmosphere of the cold war promoted fairly lax and distant congressional oversight. It was long characterized by a remark by Sen. Leverett Saltonstall (R, Mass.), a member of the Senate Armed Services Committee:

"There are things that my government does that I would rather not know about." This attitude was partially responsible for some of the abuses that investigators uncovered in the 1970s.

Working out the parameters of the new oversight system has not been easy. Successive administrations, regardless of party affiliation, have tended to resist what they have seen as unwarranted intrusions.

There is no objective way to determine the "proper" level of oversight. On the budget, Congress reviews each "line item." There is no other way to make informed judgments on how to allocate funds, which ultimately is Congress's decision. Reviewing specific covert actions may seem intrusive, but it also represents an important political step. If Congress allows the operation to proceed unquestioned, then the executive branch can claim political support should problems arise later. Similarly, serious questions raised by Congress are an important signal to rethink the operation, even if the ultimate decision is to go ahead as planned.

Does rigorous oversight require just detailed knowledge of intelligence programs, or does it require something more—such as information on alternative intelligence policies and programs? Congress has on occasion taken issue with the direction of intelligence policy and acted either to block the administration—such as the Boland amendments that blocked military support to the contras—or to demand changes, such as the purchase of the INF satellites.

SECRECY AND THE OVERSIGHT PROCESS.   The high level of security that intelligence requires imposes costs on congressional oversight. Members of Congress have security clearances by virtue of their election to office. Members must have clearances to carry out their duties. Security clearances are granted only by the executive branch, but there is no basis for the executive branch to grant or to deny clearances to members of Congress, since this would violate the separation of powers. At the same time, member clearances do not mean full access to the entire range of intelligence activities. Congressional staff who require clearances receive them from the executive branch after meeting the usual background checks and demonstrating a need to know. Congressional staff are not polygraphed as a prerequisite for clearances.

Although all members are deemed to be cleared, both the House and Senate limit the dissemination of intelligence to members who are not on the Intelligence Committees. Although this limitation replicates the acceptance of responsibility that all congressional committees have, in the case of intelligence it entails additional burdens for the committees since their information cannot be easily shared. Thus, the Intelligence Committees require special offices for the storage of sensitive material and must hold many of their hearings in closed session. Both houses have also created different levels of notification, depending on the sensitivity of the information. Intelligence officials may brief only the leadership, or the leaders and the chairman and ranking member of the Intelligence Committee, or some additional committee chairmen as well, or the full Intelligence Committees.

Despite these precautions and the various internal rules intended to punish leaks by members or staff, Congress as an institution has an image as a fount of leaks. This image of Congress is propagated mostly by the executive branch, which believes that it is much more rigorous in handling classified information. In reality, most leaks of intelligence and other national security information come from the executive, not from Congress. (In 1999 DCI George Tenet admitted before a congressional committee that the number of leaks from executive officials was higher than at any time in his memory.) This is not to suggest that Congress's record on safeguarding intelligence material is perfect, but it is far better than that of the CIA, the State or Defense Departments, or the staff of the NSC. The reason for Congress's better record is not superior behavior so much as relative levers of power. Leaks occur for a variety of reasons: to show off some special knowledge, to settle scores, or to promote or stop a policy. Other than the first motive, showing off, members of Congress—and their staffs— have much better means than leaks at their disposal to achieve ends two and three. They control spending, which is the easiest way to create or to end a policy or program. Even minority members and staff can use the legislative process, hearings, and the press to dissent from policies or to attempt to slow them down. Officials in the executive branch do not have the same leverage and so resort to leaks more frequently. However, the perception of Congress as a major "leaker" persists.

The other issue raised by secrecy is the effectiveness with which Congress can act as a surrogate for the public. The U.S. government ostensibly operates on the principle of "openness": that its operations and decisions should be known to the public. (There is nothing in the Constitution about "the public's right to know." The Constitution safeguards freedom of speech and of the press, but these are not the same as a right to information.) In the case of intelligence, the principle of openness does not apply. Some people accept the reasons for secrecy and accept the limitations that it places on public accountability. Others have concerns about Congress acting as the public's surrogate in executive oversight. Their reasons vary, from concerns about how forthcoming the executive branch is with Congress to concerns about how willing Congress may be to air information that is disquieting.

CONGRESS AND THE INTELLIGENCE BUDGET.   A recurring issue for Congress has been whether to reveal some aspects of the intelligence budget. As noted above, Article I, section 9, paragraph 7 of the Constitution requires that accounts of all public money be published "from time to time." The phrase "from time to time" is vague, and successive administrations used its vagueness to argue that their refusal to disclose the details of intelligence spending was permissible. Critics argued that this interpretation vitiated the constitutional requirement to publish some account at some point. Most advocates of publication were not asking for a detailed publication of the entire budget, but publication of at least the total spent on intelligence annually. *(See box, "Intelligence Budget Disclosure: Top or Bottom?" p. 145.)*

The argument over publishing some part of intelligence spending appeared to have ended effectively in 1997 when DCI George Tenet revealed that overall intelligence spending for Fiscal Year 1998 was $26.6 billion. Tenet revealed the number in response to a Freedom of Information Act suit, acting to end the suit and to limit the information that the intelligence community revealed. Tenet later refused to divulge the amount requested or appropriated for intelligence for Fiscal Year 1999, arguing that to do so would harm national security interests and intelligence sources and methods.

Nonetheless, it is instructive to review the arguments that both sides raised in the debate. Proponents of disclosure cited, first and foremost, the constitutional requirement for publication. They also argued that disclosure of this one number posed no threat to national security, since it revealed nothing about spending choices within the intelligence community.

Proponents of continued secrecy tended not to cite the "time to time" language of the Constitution, which was a weak argument at best. Rather, they argued that Congress was privy to the information and was acting on behalf of the public. They also raised concerns that disclosure of the overall number was just the beginning of more detailed disclosure. Noting how little this one number revealed (and implicitly accepting their opponents' argument that little security would be jeopardized by its disclosure), they argued that this initial disclosure would inexorably lead to pressure for more detailed disclosures about specific agency budgets or programs and that these disclosures would have security implications.

DCI Tenet's disclosure revealed that many public estimates of the size of the intelligence budget were fairly accurate, as was the estimate that the intelligence budget is roughly one-tenth the size of the defense budget. As disclosure proponents had long argued, national security did not unravel. However, as opponents argued, many who had advocated disclosure were left dissatisfied by how little information this one number revealed.

Disclosing the overall number entails political risks for U.S. intelligence. Relating spending to outputs is more difficult for intelligence than

---

Intelligence Budget Disclosure: Top or Bottom?

One of the curiosities of the debate over intelligence budget disclosure was the term used for the number most at issue. The overall spending total for intelligence was alternatively described as the "top line number" or the "bottom line number." It sometimes sounded as if people on the same side—those in favor of or opposed to disclosure—were at odds with themselves.

---

for virtually any other government activity. How much intelligence should we get for $26.6 billion? Do we quantify output by the number of reports produced? Number of covert actions undertaken? Number of spies recruited? Moreover, the overall number—which will not strike many people as a small sum—will inevitably lead some people to question intelligence community performance. Statements along the lines of "How could they miss that coup (or lose that spy) when they have $26.6 billion?" will ensue. Such sentiments would add little to a meaningful debate about intelligence.

REGULATING THE INTELLIGENCE COMMUNITY.   The most important piece of legislation passed by Congress on the subject of intelligence remains the National Security Act of 1947. Although it has been amended several times since, its basic provisions regarding the NSC, DCI, and CIA remain. Since the 1975–1976 investigations of intelligence, congressional efforts at major legislative change have not been notably successful. Small changes have been made, but larger legislative efforts have faced executive opposition, minimal interest in Congress, and opposition from other congressional committees. Three presidents have since issued extensive executive orders on intelligence—Gerald R. Ford in 1976, Jimmy Carter in 1978, and Ronald Reagan in 1981.

The major advantage of executive orders is that they provide presidents with flexibility to make changes in the intelligence community to meet changing needs or to reflect their own preferences about how the intelligence community should be managed or its functions limited. The major disadvantages of executive orders (or E.O.s, as they are known) are that they are impermanent, subject to change by each president (or even by the same president); they are not statutes and therefore are more difficult to enforce; and they give little role to Congress. (As a rule, the executive branch has made Congress privy to drafts of executive orders in advance of their promulgation and has given Congress opportunities to comment on them.)

Legislative changes, despite the difficulty that Congress and the executive branch have experienced in passing them, offer the advantages of being permanent, of being statutes in law and thus being more enforceable, and of allowing Congress a major and proper role. On the other hand, legislation is also more likely to raise major disputes between Congress and the executive branch and thus is more difficult to enact. Congress is also more likely to be of several points of view on major intelligence issues than is the executive branch—where the major issues are likely to be agency-parochial in nature.

Given the permanent nature of legislation, some people question whether certain regulations should not be made statutory largely because the actions they cover are embarrassing or inappropriate—such as assassinations. Moreover, if legislation lists proscribed activities, does it implicitly permit those activities that are not listed?

THE ISSUE OF CO-OPTION.   As eager as Congress is to be kept informed about all aspects of policy, Congress also incurs a cost when it accepts information. Unless members raise questions about what they are told, they are, in effect, co-opted. Their silence betokens consent, as the maxim of English law says. They are free to dissent later on, but the administration will be quick to point out that they did not raise any questions at the time they were briefed. Having been informed before the fact will tend to undercut Congress's freedom of action after the fact.

This dynamic is not unique to intelligence, but intelligence makes it somewhat more pointed. The nature of the information, which is both secret and usually limited to certain members, makes co-option more easily accomplished and more serious in consequences. It also puts additional pressure on the members of the Intelligence Committees, who are privy to the information and are acting on behalf of their entire body.

Congress has no easy way to avoid the inherent exchange of foreknowledge and consent. Congress is unlikely to revert to the trusting attitude expressed by Senator Saltonstall. Nor is it reasonable to expect Congress to raise serious questions about every issue just to establish a record that will allow it to dissent later on.

WHAT PRICE OVERSIGHT FAILURES?   Even when the intelligence oversight system is working well, most members and congressional staff have difficulty running the system so as to avoid all lapses. Most members and staff involved in the process understand the difference between small lapses and large ones. Some of the larger lapses for which Congress has taken the intelligence community to task include:

- Failure to inform the Senate Intelligence Committee that CIA operatives were directly involved in mining Corinto, a Nicaraguan port, during the contra war. The CIA let it appear that the contras had carried this out on their own. When the truth became known, not only did Vice Chairman Daniel Patrick Moynihan (D, N.Y.) resign—though he later changed his mind—Chairman Barry Goldwater (R, Ariz.) also took DCI William Casey to task in harsh and public terms.
- Failure to inform Congress on a timely basis when agents in Moscow began to disappear—which was later found to be the result of the espionage of Aldrich Ames. The House Intelligence Committee issued a public report critical of the CIA, with which the CIA agreed.

Congress has at hand some real levers to enforce its oversight. It can reduce the intelligence budget, delay nominations, or, in the case of a serious lapse, demand the resignation of the official involved. If the lapse was serious enough and was traceable back to the president, impeachment might be an option. In the two cases cited above, Congress did not impose any of these penalties.

But even without inflicting concrete penalties of the sort noted above, Congress can enforce its oversight. The loss of credibility by officials before their major committees is serious, in and of itself. As hackneyed as it sounds, much of Washington runs on the basis of trust and the value of one's word. Once credibility and trust are lost, as Casey lost his in the Corinto affair, they are very difficult to regain.

THE INTERNAL DYNAMICS OF CONGRESSIONAL OVERSIGHT OF INTELLIGENCE

Even though oversight is inherent in the entire congressional process, the way in which Congress organizes itself to handle intelligence oversight is somewhat peculiar.

WHY SERVE ON AN INTELLIGENCE OVERSIGHT COMMITTEE? Members of Congress enter office with specific areas of interest, derived either from the nature of their district or state or their own personal interests. Most members, at least early in their legislative careers, also tend to focus on issues that are most likely to enhance their careers. For most members, intelligence is unlikely to fit any of these criteria. Therefore, why would members spend a portion of their limited time on intelligence?

At first blush, the disadvantages are more apparent than the advantages. Intelligence is, for most members, a distraction from their other duties and from those issues likely to be of greatest interest to their constituents. Very few districts have a direct interest in intelligence. The main ones are those in the immediate Washington, D.C., area, where the major agencies are located, and those where major collection systems are manufactured. But these are a very small fraction of the 435 House districts among the 50 states.

Once involved in intelligence issues, members cannot discuss much about what they are doing or what they have accomplished. Co-option is also a danger. Should something go wrong in intelligence, committee members will be asked why they did not know about it in advance. If they did know in advance, they will be asked why they did not do something about it. If they did not know, they will be asked why not. These are all difficult questions to answer.

Finally, the intelligence budget is remarkably free of "pork," that is, budget projects that are earmarked to benefit a member's district or state. Therefore, members on the committees have few opportunities to help their constituents.

With all of those disadvantages, why serve? Because some advantages accrue from membership. First, service on the Intelligence Committees allows members to perform "public service" within Congress, to serve on a committee where they have few, if any, direct interests. Second, their service gives members a rare opportunity to have access to a closed and often interesting body of information. Third, it gives members a role in shaping intelligence policy and, given the relatively small size of the two committees (in the 106th Congress—1999–2001—sixteen members on the House Intelligence Committee and nineteen on the Senate Intelligence Committee), perhaps a greater role than they would have on many of the other oversight committees. Fourth, it may offer opportunities for national press coverage on high-profile issues about which very few people will be conversant. Finally, since the two intelligence committees are select committees, members are selected by the majority and minority leadership of the House and Senate. Being chosen is a sign of favor that can be very important to a member's career. (Select committees usually have limited lifespans, especially in the House. The House Intelligence Committee is called "permanent select" to denote its continued existence, even though it remains "select.")

THE ISSUE OF TERM LIMITS.   Unlike service on other committees, service on the House and Senate Intelligence Committees is limited, currently to eight years. Congress adopted term limits for committee membership based on the view that the pre-1975 oversight system had failed, in part, because the few members involved became too cozy and too comfortable with the agencies they were overseeing.

The distance that they promote between the overseers and the overseen is the major advantage of intelligence oversight term limits. Limited terms also mean that more members within the House and Senate will have served on the Intelligence Committees, thus adding to the knowledgeable body necessary for informed debate.

Term limits also carry disadvantages. Few members come to Congress with much knowledge of, and virtually no experience with, intelligence. Intelligence can be arcane and complex and requires some time to master. Therefore, members are likely to spend some portion of their tenure on the committee simply learning about intelligence. Once members have mastered it and become knowledgeable and effective, they are nearing the end of their term. Term limits also make service on the Intelligence Committees less attractive, since they reduce the likelihood that a member can become chairman through seniority.

In 1996 then-chairman of the House Intelligence Committee, Larry Combest, testified that he thought it time to reconsider term limits, and that it was to Congress's advantage to consider longer tenures on House Intelligence.

BIPARTISAN OR PARTISAN COMMITTEES?   The Senate and House Intelligence Committees are distinctly different in their composition. Typically, the ratio of seats between the parties on committees roughly reflects the ratio of seats in each chamber as a whole. The Senate Intelligence Committee has always been exempt from this practice, with the majority party having just one more seat than the minority. Moreover, the ranking minority member is always the vice chairman of the Senate committee. The Senate leadership took these steps in 1976 to minimize the role of partisanship in intelligence. When the House Intelligence Committee was formed in 1977, the House Democratic leadership rejected the Senate model, insisting that each committee reflect the parties' ratio, which reflected the will of the people in the last election.

A bipartisan committee offers opportunities for greater coherence of policy since the committee is removed—as far as is possible—from partisanship. A committee that is united on policy and is not divided by party also may be more influential with the executive branch. In the case of the Corinto mining, Chairman Goldwater and Vice Chairman Moynihan agreed that the intelligence community was guilty of a significant and unacceptable failure. Thus, the DCI had no political refuge for his failure to keep the committee informed.

A partisan committee, the House Democratic leadership believed, is a reflection of the political will of the people. But partisanship runs counter to the preferred myth that U.S. national security policy is bipartisan or nonpartisan. A partisan committee has the potential to be more dynamic than a bipartisan committee, where political compromise is more at a premium. In many ways, the compromise that a bipartisan committee engenders is equivalent to the lowest-common-denominator dynamic that one sees in intelligence community estimates.

In its own accidental way, Congress may have achieved the right balance, with a bipartisan intelligence committee in one chamber and a partisan committee in the other.

HOW DOES CONGRESS JUDGE INTELLIGENCE?   An important but little discussed issue is how Congress views and judges intelligence, as opposed to the criteria used by the executive branch. No matter how much access Congress has to intelligence, it is not a customer of the intelligence community in the same way as the executive branch. Congress never achieves the same level of intimacy with intelligence and does not have the same requirements of or demands for intelligence.

The budget is one major divide. There is no set pattern as to which branch wants to spend more or less. The Reagan administration wanted to spend more on intelligence than Congress and was allowed to, up to a point, after which Congress began to resist. However, the Reagan administration did not want to buy the additional imagery satellites demanded by the Senate Intelligence Committee. In the Clinton administration, it was Congress, after the Republican takeover in 1995, that was willing to spend more than was requested. Congress takes the firm view that all budget requests from the executive are just that—requests. These requests are nonbinding suggestions on how much money should be spent. To put it succinctly, the executive has programs, Congress has money.

The second major divide is the intimacy of the relationship that each branch has with intelligence. Executive officials may have unrealistic expectations of intelligence, but over time they will have far greater familiarity with it than will the majority of members. Thus, the possibility of even larger false expectations looms in Congress. Moreover, having provided the money, members may have higher expectations of intelligence performance. At the same time, members may also tend to be more suspicious of intelligence analysis, fearing that it has been written largely to support administration policies. Members and staff rarely hear of intelligence that questions administration policies, even when such intelligence exists. Thus, the Congress–intelligence relationship is fertile ground for doubts, whether justified or not.

Another major divide is partisanship. Whether it is the majority or the minority, a substantial group in Congress always opposes the administration on grounds of party as well as policy. Partisanship inevitably spills over into intelligence, often in the form of concerns that the executive branch has "cooked" intelligence to support policy. There may be dissent about policy within the executive over intelligence, but it is inconceivable that the dissent would be based on partisanship.

Thus, for a variety of reasons that are largely inherent in the U.S. system, the two branches do not view intelligence in quite the same way.

EXTERNAL FACTORS.   The intelligence oversight system does not take place in a vacuum. A number of other factors also come into play to affect oversight. The press is a major factor. The lingering effects of Watergate on the press, including the search for "scoops" and major scandals, have influenced reporting on intelligence. The press, as an institution, gets more mileage out of reporting things that have gone wrong than out of bestowing kudos for those that are going right. The fact that intelligence correctly predicts some major event is hardly news; after all, that is its job. Moreover, in the aftermath of the 1975–1976 investigations, the intelligence community found it impossible to return to its previous state of being largely ignored by the press. The greater coverage given to intelligence and the press's emphasis on flaws and failures influence how some in Congress approach oversight.

Finally, even intelligence has proponents and opponents who appear in the guise of lobbyists. There are groups made up of former intelligence community employees and groups that advocate strong stances and spending on national security. Similarly, there are groups that oppose certain aspects of intelligence, usually covert action, but also some aspects of espionage; groups concerned about U.S. policy in every region of the world; and groups that would prefer to see some portion of the funds devoted to intelligence spent elsewhere. Finally, there are some firms that derive large amounts of their income from work they do for the intelligence community. All of these groups are legitimate within the U.S. political system and must be taken into account when considering how Congress oversees intelligence.

COMPETITION WITHIN THE CONGRESSIONAL AGENDA.   The final issue that influences intelligence oversight is a series of debates that recur in every Congress, with varying degrees of strength. One is the debate between domestic concerns and national security concerns, which is especially important when dealing with the budget. During the cold war, national security rarely suffered. In the post-cold war period, with national security concerns more difficult to define, the intelligence community has had difficulty maintaining level spending, let alone winning increases.

A second debate is that between civil liberties and national security. This debate is almost as old as the Republic, harkening back to the Alien and Sedition Acts of 1798. Other instances of civil liberties clashing with national security concerns predate the advent of the intelligence community: President Abraham Lincoln's suspension of habeas corpus during the Civil War; the arrest of antiwar dissidents during World War I; the mass arrests and detention of Japanese-Americans during World War II; various acts aimed at rooting out communist subversion during the cold war. In each case, political leaders cited national emergencies to place temporary limitations on civil liberties.

These "precedents" notwithstanding, the intelligence investigations of the mid-1970s revealed several instances in which intelligence agencies violated constitutional guarantees, laws, and their own charters. The violations included surveillance of dissident groups, illegal mail openings, illegal wiretaps of U.S. citizens, and improper use of the Internal Revenue Service. Some of these actions were known by presidents at the time; some were not. The revelation of these activities underscored concerns about the ability of secret agencies to act without safeguards and about the need for strong executive and congressional oversight.

A third perennial congressional debate is that over the level and range of U.S. activism abroad. From World War I through the cold war, the Democrats were largely the interventionist party and the Republicans the noninterventionists. During World War II and the cold war, an interventionist consensus formed, although a Republican faction remained noninterventionist. The damage that the Vietnam War inflicted on the cold war consensus fostered a shift in the positions of the two parties. The Democrats largely became the noninterventionist party and the Republicans the interventionist. In the post-cold war period, a renascent noninterventionist faction grew within the Republican Party. This debate is of particular importance to covert actions, especially large-scaled ones and those likely to be of long duration.

Finally, the immigrant basis of the U.S. population is reflected in foreign policy debates. Every region of the world and virtually every nation are represented within the U.S. population. U.S. policies or actions—real, planned, or rumored—around the world are likely to stir reactions from some segment of the population and perhaps even several reactions, pro and con. Members of Congress who have ethnic ties to a region or who represent constituents who do are also likely to voice opinions.

CONCLUSION

The nature of congressional oversight of intelligence changed dramatically in 1975–1976. Although Congress may go through periods of greater or lesser activism, it is unlikely to return to the laissez-faire style of oversight. Congress has become a consistent player in shaping intelligence policy.

This seems novel in the case of intelligence only because it is relatively recent. Congress has played the same activist role in all other areas of policy since adoption of the Constitution, and its role is inherent in the checks and balances system that the framers of the Constitution purposefully created. The willful division of power creates a system that is a constant "invitation to struggle."

The oversight system is, of necessity, adversarial but not necessarily hostile. Any system that divides power is bound to have debates and friction. But they do not have to be played out in a manner that is antagonistic. When antagonism arises, it is more often the effect of personalities, issues, and partisanship rather than the oversight system per se.

KEY TERMS

appropriated but not authorized (A not A)
appropriation
authorization

executive order
hollow budget authority
oversight

FURTHER READINGS

The expansion of the role of Congress as an overseer has been matched by an expansion of books and articles on the topic. This chapter also discusses executive oversight issues, which are discussed in the first entry below.

Adler, Emanuel. "Executive Command and Control in Foreign Policy: The CIA's Covert Activities." *Orbis* 23 (1959): 671–696.

Cohen, William S. "Congressional Oversight of Covert Actions." *International Journal of Intelligence and Counterintelligence* 2 (summer 1988): 155–162.

Colton, David Everett. "Speaking Truth to Power: Intelligence Oversight in an Imperfect World." *University of Pennsylvania Law Review* 137 (December 1988): 571–613.

Conner, William E. *Intelligence Oversight: The Controversy Behind the FY1991 Intelligence Authorization Act.* McLean, Va.: Consortium for the Study of Intelligence, 1993.

Currie, James. "Iran-Contra and Congressional Oversight of the CIA." *International Journal of Intelligence and Counterintelligence* 11 (summer 1998): 185–210.

Gumina, Paul. "Title VI of the Intelligence Authorization Act: Fiscal Year 1991: Effective Covert Action Reform or 'Business as Usual'?" *Hastings Constitutional Law Quarterly* (fall 1992): 149–205.

Jackson, William R. "Congressional Oversight of Intelligence: Search for a Framework." *Intelligence and National Security* 5 (July 1990): 113–147.

Johnson, Loch K. "The CIA and the Question of Accountability." *Intelligence and National Security* 12, no. 1 (January 1997): 178–200.

———. "Controlling the Quiet Option." *Foreign Policy* 39 (summer 1980): 143–153.

———. "The U.S. Congress and the CIA: Monitoring the Dark Side of Government." *Legislative Studies Quarterly* 5 (November 1980): 477–499.

Latimer, Thomas K. "United States Intelligence Activities: The Role of Congress." In *Intelligence Policy and National Security,* edited by Robert L. Pfaltzgraff, Jr., et al. Hamden, Conn.: Archon Books, 1981.

Pickett, George. "Congress, the Budget and Intelligence." In *Intelligence: Policy and Process,* edited by Alfred C. Maurer et al. Boulder, Colo.: Westview Press, 1985.

Simmons, Robert Ruhl. "Intelligence Performance in Reagan's First Term: A Good Record or Bad?" *International Journal of Intelligence and Counterintelligence* 4 (spring 1990): 1–22.

Smist, Frank J., Jr. *Congress Oversees the United States Intelligence Community.* 2d ed. Knoxville: University of Tennessee Press, 1994.

Snider, L. Britt. *Sharing Secrets with Lawmakers: Congress as a User of Intelligence.* Washington, D.C.: Central Intelligence Agency, Center for the Study of Intelligence, 1997.

Treverton, Gregory F. "Intelligence: Welcome to the American Government." In *A Question of Balance: The President, the Congress and Foreign Policy,* edited by Thomas E. Mann. Washington, D.C.: Brookings Institution, 1990.

U.S. Senate Select Committee on Intelligence. *Legislative Oversight of Intelligence Activities: The U.S. Experience.* Report, 103rd Congress, 2d session. 1994.

CHAPTER 11

The Old Intelligence Agenda—
What and How Well?

Although the intelligence community was not created specifically to prosecute the cold war, the community's development, forms, structures, and practices were influenced most by that fifty-year struggle. To understand how the intelligence community developed and its nature as it tries to transform, it is important to understand how well the community performed during the cold war. The community's performance is an issue of some controversy, fueled largely by those critics who argue that the intelligence community failed to foresee the biggest story of its time, the collapse of the Soviet Union. The degree to which the intelligence community understood the failing Soviet state is an important question, but it is not the sole question upon which an assessment of its cold war role hangs.

U.S. COLD WAR POLICY VIS-À-VIS
THE SOVIET UNION—CONTAINMENT

In assessing the role of intelligence during the cold war one must return to basics and review the premises of U.S. cold war policy. Intelligence policy, to be successful, should be a reflection of broader national policy. Inspired by George Kennan, a career diplomat, the United States developed a policy of containment vis-à-vis the Soviet Union. Kennan argued, first in his famous "long telegram" from Moscow in February 1946 and then in his "Mr. X" article in *Foreign Affairs* (July 1947), that the Soviet Union was, by its nature, an expansionist state. If the Soviet Union was contained within its own geographic limits, it would eventually be forced to deal with the inconsistencies and shortcomings of its communist system and either change or collapse. Kennan saw the struggle between the United States and the Soviet Union as largely political and economic. But others responsible for shaping policy, particularly Paul

Nitze, who played a key role in drafting NSC-68 in early 1950, gave containment a more military dimension, as did the outbreak of the Korean War in June of that year.

THE INTELLIGENCE IMPLICATIONS OF CONTAINMENT. The containment policy included a role for intelligence analysis and intelligence operations. Analytically, the intelligence community was expected to know or to be able to predict:

- Likely areas of Soviet probes or expansion
- Imminence and strength of the probes
- Overall Soviet strength—military, economic, and social
- Likely Soviet allies or surrogates
- Strength of U.S. allies or surrogates
- Signs of relative Soviet strength or weakness (signs of the "contradictions" predicted by Kennan)

This is a long list and an ironic reflection of Sherman Kent's desire to "know everything."

In terms of intelligence operations, containment required:

- An ability to collect intelligence on the Soviet target to enable analysts to fulfill their requirements
- An operational ability to help blunt Soviet expansion
- An ability to weaken the Soviet Union and its allies and surrogates
- A counterintelligence capability to deal with Soviet espionage and possible subversion

Neither set of tasks, analytical or operational, arrived full-blown with the acceptance of the containment policy. Both sets evolved over time as the United States dealt with the Soviet problem.

THE DIFFICULTY OF THE SOVIET TARGET. The Soviet Union was a uniquely difficult target for intelligence collection and analysis. First, it was a very large nation, with a remote interior. Geography gave the Soviet leadership a great deal of space in which to hide capabilities they preferred to keep secret. Moreover, large portions of the Soviet Union were subject to adverse weather conditions that impeded overhead collection. Second, it was a closed and heavily policed society, which meant that large portions of the Soviet state—even in its more developed areas—were closed to foreigners, even to diplomats legally posted to the Soviet Union.

Long-standing Russian traditions compounded the geographical difficulties. Russians traditionally have been suspicious of foreigners. Prior to the reign of Peter the Great (1682–1725), foreigners were often sequestered in special areas of the Russian capital, where they could be easily watched and where their contact with Russians could be limited and controlled. Russians also have a tradition of obscuring the physical realities of the Russian state, which came to be known as *maskirovka* but which had roots going back to the tsars. The most famous—and perhaps legendary—instance of obscuring reality occurred during the reign of Catherine the Great (1762–1796). Her minister of war, Grigory Potemkin, built false villages that were only facades to impress Catherine with the success of his policies. These "Potemkin villages" presaged *maskirovka.*

As the scope of the cold war expanded from the Soviet Union to Europe to Asia and then globally, the field within which intelligence had to be collected and analyzed and within which operations might be required expanded as well. The bilateral cold war was, in intelligence terms, a global war.

THE INTELLIGENCE RECORD—THE SOVIET MILITARY

Any military establishment that is targeted by intelligence can be broken down into two broad categories—capabilities and intentions. Capabilities refer to the forces in being or being planned. The U.S. intelligence community sought out information about the quantity and quality of Soviet armed forces across the board; the directions of Soviet military research and development, and which new capabilities they might be pursuing; the degree to which current and planned capabilities posed a threat to U.S. and allied interests; and Soviet doctrine, that is, how they planned to employ their forces in combat.

With the right collection systems, much of a potential adversary's capabilities can be known. This is particularly true of deployed forces, which are difficult to conceal and which must exercise from time to time. Indeed, the regularity and precision that govern each nation's military make the military susceptible to intelligence collection. Forces tend to exercise in regular and predictable patterns. Exercises also reveal how forces are intended to be employed in combat. Research and development may be more difficult to track up to a point, but systems must be tested before they are deployed, again exposing them to collection.

Intentions—the plans and goals of the adversary—are a more amorphous subject and pose a much more difficult collection problem. They need not be demonstrated, exercised, or exposed in advance, and they may not even be revealed by regular military exercises. Stand-off or remote collection systems, which may be useful for collecting against capabilities, may not reveal anything about intentions. That collection task may require espionage.

During the mid-1970s a capabilities-versus-intentions debate about the Soviet Union took place, largely among policy makers and influential individuals outside of government, but involving the intelligence community as well. U.S. intelligence knew Soviet military capabilities fairly well, but not Soviet intentions. The question at issue was whether Soviet intentions mattered. U.S. officials engaged in long and sometimes heated debates about whether the Soviet Union planned to conduct large-scale offensive conventional operations pre-emptively or at the very outset of a war with NATO; whether it could carry out such operations from a "standing start," that is, with forces already deployed and supplied and without bringing up telltale reserves and additional supplies, and thus with little or no warning; and whether the Soviet Union thought a nuclear conflict was "winnable."

Those who believed that intentions mattered argued that simply keeping track of the numbers of military forces was not enough to gauge the threat they posed. Only intentions made it possible to gauge the true level of threat. For example, Britain has a substantial nuclear force but is of no concern to the United States because the two nations are close allies. By taking into account Soviet intentions, the United States would have a much clearer picture of the true nature of Soviet policy, which was central to U.S. and Western security concerns. Proponents of the view that intentions mattered believed that the Soviet threat was being underestimated because intentions were not a factor in national estimates.

Those who were less concerned about intentions argued that if one knew there was a certain level of hostility and also knew the adversary's capabilities, then knowing specific intentions was not that important. Indeed, they argued that a "worst case" based on capabilities could serve as a planning yardstick. Finally, intentions (that is, plans) may be changed at will, making them a highly elusive target. Differences over the importance of intentions led to the Team A–Team B competitive analysis discussed earlier.

How, then, did the intelligence community do against the Soviet military target? In the area of capabilities, the intelligence community did quite well. This activity is often derogatorily referred to as "bean counting." Despite the importance of the task, it is not seen, even within the intelligence community, as one of the highest callings. The community did, of course, make mistakes, including both overestimates and underestimates, as in estimating the missile gap. The bomber and missile gaps took place before or just after the advent of satellite imagery, when collection was still limited. But the window of vulnerability debate (circa

1976–1981) took place amid a wealth of data. However, the debate centered on 1) a bean-counting issue that could be estimated but not known—how many warheads were on each Soviet missile; and 2) Soviet strategic intentions, an even more difficult collection task.

The fairly continuous capability assessments also had political implications, since they highlighted the need for countervailing U.S. and allied forces. The level, nature, and intent of Soviet forces—as well as the appropriate response—were often subject to debate in Congress and within NATO, perhaps most famously over the decision taken in the mid-1980s to deploy U.S. intermediate nuclear forces to Europe in response to Soviet SS-20 IRBM deployments.

Some discounted the bean counts, arguing that they were undertaken largely to justify larger defense budgets. The logic of this view was difficult to follow, since the intelligence community had little institutional interest in larger military forces. Indeed, within the national security sector of the budget, every dollar that went to defense was one less dollar available for intelligence, which was always funded at significantly lower levels than defense.

The track record for Soviet intentions is much less certain. The United States was never able to ascertain, for example, whether the Soviets subscribed to the nuclear doctrine of mutual assured destruction (MAD), which provided the basis for the size of U.S. strategic nuclear forces. MAD was based on the view that the prospect of nuclear devastation was so awesome as to make nuclear forces almost unusable, the two forces holding each other in check. The United States spent many rounds of the early strategic arms control talks proselytizing the Soviets on the importance of MAD. Did the Soviets really agree, at last, or give lip service to the idea of MAD merely as a way to get on to negotiations? Did it matter? Similarly, did the Soviets think that nuclear war was winnable? Did the Soviets plan to invade Western Europe? Soviet doctrine certainly emphasized keeping war away from the homeland, but most doctrines do.

Mirror-imaging underlay much of the debate over Soviet intentions. Did U.S. analysts impose their own views of Soviet intentions in lieu of knowing them? Another question was the utility of worst-case planning. Is it a useful analytical tool? For defense planners, the answer is "yes." If they are going to commit forces to combat, they need to be able to gauge the worst level of threat they are likely to face. For other planners and analysts, the worst case may be an overestimate that is much less useful.

Finally, some people question whether the intelligence products themselves affected the intelligence process. Each year the intelligence community completed a national estimate on Soviet strategic military capabilities (NIE 11-3-8). U.S. policy makers saw this estimate as necessary for U.S. strategic planning, including preparation of forces and budgets. But did the preparation of an annual major estimate also affect intelligence? Did it lock intelligence into set patterns, making it more difficult for the community to make major changes or shifts in analyses? In other words, once the community had produced NIE 11-3-8 for several years, how easy was it for analysts to propose dissenting, iconoclastic, or wholly new views? One remedy for these possible flaws was competitive analysis, tried most prominently in the Team A–Team B exercise.

Direct comparison of forces, a legitimate intelligence activity, often took place in a politicized atmosphere. Policy makers in successive administrations and Congresses tended to have preconceptions about the nature of the Soviet threat and viewed intelligence, in light of their views, as being either supportive or mistaken. They engaged in long debates about quality (a U.S. advantage) versus quantity (a Soviet advantage) of weapons systems. The inconclusive nature of the debates led many to seek other means of comparison. One means was defense spending, both in direct costs and in the percentage of GNP devoted to defense, which were taken as signs of intentions as well as capabilities.

The U.S. intelligence community devoted a great deal of time and energy—perhaps too much—to a variety of efforts to compare Soviet defense spending to that of the United States. Some analysts converted the cost of U.S. defense into rubles; others converted assessed values for the Soviet defense establishment into dollars. Each of these methodologies was artificial, and their respective proponents usually ended up preaching to the converted or the stubbornly unbelieving regarding the Soviet threat.

THE INTELLIGENCE RECORD—THE SOVIET ECONOMY

Gauging the strength and nature of the Soviet economy was another major intelligence facet of the cold war. The intelligence community and its policy customers wanted to know the size of the Soviet economy, its strength relative to the U.S. economy, and the amount or percentage of the economy devoted to the military. Economic intelligence was long a part of the U.S. intelligence agenda, not something that policy makers discovered amid the cold war.

A major problem in assessing the Soviet economy was its alien and artificial nature. Not only were all Soviet economic data suspect, but the measures that economists use to gauge economic strength and performance in the U.S. and abroad—employment; inflation; gross national and domestic product; the value and state of stocks; the cost of goods and services; currency exchange rates; trade balances; and so forth—had no meaning in the context of the Soviet state.

The intelligence community's track record on the Soviet economy was mixed. It grossly overestimated the relative size and health of the Soviet economy. At the same time, it grossly underestimated the percentage of the Soviet economy devoted to the military, perhaps by a factor of 100 percent.

There are several reasons why U.S. intelligence did not do a better job of assessing the Soviet economy. First, data published by the Soviet Union itself were highly unreliable, and few alternative sources of data existed. Second, the Soviet economy bore no relationship to any other economy for which models and analyses existed. Although the intelligence community understood the economic premises and practices of the Soviet state, it was impossible to comprehend how the economy actually functioned or failed to function. Western observers of the Soviet economy knew that prices and exchange rates were wholly artificial. They knew that the Soviet state experienced hidden inflation (despite the fact that inflation ran counter to official Soviet doctrine) and that a "second economy" consisting of large-scale and small-scale barter thrived, as did a large black market.

In retrospect, Western analysis of the Soviet economy was a classic case of flawed and incomplete data. In such cases, the community's first recourse should be to find alternative sources of data, which was impossible in the case of the Soviet economy. A second step would be to estimate in lieu of data, although that would make the basis for intelligence less certain. Finally, intelligence producers should be very clear with policy makers about the state of intelligence and intelligence uncertainties.

Part of what went wrong with U.S. intelligence on the Soviet economy was that the one area of certainty—Soviet military production—became the basis for much of the subsequent economic analysis, based on faulty premises. U.S. intelligence assumed, incorrectly, that rational leaders would not devote above a certain level of the nation's economic output to the military. When they estimated the size of the Soviet economy on this incorrect premise, they grossly overestimated its size. Moreover, even though intelligence understood the inefficiencies of the Soviet system in broad terms, if not in detail, it still assumed that the overall system was more efficient than it actually was, further inflating the economy's size.

Estimates of the amount of the Soviet economy devoted to defense crept up over time, from some 6–7 percent of GNP at the end of the Ford administration (1974–1977), to 13–14 percent in the Carter administration (1977–1981), to 19–20 percent by the end of the Reagan administration (1981–1989). U.S. cold war outlays, by contrast, peaked at 14.5 percent during the Eisenhower administration (1953–1961). Even during the

Reagan administration defense build-up, the percentage of U.S. GNP devoted to defense never rose above 6.8 percent.

The reality of Soviet defense spending as a percentage of GNP, as revealed in the aftermath of the cold war, was staggering, estimated by some to be as high as 40 percent annually—year in, year out. The highest U.S. defense spending ever was in 1943 and 1944 (39–40 percent) during two years of global warfare. This incredible Soviet effort not only reveals much about the Soviet state—its insecurity and its economic unreality—but also raises questions about the limits of intelligence. Had a U.S. analyst come close to estimating Soviet defense efforts, what would have been the reception in any administration? No U.S. administration could hope to match the Soviet effort—although given the great disparities in the size of the two economies, a lesser effort by the United States (in percentage terms) would have sufficed. But the political effects of this intelligence would have been profound—if policy makers in the executive branch and Congress could have believed it at all.

The amazing if not insane level of Soviet defense spending helped undermine an already flawed economic system. To some extent, the Soviet Union spent itself into the ground regardless of the state of U.S. defense policy.

THE INTELLIGENCE RECORD— ## THE COLLAPSE OF THE SOVIET UNION

Much of the controversy surrounding the U.S. intelligence record on the Soviet Union stems from the sudden Soviet collapse. Critics of intelligence performance argue that the intelligence community was deeply surprised by the collapse, overestimating the strength of the Soviet state and thus "missing" the biggest story in the history of the intelligence community. Some even argue that this intelligence "failure" is sufficient reason for a profound reorganization of U.S. intelligence. Defenders of intelligence performance argue that the intelligence community had long reported the inner rot of the Soviet system and the weakness of its hold on its satellite states and its own people.

The defenders of U.S. intelligence performance are correct, in part. Intelligence provided numerous stories about the gross inefficiencies of the Soviet system, many of them anecdotal, but too many to ignore. Insights into the sad realities of the Soviet system grew with the beginning of on-site inspections of Soviet INF bases in 1988. But few, if any, analysts compiled these anecdotal accounts into a prediction that the Soviet state was nearing collapse. It was weak; it might even be tottering. But no one expected that the Soviet Union would suddenly—and peacefully—pass from the scene. At least two factors were at work. First, most U.S. analysts working on the Soviet Union could not bring themselves to admit that the center of their livelihood might disappear, or that it was as weak politically as it turned out to be. Such a conclusion was inconceivable. They concentrated on the perils and pitfalls of reform but did not consider the possibility of collapse. Second, analysts failed to factor into their calculations the role of personalities, particularly that of Mikhail Gorbachev.

The difficulty in assessing Gorbachev should not be underestimated. Gorbachev came to power through the usual Politburo selection process. Like each new Soviet leader, Gorbachev promised reforms to make the admittedly inefficient state more efficient. Eduard Shevardnadze, Gorbachev's foreign minister, reveals that at a certain point they both admitted that to fix the economy would require something more basic than tweaking reforms. Even while accepting this fact, Gorbachev remained committed to the basic forms of the Soviet state, not understanding that any true reform was, by definition, revolutionary. Gorbachev himself came to these conclusions only over time, and he could not accept their ultimate implications. In other words, Gorbachev did not know where his reforms would lead. Should the intelligence community have known better than Gorbachev himself?

Many intelligence analysts were also slow to pick up on Gorbachev's approach to most of his foreign policy problems—arms control, Angola, even Afghanistan—which was to liquidate them as quickly as possible so as to be free to concentrate on more pressing domestic problems. Nor did many correctly analyze that the Soviet Union would acquiesce in the collapse of its European satellite empire. Czechoslovakia, maybe. But East Germany? Never! Again, the degree to which this was knowable remains uncertain. Ironically, Gorbachev succumbed to the premises of containment as described by George Kennan forty years earlier. Stymied abroad, Gorbachev had to face the manifold problems he had at home.

We still do not know all of the factors that went into Gorbachev's thinking or into the sudden Soviet collapse. Did the U.S. defense build-up convince Gorbachev that he needed to strike some deals with the United States or be outpaced and outspent and face even deeper economic ruin? Shevardnadze suggests that the answer is "yes." There is reason to believe that President Reagan's Strategic Defense Initiative was an important spur to arms control, not because of any near-term change that SDI might effect in the military balance but because it brought home to the Soviet leadership all of their weaknesses in technology, in computers, in wealth. One of the ways to avoid economic ruin was to strike arms control deals.

We also do not know what effect, if any, the so-called Reagan Doctrine—a U.S. effort to aid anti-Soviet guerrillas—had on Soviet thinking. The effort to aid the contras became a political liability for the Reagan administration. But aid to the Mujaheddin in Afghanistan and the stale-mate of that war shook the Soviet leaders. They were unable to win a war just over their border. All of their military prowess was meaningless. Some analysts believe that a rift developed between the General Staff in Moscow and the Afgantsy—Soviet field commanders in the war, many of whom rallied to Boris Yeltsin in August 1991 when opponents of radical reform attempted to overthrow Gorbachev.

Gorbachev clearly thought that the price of empire was too high, not only overseas but even in Eastern Europe. What neither Western analysts nor Gorbachev himself understood was that piecemeal liquidation of these problems could not save the Soviet state.

CONCLUSION—INTELLIGENCE AND THE SOVIET PROBLEM

No U.S. intelligence estimate boldly predicted the peaceful collapse of the Soviet Union and its dissolution into several independent republics. Indeed, U.S. intelligence assumed that the Soviet state would go on, per-haps ever weaker but still intact. At the same time, the community pro-duced numerous reports about how inefficient, how weak, and how unsustainable (over some unknown period of time) the Soviet Union was.

There are two key questions. Should intelligence have done better? Did intelligence matter in our final cold war victory?

Those who argue that intelligence should have done better do so on the grounds that the Soviet Union was the central focus of U.S. intelli-gence and that all of the expertise and spending over five decades should have provided greater insight into the true state of affairs. But there is a large gap between knowing that a state has fundamental weaknesses and foreseeing its collapse. To a large extent, the collapse of the Soviet Union was unprecedented. (In the past, some once-great empires, such as the Ottoman Empire, had suffered long, lingering demises. Other great empires had suffered sudden collapses, but usually in the context of war—as the German, Austrian, and Russian Empires had after World War I.) Nor was there anything in Soviet behavior—which had shown its bru-tal side often enough—to lead analysts to expect that the Soviet elite would acquiesce to their own fall from power without a struggle. Indeed, it is one of the ironies of history that an attempt by the so-called "power ministries" of the Soviet state (the military, the defense industrial com-plex, the KGB) to derail Gorbachev revealed how little support the Sovi-et system really had. (Rumors persist that Gorbachev knew about the coup or actually abetted it as a means of isolating his opposition.)

The debate over the performance of U.S. intelligence in the final stages of the cold war continues. Perhaps some analyst should have made the leap from the mountain of anecdotal evidence to a better picture of the true state of Soviet staying power. But much that happened from 1989 to 1991 was unknowable, both to U.S. analysts and to those taking part in the events.

Finally, how do we assess the role of intelligence overall on the Soviet problem? In collection, U.S. intelligence performed some remarkable feats, finding sophisticated technical solutions to the problems posed by the remote and closed Soviet target. In analysis, U.S. intelligence very accurately tracked Soviet military numbers and capabilities. This was important not only on a day-to-day basis but during periods of intense confrontation, such as in Cuba in 1962, when President John F. Kennedy acted confidently, knowing a great deal about the true state of the U.S.-Soviet military balance. Discussion of Soviet intentions veered off quickly to the political realm, where convinced and unconvertible hawks and doves dominated the debate, often freed from the constraints of intelligence by its unavailability. Operationally, the record is much less clear. Early efforts to foment rebellion within Soviet domains were disasters. Operations to limit Soviet expansion were uneven. U.S. intelligence operations were successful in Western Europe, Guatemala, and Iran and were failures in Cuba and Southeast Asia. The contra war likely could have been dragged out inconclusively forever. But the intervention in Afghanistan was a major and telling success. In espionage, U.S. intelligence scored major successes, such as Col. Oleg Penkovsky, and suffered a number of Soviet penetrations as well, some of which—such as Aldrich Ames—bridged the Soviet and post-Soviet Russian states.

In short, the record of intelligence in the cold war is mixed. Perhaps a better way to pose the original question might be: Would the United States have been better off or more secure without an intelligence community during the cold war?

KEY TERMS

bean counting
capabilities versus intentions
containment
maskirovka

Potemkin villages
Reagan Doctrine
worst-case analysis

FURTHER READINGS

As might be expected, the literature on U.S. intelligence vis-à-vis the Soviet Union is rich. The readings listed here include some older pieces that are of historical value.

Berkowitz, Bruce D., and Jeffrey T. Richelson. "The CIA Vindicated: The Soviet Collapse Was Predicted." *National Interest,* no. 41 (fall 1995): 36–47.

Burton, Donald F. "Estimating Soviet Defense Spending." *Problems of Communism* 32 (March–April 1983): 85–93.

Firth, Noel E. *Soviet Defense Spending: A History of CIA Estimates, 1950–1990.* College Station: Texas A & M University Press, 1998.

Freedman, Lawrence. "The CIA and the Soviet Threat: The Politicization of Estimates, 1966–1977." *Intelligence and National Security* 12, no. 1 (January 1997): 122–142.

———. *U.S. Intelligence and the Soviet Strategic Threat.* Boulder, Colo.: Westview Press, 1977.

Koch, Scott A., ed. *Selected Estimates on the Soviet Union, 1950–1959.* Washington, D.C.: History Staff, U.S. Central Intelligence Agency, 1993.

Lee, William T. *Understanding the Soviet Military Threat.* New York: National Strategy Information Center, 1977.

Lowenthal, Mark M. "Intelligence Epistemology: Dealing with the Unbelievable." *International Journal of Intelligence and Counterintelligence* 6, no. 3 (1993): 319–325.

MacEachin, Douglas J. *CIA Assessments of the Soviet Union: The Record vs. the Charges.* Langley, Va.: Central Intelligence Agency, Center for the Study of Intelligence, 1996.

Moynihan, Daniel Patrick. *Secrecy: The American Experience.* New Haven, Conn.: Yale University Press, 1998.

Pipes, Richard. "Team B: The Reality Behind the Myth." *Commentary* 82 (October 1986): 25–40.

Prados, John. *The Soviet Estimate: U.S. Intelligence and Russian Military Strength.* New York: Dial Press, 1982.

Reich, Robert C. "Re-examining the Team A–Team B Exercise." *International Journal of Intelligence and Counterintelligence* 3 (fall 1989): 387–403.

Steury, Donald P., ed. *Intentions and Capabilities: Estimates on Soviet Strategic Forces, 1950–1983.* Washington, D.C.: History Staff, U.S. Central Intelligence Agency, 1996.

U.S. Congress. Senate Select Committee on Intelligence. *The National Intelligence Estimate A–B Team Episode Concerning Soviet Strategic Capability and Objectives.* 95th Congress, 2d session. 1978.

U.S. General Accounting Office. *Soviet Economy: Assessment of How Well the CIA Has Estimated the Size of the Economy.* GAO Report NSIAD 910274. Washington, D.C., September 1991.

CHAPTER 12

The New Intelligence Agenda

The end of the cold war was not the end of history, as political scientist Frank Fukuyama suggested. (Fukuyama posited that, since the struggle to advance democratic values had been the major development of the last several centuries, the collapse of the Soviet Union would bring an "end" to "history.") But the end of the cold war did remove the most central national security issue that the United States faced. In the aftermath of the cold war, what role should intelligence play? What issues should it be pursuing in support of U.S. policy makers?

U.S. NATIONAL SECURITY POLICY AFTER THE COLD WAR

The cold war gave U.S. national security policy an easily understood point of reference. Diplomacy, defense policy, intelligence, and all else followed from the fundamental, bilateral struggle with the Soviet Union. Admittedly, serious debates arose in the United States over the nature of the Soviet threat, how the United States should deal with the threat overseas, defense spending levels, arms control agreements, and other major facets of the bilateral competition. But there was little doubt that the antagonistic and hostile relationship with the Soviet Union was the foremost issue in U.S. national security policy. As the previous chapter indicated, U.S. analyses of the subtler aspects of the Soviet problem suffered significant flaws. But the issues of what the intelligence community should be doing and why were rarely in doubt.

The post-cold war period offers no such clarity. The administrations of George Bush (1989–1993) and Bill Clinton (1993–) have either failed or not tried to define U.S. national security interests in the aftermath of the cold war. The Bush administration tried the concept of "new world order," which was never clearly defined and became irrelevant after President Bush's defeat at the polls in 1992. The Clinton administration largely avoided such grandiose conceptions—despite brief forays into the concepts of "preventive diplomacy," "engagement," and "enlargement"—taking a more ad hoc approach to shaping policy. Some suggested that the concept of national security, which had been comfortably vague to most of its practitioners, should be redefined, although few offered concrete, useful suggestions. In short, the core of U.S. national security policy has remained vague since the fall of the Soviet Union. This vagueness as to our major national security concerns raises several questions for U.S. intelligence. Has the mission of the intelligence community changed? How do policy makers and intelligence officials create and define intelligence requirements—and all that flows from them—in the absence of guiding national security concepts or policies?

THE QUESTION OF THE INTELLIGENCE MISSION

At a basic level, the answer to the question of whether the mission of the intelligence community has changed in the aftermath of the cold war is "no." The mission of the intelligence community remains what it was: to collect and analyze information that policy makers need, and to carry out covert actions as lawful authorities direct. This mission is—or should be—independent of any particular target, relationship, or crisis. This mission is the reason why the United States has an intelligence community and should not be subject to the vagaries of international politics. U.S. intelligence targets and priorities have changed, but the community's mission has not.

THE QUESTIONS OF INTELLIGENCE AGENDA AND PRIORITIES

Agenda and priorities are much more vexing questions. DCI Robert Gates (1991–1993) estimated that at the height of the cold war, some 50 percent of the intelligence budget went to the Soviet Union and related issues. Everything else was secondary. That clarity of priorities is gone.

Numerous issues now jostle for pride of place on the U.S. national security agenda: international economics; proliferation of weapons of mass destruction; narcotics; crime; terrorism; ecological and health issues; the post-Soviet transition in Russia; peacekeeping operations; and a variety of regional issues—the Balkans, the Middle East, central Africa, North Korea, and so on. Any one of these issues can be the most important for some period of time. None maintains the dominance that the Soviet Union once had.

The lack of a clear focus poses a severe problem for policy makers and intelligence managers. Requirements can be uncertain or subject to rapid shifts. A greater diversity of talent is likely required. Very few of these issues are "new" to the U.S. national security agenda. Economic issues, narcotics, terrorism, proliferation, and regional stability were all being addressed during the cold war. Health and ecological issues are somewhat new. All of these issues are more difficult to analyze than were the cold war political-military issues, and they are much less susceptible to "bean counting."

In most cases, policy makers also find them more difficult to deal with than the old Soviet issues. The cold war had a certain comforting pattern of action/reaction. The United States and the Soviet Union each assumed, often correctly, that it could influence the behavior of the other through certain actions. On many of these new issues, there are no clear actions to take and sometimes no actors whom one can hope to influence. In some cases, the available intelligence outruns available or acceptable policy options. This often leads to frustration on the part of policy makers because they seek intelligence that is "actionable," that is intelligence with which they can "do something." But they find it difficult to do something when they do not know what it is they want to do.

Finally, several of these issues spill into the domestic realm—economics, narcotics, crime, terrorism—thus curtailing the activities of much of the intelligence community and creating confusion and competition between intelligence and law enforcement. This problem may be unique to the U.S. system, which draws a sharp distinction between foreign and domestic intelligence. As has been noted, the CIA is restricted in its work—analytical and operational—to foreign intelligence issues. The FBI is responsible for intelligence issues in the United States. The Drug Enforcement Administration (DEA) has responsibility for narcotics. The FBI has an advantage over the CIA in that it posts some people—the legal attachés—in embassies. The capture of an individual overseas, known as a "rendition," requires the presence of U.S. law enforcement personnel even if it is primarily an intelligence operation. The main problem that arises as the foreign and domestic communities grapple with these so-called transnational issues is attempting to define the point at which the CIA must hand off a case to the FBI, or vice versa. No firm lines divide one sphere from the other. During the late 1990s, the FBI became very aggressive, particularly in its overseas activities related to terrorism and crime, much to the discomfort of the CIA.

A second problem that arises is the very different ways in which the CIA and the FBI use intelligence. The CIA is an intelligence organization and disseminates its intelligence and analysis to its policy customers. Without the customers, the intelligence has no use. The FBI is essentially a law enforcement organization and sometimes uses its intelligence to help the Justice Department prosecute criminal cases. For legal reasons, intelligence may have to be kept confidential from policy makers or overseers, lest it jeopardize a developing case.

The Clinton administration attempted to define intelligence priorities by issuing Presidential Decision Directive 35 (PDD-35). PDD-35 divided intelligence priorities into two groups: hard targets and global coverage. Hard targets (or upper-tier issues) are the most pressing priorities: the so-called rogue states (Iran, Iraq, Libya, Cuba, North Korea) and the transnational issues (terrorism, weapons proliferation, narcotics, international crime, ecological issues). Global coverage (the lower tiers) is everything else.

Clinton administration officials envisioned PDD-35 as a way of allocating resources across all intelligence needs. Critics argued that, inevitably, the lion's share of resources would go to the hard targets, leaving little at all for global coverage. This proved to be the case; the intelligence community admitted that it had the resources to cover the hard targets but not global coverage.

The other flaw in PDD-35 lay in the fact that over the course of a year some global-coverage issues would inevitably become more critical, moving into the upper tier. Although the intelligence community regularly checks the status of issues to determine if they are becoming more pressing, issues still receive significant attention only once they have moved into the upper tier. Moreover, the absence of a collection or analytical surge capacity in the intelligence community means that when an issue moves from global coverage to hard targets, it sets off a sudden scramble for resources.

INTELLIGENCE AND THE NEW AGENDA

An examination of some of the issues that have risen in priority in the post-cold war period give some sense of the difficulties that the intelligence community faces.

ECONOMICS.   Economics can be subdivided into several issues: U.S. economic competitiveness overseas, U.S. trading relations, foreign economic espionage and possible countermeasures, and the intelligence community's ability to forecast major international economic shifts that may have serious consequences for the U.S. economy.

During the late 1980s it appeared to some people that several of these issues (overseas competitiveness, trading relations, foreign economic espionage undertaken by nations, industrial espionage undertaken by businesses, and possible countermeasures) could be addressed, in part, through a closer connection between intelligence and U.S. businesses. Few advocates of closer intelligence–business collaboration, however, had substantial answers for some of the more compelling questions that it raised (which is one reason why this approach was quickly rejected):

- If the intelligence community were to share intelligence with businesses, how would they safeguard the sources and methods by which they had obtained it? If the underlying sources and methods could not be shared, would businesses accept the intelligence?

- With whom would the intelligence be shared—or, in other words—what constitutes a "U.S. company?" In an age of multinational corporations, the concept is not easy to define.

- Given that every business sector has many competitive businesses, which ones would the community provide with intelligence? What would be the basis for selecting recipients and nonrecipients of the intelligence?

- Would the provision of intelligence be part of an implicit quid pro quo on the part of the government—that some action should be (or should not be) taken by industry in exchange for access to intelligence?

The collection of foreign economic intelligence by other nations was also very controversial. An aggressive collection policy was at the heart of the concept of greater intelligence support to business. Supporters of the policy cited cases in which supposed "friends" of the United States, such as France, were caught engaging in such activity. Advocates saw similar activity by the United States as "fighting fire with fire." Critics argued that to do so would justify the initial hostile action. They also raised some of the arguments noted above about the limits on how such information might be used. But DCI Robert Gates put it best when he said that no U.S. intelligence agent was "willing to die for General Motors."

U.S. policy makers saw foreign economic counterintelligence to be largely noncontroversial. Most saw it as a proper response to foreign economic intelligence, although some questioned how extensive the problem was. Press accounts of the issue often cited the same shopworn cases, creating "echo"—the impression of a larger problem through repetition. But the problem may actually be under-reported, since many businesses do not want to admit that they have been the victims of successful foreign intelligence operations. There are also those who argue that foreign economic counterintelligence, although necessary, treats the symptom but not the cause. They acknowledge that blunting attempts at economic intelligence collection may be important but argue that the issue should be addressed at a political level—perhaps by negotiations that offer per-petrating nations the choice of cessation or countermeasures.

Legislation passed during the 105th Congress (1997–1999) extend-ed the role of FBI/Counterintelligence in the business information area, which has been very controversial. This legislation also reflects a contin-uing expansion of FBI authority in the gray areas between foreign and domestic intelligence and between intelligence and law enforcement.

PROLIFERATION.   Proliferation is now a more important issue in U.S. foreign policy, with added dimensions. The basic goal is what it always was: preventing the spread of weapons capable of inflicting mass destruc-tion. The United States has always emphasized nuclear weapons first, given their relative lethality and the fact that they were central to the U.S.-Soviet relationship. But even during the cold war, the United States worked to contain the spread of chemical and biological weapons (CBW or CW and BW) as well.

Two major shifts have occurred in U.S. nonproliferation policy in the post-cold war era. First, policy makers and intelligence officials have given CW and BW increased attention. Second, the collapse of the Soviet Union has added the problem of "loose nukes," a catch phrase used to connote the possibility of both weapons and expertise leaving former Soviet states for nations eager to create an indigenous nuclear weapons capability.

The role of intelligence in this policy area is fairly obvious: identify proliferation programs early enough to stop them before they are com-pleted. Intelligence also targets the clandestine international commerce in some of the specialty items required to manufacture weapons of mass destruction. The problems this entails are obvious as well. Proliferation programs are, by their very nature, covert. Thus, the types of collection that the United States must undertake tend to come from the clandestine side of the intelligence community. The evidence that U.S. intelligence might obtain of nascent programs may be ambiguous. Indeed, the same may be true even of mature programs. Fuzzy information complicates the ability of policy makers to confront with confidence potential prolifera-tors or to convince other nations that there is a problem.

Beyond the problem of amassing convincing evidence lies the policy question: How do you stop a would-be proliferator? The preferred means is diplomacy, but the track record of diplomacy is unimpressive. No nation has been talked out of developing nuclear weapons by diplomacy alone. The United States has used its influence, and its leverage as the guarantor of a state's national security, to pressure a state into desisting from nuclear weapons development. Press accounts allege that the Unit-ed States did just that with Taiwan in the 1980s. Some other nations—for reasons of their own—decided to abandon nuclear programs. Sweden and

The Iraqi Nuclear Program—
A Cautionary Tale

During the 1980s, Iraq was one of those nations whose nuclear weapons program was closely watched by U.S. experts. The existence of a program was not in question; its status was.

On the eve of the Gulf War, the considered analytical judgment, according to subsequent accounts, was that Iraq was at least five years away from a nuclear capability. After Iraq's defeat in the Gulf War, analysts learned that Iraq had been much closer to success, even though Israel had attacked and destroyed some of their facilities some years earlier.

What had gone wrong with U.S. estimates?

Iraq was and is a closed target, one of the most repressive and heavily policed states in the world. The state's nature makes collection more difficult, but that is not the answer to the question.

The answer lies again in an analytical flaw, namely, mirror imaging. In order to manufacture the fissionable material it required, Iraq chose a method abandoned by the United States in the early days of its own nuclear program after World War II. The method works, but it is a very slow and tedious way to produce fissionable material.

For Iraq, however, it was the perfect method, not because it was slow, but because foreign analysts disregarded it. The method allowed Iraq to procure materials that were more difficult to associate with a nuclear weapons program, to mask its actual status. A program of this sort was also more difficult for Western analysts to spot because they largely dismissed this approach out of hand, assuming that Iraq would want—just as the United States and others had—to find the fastest way to produce fissionable material.

Japan chose not to develop programs. Argentina and Brazil agreed bilaterally to abandon their fledging efforts. The white South African government gave up its nuclear weapons and its capabilities on the eve of the advent to power of the black majority. But many other states—Israel, India, Pakistan, Iraq, and, reportedly, North Korea— remain unconvinced by U.S. diplomacy. Given the minimal success of moral suasion, some have argued that only an active nonproliferation policy—intervening to destroy the capability, as both Israel and the Gulf War allies did with Iraq—will work. (See box, "The Iraqi Nuclear Program—A Cautionary Tale," this page.)

The "loose nukes" aspect of the issue adds a new and more difficult complication. The Soviet Union agreed with the goal of nuclear nonproliferation, recognizing that it could be a target of would-be proliferators. But tracking unknown quantities of weapons-grade material (which even Russian and other authorities have been unable to account for with accuracy) and tracking the international movement of experts from former Soviet states is all much more daunting. The collapse of the post-Soviet economy and the end of the privileged status these scientists once enjoyed are frightening incentives to would-be proliferators.

CW and BW proliferation require much less expertise and technical capability than nuclear proliferation requires. CW and BW weapons are far less accurate than nuclear weapons, but the random terror they portend is part of their appeal to nations and terrorists. These types of programs are more difficult than nuclear programs to identify and to track.

NARCOTICS.   Narcotics policy is a difficult area in which to work. The main policy goal is to prevent—by a variety of means—individuals from using drugs that the government deems addictive and harmful. But, as almost everyone who has ever worked on the narcotics issue has said, this is not a foreign policy issue. It is a domestic issue. Also, given the variety of reasons for which individuals use drugs, it is a very difficult goal to attain. For both practical and political reasons, narcotics has become in part a U.S. foreign policy problem, since the United States attempts to reduce the overseas production of illegal drugs and to intercept the drugs before or just as they arrive in the United States.

The intelligence community is quite capable of collecting and analyzing intelligence related to the illicit trade in narcotics. The plants from which certain narcotics derive can be grown in large quantities only in certain parts of the world. Coca is produced in the Andean region of South America. Poppies, from which heroin is made, are grown predominantly in two parts of southern Asia, centering roughly on Afghanistan and Myanmar (formerly Burma). Areas where these plants are processed into narcotics are also fairly well known, as are the routes customarily used to ship the finished products to customer areas.

The real problem lies in converting this intelligence into successful policy. Efforts at crop eradication and substitution stumble on the simple economic choices facing local farmers. Narcotics crops pay more than food crops. Processing facilities, although U.S. intelligence can locate them, tend to be small and numerous. Drugs are so profitable that small amounts, which are easily shipped, are economically attractive. This fact allows shippers to use a variety of routes, which they can change in response to pressure and efforts at interdiction. Finally, narcotics activities yield money in sufficient amounts to subvert the local authorities—civil, military, and police.

All experienced policy makers point to the importance of a domestic answer. If people do not have an interest in using illegal drugs, then all of the rest—growth, processing, shipping, and even price—become irrelevant. The drugs become valueless commodities. But the elusiveness of a successful domestic response leads policy makers back to foreign policy. (Legalizing drugs might not have the same effect on production and distribution as eliminating demand, since a black market might arise to compete with government-approved providers.)

The conjunction of the narcotics trade with international crime and possibly with terrorism as well adds a new dimension to the intelligence-gathering and policy-making problem. The profits from sales of narcotics, rather than being an end in themselves, now become the means to fund a different end. This also puts new and more difficult demands on intelligence, since terrorists and criminals operate clandestinely. The United States must be able to establish intelligence about networks, contacts, relationships among individuals and groups, flows of capital, and so forth.

Finally, narcotics crosses the line established in the United States between foreign and domestic intelligence and between intelligence and law enforcement. As noted earlier, the point at which an issue is handed from one agency to another is not always clear but is important, raising both practical and legal questions—some of which can impede prosecution.

TERRORISM.   Terrorism is a very demanding issue for intelligence because the political system will not tolerate even one terrorist attack on U.S. interests—either within the United States or overseas. Thus, in some respects intelligence is expected to operate perfectly when dealing with terrorism.

To combat terrorism, U.S. intelligence must identify known and likely terrorist threats; identify connections among groups, among primary participants and secondary supporters, and so forth; locate the primary bases out of which terrorists operate; and forestall hostile operations against U.S. and allied interests. Terrorists operate clandestinely; terrorist groups are usually small in terms of the number of people involved. The intelligence requirements are fulfilled mostly by clandestine collection and clandestine services. HUMINT becomes increasingly important, since penetrating terrorist groups is a means of obtaining the necessary information. This last aspect often means giving money to terrorists as a means of turning them into assets who will provide information. As will be discussed in the next chapter, paying terrorists raises ethical and moral issues for some Americans.

Although the intelligence community has not achieved the perfection vis-à-vis terrorism that the political system requires, the number of successful terrorist attacks made against the United States by foreign terrorists has been quite small. This suggests that the threat is less than has been supposed, that U.S. intelligence has been fairly successful in blunting attacks, or both.

The willingness of the United States to retaliate for terrorist attacks adds to the intelligence task. If those responsible for the attack do not identify themselves, the intelligence community is expected to identify them. (Even if some group claims responsibility, the claims still must be authenticated.) The certainty of intelligence about likely perpetrators becomes more important when policy makers decide to retaliate. No one wants to attack the wrong target. This became an issue in 1998, for example, after a terrorist network headed by Osama bin Laden attacked two U.S. embassies in east Africa. One of the targets against which the United States retaliated was a chemical factory in Sudan that the United States claimed was producing chemical weapons for the terrorists who participated in the attack. According to press accounts, the allegation seemed to be based to a large extent on soil samples provided by U.S. agents who went to the site. The Sudanese government refuted the charges. Even in the United States, some felt that the physical evidence was questionable and was, at any rate, a thin basis for a U.S. cruise missile attack.

HEALTH AND ENVIRONMENT.   These issues are relatively new to the intelligence agenda. They are sometimes treated as one issue, and sometimes as two. The health issue owes much of its status to the AIDS pandemic and some recent smaller outbreaks of deadly diseases such as Ebola virus. The intelligence task is largely one of tracking patterns of infection, but the gap between intelligence and policy is large. Take AIDS as an example. The causes, means of infection, and results of AIDS are very well known. Although AIDS strikes people worldwide, there are some very high concentrations of AIDS cases, especially in eastern and central Africa. The ability of the intelligence community to track rates of infection and mortality has little effect on any useful international policy. Many of the African governments that face the highest rates of AIDS infection have chosen, for a variety of reasons, to ignore or even to deny their health crisis. Local culture is a major factor in the spread of AIDS in Africa: toleration of polygamous relationships; low literacy rates, thus making even minimal efforts at education about prevention more difficult; and minimal use of prophylactics. Nor is it clear what these nations or the international community should be doing in the absence of any cure for the disease. Outsiders' attempts to change the cultural factors that allow AIDS to spread not only would be difficult to make but likely would be resisted as external interference.

The environment issue is also somewhat amorphous. The basic goal —preserving a healthier global ecology—stumbles when it comes down to practicalities. As has been found with international efforts to deal with

---

A New Intelligence Task: Environmental Verification

One of the most compelling and difficult tasks of the intelligence community during the cold war was monitoring Soviet compliance with arms control agreements. With the advent of the Kyoto Treaty on the environment, the intelligence community now faces the prospect of a similar, if not more daunting task.

The Kyoto Treaty establishes levels of pollution that nations are allowed to generate via their industrial activities. The limitations are more onerous for the industrialized nations. However, nations may "buy" the pollution rights of other nations—presumably the less industrialized ones.

The United States will "self-police," that is, voluntarily keep within its limits. But U.S. policy makers are likely to want to know whether other nations are also complying. The issue will take on a regional aspect in the United States, since states in the so-called Rust Belt face the loss of jobs.

It will fall to the intelligence community to track other nations' compliance, but doing so will be even more difficult than tracking the production and deployment of nuclear systems. As with arms control, policy makers will have to decide how and when to use intelligence indicating noncompliance. The call will never be straightforward. Other factors—the state of relations, trade issues, national security issues, to name a few—will also intrude.

AIDS, the nations at the center of the issue have different interests and preferences. The international community may believe that it has a vested interest in the preservation of some local ecological habitat, such as a rain forest. But the nation whose land it is may be more interested in its own economic development than in the stewardship of a world ecological resource.

The basic intelligence tasks are identifying major threats to the environment; identifying states whose policies may be harmful to the environment; and tracking major changes in the environment. Again, a gap separates intelligence from what policy makers are supposed to do with it. Substantial intelligence community involvement in this issue dates back only to the very late stages of the cold war. (See box, "A New Intelligence Task: Environmental Verification," this page.)

The health and environment issues also share in common the fact that much of the intelligence can be carried out through open sources. Commercial infrared satellites can track environmental changes. The spread of disease also can be tracked overtly. Intelligence on these issues has tended to suffer from the inattention of policy makers and from the fact that the overt means of collecting intelligence have not been as fully developed as the clandestine means.

PEACEKEEPING OPERATIONS.   Since the end of the cold war, international peacekeeping operations have expanded dramatically. Regional outbursts of violence, most of them within the borders of one country (or former country), have required the imposition of external troops to restore and then maintain peace. These external troops have customarily formed into multinational units. Although many of the participant nations have experience in allied operations—at least training operations—the participants tend to cross the boundaries of old alliances. Thus, for example, UN-mandated forces in Bosnia include NATO allies (United States, Britain, France, Italy, Spain) and their former Warsaw Pact foes (Russia, Ukraine), along with other nations. Successful military operations require strong intelligence support; multinational operations require intelligence sharing. But even in the aftermath of the cold war, some U.S. policy makers and intelligence officials are reticent about sharing intelligence with former foes, with nonallies, and even with some allies. Responsible civil and military officials may find themselves torn between the need to keep peacekeeping partners well informed so as to carry out successful operations and the recognition that sources and methods may be compromised even beyond the limited theater in which the peacekeeping is being carried out.

The use of peacekeeping or other internationally sanctioned operations for unilateral, U.S. intelligence purposes became an issue in 1999. A former member of UNSCOM—the U.N. group responsible for monitoring Iraqi destruction of its weapons of mass destruction—alleged that the United States used an UNSCOM inspection team to plant intelligence collection devices. Some saw the U.S. action as a necessary precaution against a hostile state; others believed it violated the basis of the UNSCOM mission.

INFORMATION OPERATIONS.   This is a new issue on the intelligence agenda, dealing with the use of computer technology to wage war and also to protect the United States from similar attacks. The Gulf War gave a great boost to this operational concept. Intelligence officers find that information operations allow them to be combatants rather than just combat supporters.

The parameters of information operations have yet to be fully defined. The technology to disrupt communications and infrastructure, send false messages, and destroy vital information exists; firm operational concepts for using the technology do not. The same was true of virtually every other military technology—firearms, tanks, airplanes, and so on. Only through operations do military and intelligence officials learn the best ways to employ—and defend against—new technologies.

The widespread use of computers and the increasing dependence of all nations and their militaries on computers underscore the attractiveness and the threat of information operations. Information operations can weaken an opponent and lessen the chance of U.S. casualties in combat.

At this point, the doctrinal questions outnumber the accepted doctrinal precepts. Should information operations be used pre-emptively, before hostilities begin? Pre-emptive use would tend also to pre-empt potential diplomatic solutions, which depend on the ability of leaders and diplomats to communicate authoritatively between capitals. One can easily envision heated debates between diplomats seeking to forestall information operations in order to keep lines of communications open, and military officers arguing about the need to begin preparing the electronic battlefield. On the other hand, a broad and successful information operation attack might induce a hostile state to agree to end a crisis. It would not entail civilian casualties, as would a classic military attack. But is this the way the United States wants to behave? Would U.S. leaders feel compelled, for legal reasons, to consider information operations to be a covert action, launched with a presidential finding, rather than a military operation? The agency largely responsible for information warfare, the National Security Agency, is both an intelligence agency and a combat support agency, so it bridges the gap. But this fact does not, in and of itself, answer the question.

Battle damage assessment (BDA), which became a major intelligence issue during the Gulf War, would be difficult to perform in an information operation. Analysts in Washington (mostly at the CIA) differed with analysts in the field as to the efficacy of the air campaign in the Gulf War. How would you carry out BDA in the even more opaque area of information operations? How would you know if an enemy's computer system had been successfully disrupted, or if the enemy had just shut it down when it recognized that an attack was under way? How would you know if your enemy had back-up systems? If a successful information warfare attack is a precondition for some type of overt military operation, can we be sure that the precondition has been satisfied? How much disruption do we want to cause? Disrupting enemy communications is useful, but do we want to preclude, for example, the ability of an enemy headquarters to signal its troops authoritatively that hostilities are to cease? Or, having disrupted the enemy's ability to communicate, how do we verify an enemy's offer to cease hostilities, to negotiate, and so on.

Turning to the defensive problem, how do we verify the state or group responsible for an information operations attack? As with terrorism and retaliation, the source of the attack is an important question. More-over, if the United States were subject to such an attack, what would the proper response be? Do we retaliate via computers or with weapons? Again, is our response an intelligence action or a military one?

DOMINANT BATTLEFIELD AWARENESS.   As noted earlier, support to military operations (SMO) is one of the highest intelligence priorities under PDD-35. A key aspect of SMO is the concept of dominant battle-field awareness (DBA). At the National Defense University in June 1995, former DCI John Deutch defined DBA as the integration of IMINT, SIG-INT, and HUMINT to give "commanders real-time, or near real-time, all-weather, comprehensive, continuous surveillance and information about the battlespace in which they operate. . . . Dominant battlefield awareness, if achieved, will reduce—never totally eliminate—the 'fog of war,' and provide you, the military commanders, with an unprecedented combat advantage."

DBA reflects at least two impulses. The first is the very great strides that U.S. intelligence has made in collecting and disseminating intelligence to commanders in the field. U.S. military commanders believe that this superiority will allow them to use forces more effectively, so as to achieve ends quicker and with fewer casualties. The second impulse behind DBA is the so-called lessons learned from the Gulf War about the problems in bringing intelligence to the field and getting the right intelligence to the right military user.

Although Deutch raised the caveat that the "fog of war" (the term coined by nineteenth-century Prussian general Carl von Clausewitz for the confusion and uncertainty that are inevitable in any combat) will never be totally eliminated, many advocates of DBA seem not to have heard him. DBA is often oversold as the ability to bring near-total intelligence to com-manders. This hyperbole puts intelligence on the spot for capabilities it does not have. Unrealistically high expectations may lead commanders to rely more on intelligence that is not forthcoming and less on their own instincts when dealing with the fog of war—which is the ultimate skill of a combat commander. (Gen. William T. Sherman observed that Gen. Ulysses S. Grant was the superior commander because Grant was uncon-cerned about what the enemy was doing when out of sight.)

Another problem with DBA is that delivering on its promise could require the intelligence community to allocate a very large percentage of collection assets to the task, to the detriment of other priorities elsewhere in the world. As with SMO, the question of "How much is enough?" is pertinent. Finally, an essential ingredient in successful DBA is getting the right type and amount of information to the right user. An army com-mander's intelligence needs differ from those of an infantry squad leader or a combat pilot. Some critics are concerned that too much information will be pushed down to users who have no need for it, flooding them with irrelevant intelligence simply because we have the means to do so and making their jobs more difficult.

As with intelligence operations, much in DBA remains to be worked out.

CONCLUSION

A decade after the end of the cold war (using as a benchmark the breaching of the Berlin Wall in 1989), the U.S. national security agenda remains unformed, not in terms of which issues matter, but in terms of which matter the most, which will receive the highest priority over time (as opposed to immediate reactions to events), and what the United States is willing to do to achieve its preferred ends. In the absence of clear definition, the intelligence community finds it difficult to perform. Intelligence officials have a broad understanding of policy makers' preferences and immediate interests, but these do not form the basis upon which to make a coherent set of plans for investments, collection systems, personnel recruitment, and training.

Many of the issues discussed in this chapter share an important hallmark: the gap between the intelligence community's ability to provide intelligence and the policy makers' ability to craft policies to address the issues and to use the intelligence. If this gap persists, it has the potential to disaffect the intelligence community and their policy customers. Policy customers want to be more than just informed; they want to act. And intelligence is not meant to be collected and then filed away; it is intended to assist people in making decisions or taking action. This is not to suggest that the intelligence community will suddenly disappear. But it may come to be seen as less central and necessary—a provider of information that is interesting but not as useful as it had been in the past because of the changed nature of the issues.

KEY TERMS

actionable intelligence	hard targets
battle damage assessment	industrial espionage
dominant battlefield awareness	information operations
foreign economic espionage	surge capacity
global coverage	

FURTHER READINGS

Writings on the post-cold war intelligence agenda remain somewhat scattered across issue areas, reflecting the nature of the debate itself.

General

Colby, William. "The Changing Role of Intelligence." *World Outlook* 13 (summer 1991): 77–90.

Goodman, Allan E. "The Future of U.S. Intelligence." *Intelligence and National Security* 11, no. 4 (October 1996): 645–656.

Goodman, Allan E., and Bruce D. Berkowitz. *The Need to Know.* Report of the Twentieth Century Fund Task Force on Covert Action and American Democracy. New York: Twentieth Century Fund, 1992.

Goodman, Allan E., et al. *In from the Cold.* Report of the Twentieth Century Fund Task Force on the Future of U.S. Intelligence. New York: Twentieth Century Fund, 1996.

Johnson, Loch K., and Kevin J. Scheid. "Spending for Spies: Intelligence Budgeting in the Aftermath of the Cold War." *Public Budgeting and Finance* 17 (winter 1997): 7–27.

Dominant Battlefield Awareness

Deutch, John M. Speech at National Defense University, Washington, D.C., June 14, 1995. Transcript at http://www.fas.org/irp/cia/product/dci—speech—61495.html.

Economics

Fort, Randall M. *Economic Espionage: Problems and Prospects.* Washington, D.C.: Consortium for the Study of Intelligence, 1993.

Hulnick, Arthur S. "The Uneasy Relationship between Intelligence and Private Industry." *International Journal of Intelligence and Counterintelligence* 9 (spring 1996): 17–31.

Lowenthal, Mark M. "Keep James Bond Out of GM." *The International Economy* (July/August 1992): 52–54.

Zelikow, Philip. "American Economic Intelligence: Past Practice and Future Principles." *Intelligence and National Security* 12, no. 1 (January 1997): 164–177.

Information Operations

Aldrich, Richard W. *The International Legal Implications of Information Warfare.* Colorado Springs, Colo.: U.S. Air Force Institute for National Security Studies, 1996.

Law Enforcement

Hulnick, Arthur S. "Intelligence and Law Enforcement." *International Journal of Intelligence and Counterintelligence* 10 (fall 1997): 269–286.

Snider, L. Britt, with Elizabeth Rindskopf and John Coleman. *Relating Intelligence and Law Enforcement: Problems and Prospects.* Washington, D.C.: Consortium for the Study of Intelligence, 1994.

Narcotics

Best, Richard A., Jr., and Mark M. Lowenthal. "The U.S. Intelligence Community and the Counternarcotics Effort." Washington, D.C.: Congressional Research Service, 1992.

Peacekeeping

Best, Richard A., Jr. "Peacekeeping: Intelligence Requirements." Washington, D.C.: Congressional Research Service, 1994.
Johnston, Paul. "No Cloak and Dagger Required: Intelligence Support to UN Peacekeeping." *Intelligence and National Security* 12, no. 4 (October 1997): 102–112.
Pickert, Perry L. *Intelligence for Multilateral Decision and Action,* edited by Russell G. Swenson. Washington, D.C.: Joint Military Intelligence College, 1997.

CHAPTER 13

Ethical and Moral Issues in Intelligence

This chapter is not as oxymoronic as it may appear to some. There are important ethical standards and moral dilemmas in intelligence with which intelligence officers and policy officials must and do grapple. As with most discussions of ethics and morality, some of the questions have no firm or agreed upon answers.

GENERAL MORAL QUESTIONS

The very nature of intelligence operations and issues and the basis upon which they are created raise a number of broad moral questions.

SECRECY.   At the outset of this book we accepted that much intelligence work is done in secret, although the definition of intelligence in chapter 1 did not include secrecy as a necessary precondition. The question remains: Is secrecy necessary in intelligence? If so, how much secrecy? And at what cost?

If intelligence needs secrecy, what causes or drives the need? Governments have intelligence services because they seek information that others would deny them. Thus, secrecy is inherent not only in what our intelligence service is doing (collection and covert action) but in the information being denied us by others. We also do not want to let the other state know our areas of interest. Is this "second level" of secrecy necessary? After all, those keeping information from us often know—or at least presume—that we want it. That is one reason why they hide it from us (although many dictatorial states attempt to control all information, understanding the threat it poses to their regime). Or is secrecy driven primarily by our attempts to gain access to hidden information? Is the nub of our secrecy in not allowing those who are attempting to deny us information to know that, to some degree, they have failed? How necessary is that? After all, we will act on the intelligence we have collected, although we will attempt to mask the reasons for our actions. Will not our opponents at least guess, based on decisions we make and actions we take, that we have gained some access to the information they were safeguarding?

Beyond the causation and drivers behind the secrecy are the costs it imposes. Here we are not discussing the monetary costs of secrecy—background checks, a variety of control systems for access, and so forth—which are quite real. The issue here is the effect on people of operating in a secret milieu. What effect, if any, does this have? Does secrecy in and of itself lead to a lowering of guards or a willingness to cut corners or take steps that might be deemed unacceptable if they were not cloaked in secrecy? This is not to suggest that thousands of people are morally compromised because they work in organizations that prize secrecy. But the nature of some aspects of intelligence—primarily collection and covert action—combined with the fact that these are undertaken in secret may lower an intelligence official's inhibitions to commit questionable actions. These factors put a premium on the careful selection and training of officers and on vigorous oversight.

WAR AND PEACE.   Moral philosophers and states have long presumed that the conditions of war and peace are different and allow different types of activity. The most obvious wartime activity is organized violence against the territory and citizens of other states. During peacetime, overt conflict is obviously precluded. Does this division between acceptable peacetime and wartime norms extend to intelligence activities? Are efforts to subvert and overthrow the governments of enemy states acceptable in peacetime, as they are in wartime?

Even during periods of peace the United States has relations with states that are hostile. The cold war between the United States and the Soviet Union may have been the epitome of such relations: hostile at virtually all levels but never reaching the level of overt conflict between the two primary antagonists (as opposed to some of their surrogates).

A relationship such as that between the two cold war antagonists occupies a gray middle ground between peace and war. Intelligence activities—both collection and covert action—became one of the main means by which the two countries could attack one another. Even in this unique situation, however, the United States and Soviet Union accepted some limits. The two sides did not kill one another's nationals who were caught spying. Rather, they jailed the spies and sometimes exchanged them, as they exchanged Col. Rudolf Abel and U-2 pilot Francis Gary Powers.

(One's own national caught spying for the other side could be executed, as were Julius Rosenberg and Col. Oleg Penkovsky.) The national leadership of each side was safe from physical attacks. But did these unwritten rules create necessary boundaries, or did they serve to allow a great many other activities, including propaganda and subversion?

If a country threatens to make war or war seems imminent, does the concept of self-defense allow states to engage in certain activities—including intelligence operations—pre-emptively? As noted earlier, in an age of information operations, this question is increasingly important.

ENDS VERSUS MEANS.   The usual answer to the question, "do the ends justify the means?" is "no." Alternatively, if the ends do not justify the means, what does? Policy makers face difficult choices when means and ends are in conflict. For example, during the cold war was it proper for the United States, which advocated free elections, to interfere in the West European elections in the late 1940s in order to preclude communist victories? Which was the preferable choice: upholding moral principles or allowing a politically unpalatable and perhaps threatening outcome? How does U.S. interference in postwar European elections compare with the subversion of the Chilean economy as a means of undermining the Allende government?

Within the U.S. political experience, questions like these represent two deeply rooted themes: realpolitik and idealism. In the milieu of the cold war, realpolitik predominated. The moral aspect of the cold war (Western democratic ideals versus Soviet communism) made choices like those described above easy for policy makers. Would policy makers make the same choices in the post-cold war world, in the absence of such a moral imperative?

THE NATURE OF THE OPPONENT.   For nearly half a century the United States faced successive totalitarian threats: the Axis and then the Soviet Union and its satellite states. The gulf between the accepted values and behavioral norms of the United States and its allies and their opponents was vast. Do the actions of your opponents affect the actions you may undertake? Are they a useful guide to action?

"All's fair, . . ." is one response. It would be foolish for a state to deny itself weapons or tactics that an opponent bent on the state's destruction is using. On the other hand, does a state not lose something important when it sinks to the level of an opponent that is amoral or immoral? For example, John Le Carre argued in his George Smiley novels that there was little difference between the actions of the United States and the Soviet Union during the cold war, that a certain moral equivalence existed. Was Le Carre correct, or can one argue that, even if there were similarities in some types of intelligence operations, the moral distinctions between the two states remained strong and important?

NATIONAL INTEREST.   The concept of national interest is not new. In the period that historians call "early modern Europe," roughly the seventeenth century, all statesmen agreed that *raison d'etat*—literally "reason of state"—guided their actions. *Raison d'etat* implied two arguments: first, that the state embodied its own ends; and second, that the interests of the state were the only guides for actions, rather than resentments, emotions, or other subjective impulses. *Raison d'etat,* as practiced in early modern Europe, also implied the use of intrigue by one state against another and the ultimate sanction: the use of force.

In the late seventeenth and eighteenth centuries, international relations were, beneath a refined veneer, rather brutal. One could argue that even the creation of an international body, the United Nations, has done little to modify the behavior of states in the late twentieth century; witness the brutality of many parties in the dismemberment of Yugoslavia, or of the Khmer Rouge in Cambodia, for example. One can see a lineal descent from seventeenth-century *raison d'etat* to twentieth-century national interest.

Is national interest a sufficient guide to the ethics and morality of intelligence? On the one hand, it is the only guide. If intelligence activities are not undertaken in support of the policies of the legitimate government, then they are meaningless at best or dangerous rogue operations at worst. On the other hand, we know from experience that legitimate governments—even those that adhere to democratic ideals and principles—can sometimes reach decisions and take actions that are morally or ethically questionable.

Thus, national interest is a difficult guideline, both indispensable and insufficient at the same time.

CHANGES IN ETHICS AND MORALS OVER TIME.   Ethics and morals change over time. For example, slavery was an acceptable condition in Britain as late as the 1830s, in some parts of the United States as late as the 1860s, and in Brazil as late as the 1880s. Slavery reportedly continues in Sudan in the late 1990s. As late as the 1910s the issue of women's suffrage was still being vigorously debated in Britain and the United States.

Assuming, as we must, that intelligence activities are undertaken on lawful authority, should they keep abreast of changes in ethics and morality? As citizens, we want to say, "yes." But who decides when these changes have come? How quickly do changes in ethics and morals get translated into policies and actions? For example, political intervention of the sort undertaken in Europe during the cold war is probably insupportable today (with the Iraq Liberation Act a notable exception to this view). But when did that change come? When the Soviet Union collapsed or earlier? In 1975 the United States faced the prospect of one of its NATO allies, Portugal, electing a communist government. After a strenuous debate between the U.S. ambassador (con) and the National Security Adviser (pro), the United States did not intervene in the Portuguese elections, which turned out all right, from the U.S. perspective. The U.S. decision was based not on a new morality but on the view that the United States had more to lose by intervening and possibly being exposed than by allowing the elections to take their course, the outcome of which the ambassador felt would be favorable, as it was.

A second important question prompted by changes in values over time is whether new standards should be imposed after the fact. For example, during the cold war the United States often supported regimes that were undemocratic and sometimes brutal, but were anticommunist. Although some in the United States found these relationships objectionable at the time, many accepted their apparent necessity. In the mid-1990s DCI John Deutch ordered the CIA to review all of its contacts and operations to see if any involved links to human rights abuses. Many in the CIA felt that this review, and some of the actions that the CIA leadership took against some officers, was an unfair ex post facto imposition of standards. (Interestingly, the Constitution bars laws that are ex post facto in nature.) Was Deutch's action a necessary cleaning up of past errors or an unfair imposition of new standards on officers who had acted in good faith under old standards?

Another interesting case is that of Markus Wolf. Wolf ran East German intelligence operations for years, successfully penetrating many levels of the West German government, including the chancellor's office. When East Germany collapsed and was absorbed by West Germany, the German government put Wolf on trial for treason. Its rationale for doing so ran as follows: the constitution of West Germany had proclaimed that it was the one legitimate government of all Germany; Wolf had carried out espionage against that government. (Despite its constitutional claims, West Germany had granted East Germany diplomatic recognition and the two states had exchanged ambassadors.) Wolf argued that he had been the citizen of a separate state and therefore could not be guilty of treason. In 1993 he was convicted of espionage, but in 1995 the highest German court voided the verdict, accepting Wolf's argument that the charge should not have been made in the first place since Wolf had not broken the laws of the state he had served, East Germany. After receiving a suspended sentence for kidnappings carried out by agents under his authority, Wolf, in 1998, was jailed for refusing to identify an agent he had referred to in his memoirs.

COLLECTION- AND COVERT ACTION-RELATED ISSUES

Many ethical and moral issues arise from collection and covert action. As with the broad issues discussed above, there are many questions and few agreed answers.

HUMINT.   HUMINT collection involves the manipulation of other human beings as potential sources of information. The skills required to be a successful HUMINT collector are acquired over time with training and experience. They basically involve psychological techniques to gain trust—including empathy, flattery, sympathy. There are also more direct methods of gaining cooperation, such as bribery, blackmail, or sex.

Two issues predominate. The first is the morality of the manipulation itself. One might argue that the various psychological techniques are played against someone who is already susceptible to manipulation. An unwilling subject will likely terminate the relationship. ("Walk-ins," that is, volunteers, are different by virtue of the fact that they offer their services.) Are these legitimate activities to be undertaken by a government against the citizens of another country, whether enemy or not?

The second issue is the responsibility of the government doing the recruiting to the source:

- How far does the government's responsibility go?
- How deep an obligation, if any, does the government incur in the recruitment?
- If the HUMINT asset is compromised, how far should the recruiter go to maintain the asset's safety? Does this obligation extend to his or her family as well?
- What if the asset has not been productive for some time? For how long a period is the government obliged to protect the asset once the relationship has ended?
- What if the asset proves not to be productive at all? Perhaps the asset has misrepresented his or her access and capabilities. Is there still an obligation?

One of the most compelling arguments in favor of strong and continued responsibility for recruited sources has little to do with morality and ethics. It is the more practical concern that recruitment of new sources will become more difficult if word gets out that current or former sources are not given the support and protection they need. In other words, failing to protect your sources is bad for business.

A third issue that arises in HUMINT tends to be specific to certain issues, such as terrorism and narcotics, that depend heavily on HUMINT for good intelligence. To collect that intelligence U.S. officials must develop contacts with—and, usually, pay money to—members of terrorist or narcotics-trafficking organizations. After all, such people are the ones who have the required intelligence. Such a case arose in 1995, when the press reported that a CIA-paid asset was instrumental in the arrest of the terrorist known as Carlos. The asset was also a terrorist, a member of Carlos's group.

Some people find these types of relationships morally objectionable because of the past activities of the sources, some of which may have been directed against U.S. interests. Policy and intelligence officials must make a difficult choice between access to useful information that cannot be obtained through other means and the distasteful prospect of paying money to a terrorist or narcotics trafficker.

COLLECTION.   Intelligence officials use a variety of techniques to collect intelligence beyond the recruiting of human assets. These include the theft of material and various types of eavesdropping. These activities are deemed unlawful in everyday life. What legitimizes them as intelligence operations of the state? In the United States, intelligence and law enforcement officials require court orders for eavesdropping and other techniques, and various procedures are in place to prevent intelligence collections from including information about U.S. citizens.

The same issues arise in counterintelligence, when a potential suspect has been identified. In the United States, unlike in many other countries, the law requires that intelligence officials obtain a court order before performing these activities against a possible spy.

One other moral question raised by collection is that of responsibility for the knowledge that is gained. Do intelligence officials or policy makers incur any obligations by discovering some piece of intelligence? For example, during World War II, British and U.S. intelligence became aware, via SIGINT, of the mass killing of the Jews by the Germans. The Allies did not carry out military action (bombing rail lines and camps) for two reasons. One was the belief that attacking purely military targets would end the war sooner and thus save more people in the concentration camps than would direct attacks on the camps. Another reason was concern over safeguarding the sources and methods by which the Allies had learned about the camps. What are the ethical and moral implications of the decision to desist?

COVERT ACTION.   Covert actions are interventions by one state in the affairs of another. The basic ethical issue is the legitimacy of such operations. As noted earlier, concepts of national interest, national security, or national defense are most commonly used to support these operations. But, taken to the extreme, *every* nation could be both a perpetrator and a target, creating Hobbesian anarchy. In reality, many states have neither the capability, the need, nor the will to carry out covert actions against other states. But those states that do have the need and the ability believe their covert actions to be legitimate.

Covert actions also may conflict with personal goals or beliefs. Across the range of covert actions, from purely political (electoral aid, propaganda) to economic subversion and then to coups, innocent citizens in the targeted state can be affected, and perhaps put in jeopardy. We long ago accepted military attacks on civilians in wartime to be a legitimate activity, as in the large-scale bombings of cities. Are peacetime covert actions different?

As discussed in chapter 8, propaganda operations raise concern in the United States over "blowback," the danger that a false story planted in the foreign press by U.S. intelligence might be picked up by U.S. media outlets. If U.S. intelligence informs U.S. media of the true nature of the story, it runs the risk of a leak, thus undoing the entire operation. How serious a concern should blowback be? Is it a major threat to the independence of the press?

What are the moral limits of operations? During the Soviet invasion of Afghanistan, some Soviet troops, dispirited by the interminable war, succumbed to the ready availability of narcotics, as had U.S. troops in Vietnam. The United States supplied arms to the anti-Soviet Mujaheddin, including sophisticated Stinger missiles. Would it have been legitimate and acceptable to take steps to increase drug use by the Soviet troops as a means of undermining their military efforts?

Paramilitary operations—the waging of war via surrogate forces, placing them somewhat beyond the norms of accepted international law—raise a number of ethical and moral issues. Are they legitimate? They raise the prospect of innocent civilians being put in jeopardy. Are there bounds for paramilitary operations? For example, does the nature of the regime that is being fought matter? Are such operations legitimate against oppressive, undemocratic regimes but illegitimate against governments that do not meet these criteria?

As with HUMINT, paramilitary operations raise questions about the obligations of the sponsoring power to the combatants. This is a problem particularly for operations that are unsuccessful or appear to be inconclusive. In the case of a failed operation, does the supporting power have an obligation to help extricate its surrogate combatants to a safe haven? In the case of an inconclusive operation, the choices are even more difficult. The supporting state may be able to continue the paramilitary operations indefinitely, perhaps knowing that there is little chance of success, but also little prospect of defeat. Should the supporting power continue the operation, despite its near-pointlessness? Or does it have a responsibility to terminate the operation? If it decides to terminate its support, does it have an obligation to extricate the fighters it has supported?

Even a successful operation can raise ethical and moral issues. In the aftermath of the Soviet withdrawal from Afghanistan, one faction, the Taliban, eventually took over much of the country. The Taliban imposed a strict Muslim regime on Afghanistan, much at odds with Western notions of civil liberties and the rights of women. Did the United States and its anti-Soviet partners in Afghanistan (Pakistan, Saudi Arabia, China) bear some responsibility to attempt to moderate the rule imposed by the Taliban?

ASSASSINATION.   The issues raised by assassination and the U.S. ban on its use were discussed in chapter 8. Most people would, and official U.S. policy does, draw a distinction between casualties inflicted as a result of military operations and the targeting of a specific individual. At the same time, the formerly broad support for the assassination ban has apparently eroded among the public and some in the press, perhaps reflecting some of the difficulties the United States has encountered in imposing its will since the end of the cold war.

Even if the ban were to be lifted selectively, it is difficult to imagine how useful criteria for implementing assassination could be drawn up. What level of crime or hostile activity would make someone a legitimate target? As noted in the discussion about Adolf Hitler, it is not easy to identify a potential target at the right time. Also, some possible targets are former partners. Saddam Hussein, for example, received U.S. backing in his war with Iran (1980–1988), which was then seen as the bigger foe. His behavior became problematical only after he invaded Kuwait.

Assassination is also a remarkably sloppy tool. Without absolute assurances about who will follow the victim into power and how the successor will behave, assassination provides no guarantee of solving the problem. The leaders we would consider as targets are not in democracies; they are in states where the mechanisms for political succession are ill-defined or subject to contest. It is entirely possible to replace one thug with another, gaining little while risking your international reputation.

Assassination also raises the risk of reprisal. An absence of rules cuts both ways.

A FINAL LOOK AT OPERATIONAL ETHICS.   Author James Barry ("Covert Actions Can Be Just") has argued that it is possible to establish criteria for making morally guided decisions about intelligence operations. Barry suggests the following:

- Just cause
- Just intention
- Proper authority
- Last resort
- Probability of success
- Proportionality
- Discrimination and control

In the abstract, this is a compelling list of checkpoints for a policy maker to consider before launching an operation. But policy makers do not act in the abstract. And once they have decided upon the necessity for an operation, they can find ways to rationalize each of the succeeding steps.

ANALYSIS-RELATED ISSUES

The ethical and moral issues surrounding analysis largely center on the many compromises that analysts must confront as they prepare their product and as they deal with policy makers.

Is INTELLIGENCE "TRUTH-TELLING?"   One of the common descriptions of intelligence is that it is the job of "telling truth to power." (This sounds fairly noble, although it is important to recall that court jesters once had the same function!) In chapter 1 we took issue with the idea that intelligence was about "truth." Yet the image persists and carries with it some important ethical implications. If "truth" is the objective of intelligence, does that raise the stakes for analysis? Are analysts working on more than a well-informed and, they hope, successful policy? Moreover, does a goal of truth allow them greater latitude to pursue and to defend their views of likely outcomes?

A problem with setting "truth" as a goal is that it has a relentless quality. Most individuals understand the importance of being honest most of the time (and acknowledge the occasional need to at least shade the truth). But if an analyst's goal is to "tell the truth"—especially to those who might not want to hear it, as "telling truth to power" implies—then there is no room for compromise, no possible admission of alternative views. After all, if one has the truth, then those who disagree must have falsehood. Thus, analysts cannot compromise with other analysts whose views may differ, even slightly. Moreover, what should a "truth teller" do if the powerful reject his or her analysis, as they are free to do? Once the powerful have failed to accept the truth, is their legitimacy at stake?

These questions may seem far-fetched, but they underscore the problems raised by "truth telling." As noble as "truth telling" may be as a goal, it raises many problems as a practical matter in an already complex intelligence and policy process.

ANALYTICAL PRESSURES.   Let us step back from "truth telling" and ascribe to intelligence the role that we have assumed throughout this book: providing informed analysis to policy makers to aid their decision making.

Even with this less demanding role, analysts can reach judgments about which they have deep and strongly held beliefs. They may be convinced not only of the conclusions they have reached but also of the importance of the issue for the nation. What should they do if their views are rejected, disregarded, or ignored by their policy customers?

- Accept that this is the policy maker's prerogative and move on to the next issue?

- Attempt to raise the issue again with the policy maker, based on the possibility that the policy maker misunderstood the importance of the issue and the analysis? How often can analysts do this—either on one particular issue or as a regular practice? How does this behavior affect their credibility?

- Try to take their analysis to other policy makers—either above the head of their original customer or elsewhere in the policy process? Even if this ploy is successful, what is the cost to the analysts' relationship with the original policy customer and all policy customers?

- Threaten to quit? Is the issue that important? Are the analysts willing to carry out the threat or risk the loss of credibility? What does quitting accomplish beyond a protest?

The multioffice or multiagency nature of intelligence analysis raises the many issues of group dynamics noted in chapter 6. Analyses are often the product of negotiation and compromise among several analysts with differing views, but:

- How far should an analyst be willing to compromise with other analysts? What types of trades are acceptable and which are not?

- At what point do the compromises affect the integrity of the document? If a document reaches the point where compromises appear to have jeopardized its utility or its integrity, can an analyst go back on previous compromises?

- Can an analyst warn policy makers that, in his or her view, an analysis has been overly compromised?

Finally, the nature of the relationship between the intelligence officer and the policy maker is an issue. When Sherman Kent spoke about the analyst wanting to be believed or listened to, he was talking mostly about the quality of the analysis. However, an analyst's access also depends on the nature of the relationship itself.

- How great a concern, if any, should the relationship be for analysts? Should they avoid stands that would alienate the policy makers so as to keep open the best lines of communication?
- What if the analyst strongly believes that he or she must make a stand? Again, should the stand be tempered for the broader sake of the long-term relationship with policy makers?
- Alternatively, what should an analyst do in the face of pressure to produce intelligence that is, perhaps, "more supportive" of policy? Such a request may not be overt; it may be subtle. Can the intelligence officer resist outright? Should he or she? How many small compromises add up to large ones that politicize the product? What if the analyst knows that the policy maker will write a memo with contrary views and will ultimately prevail? Is it still worth resisting blandishments, knowing one will lose both the argument and perhaps access to a key policy customer as well?

Many games are being played simultaneously. There is the intelligence process itself, and the policy process, and the desire of the intelligence officers to have access to policy makers and to keep their funding levels safe and preferably growing. It is easy, in the abstract, to declare that the integrity of the intelligence process is primary. But in the "trenches," this is not always so obvious or so appealing.

ANALYSTS' OPTIONS.   An intelligence analyst may believe that something fundamental is at stake, that neither compromise nor silence is possible. What are his or her options then? They boil down to two: continue the struggle from within the system or quit. (See box, "Analysts' Options: A Cultural Difference," p. 197.) Continuing the struggle from within is appealing in that one's professional standards are preserved. But is it a realistic choice or a rationalization? Are there real prospects of continuing to fight for that viewpoint from within the bureaucratic system? For whatever reason, the viewpoint did not prevail either in the intelligence community or with policy makers. Short of capitulation, the analyst is now tagged with a certain view that has been found wanting. How influential will he or she be on this issue in the future? Or is the analyst simply putting the best gloss on having lost, since he does not want to abandon his career? If an analyst has to make such choices, he or she can only hope that they come over an issue of some significance. Not every issue is worth engaging at this level.

Alternatively, the analyst can quit. Honor and professional standards are preserved intact. But by quitting, the analyst abandons all hope of further influencing the process. Yes, there are ways in which one can attempt to influence policy from outside the government, but they are rarely very effective. The analyst who quits has, in effect, conceded the field to those with whom he or she has disagreed.

OVERSIGHT-RELATED ISSUES

The demands of oversight raise ethical issues for witnesses before Congress and for the members and staff as well.

THE HELMS DILEMMA.   In 1973, while testifying before the Senate Foreign Relations Subcommittee on Multinational Corporations in an open session, DCI Richard Helms was asked if the CIA had been involved in operations to overthrow the Allende government in Chile. Helms said that CIA had not been involved. In 1977 the Justice Department considered a charge of perjury against Helms for his false testimony. After negotiations, Helms agreed to plead guilty to a misdemeanor and was fined $2,000 and given a suspended two-year term in jail.

Helms believed his testimony to have been accurate, since the CIA had tried to prevent Allende's election but had not been part of the plot to overthrow him once he was in office. This fine line notwithstanding, what options did Helms have when he was asked about CIA activity in Chile?

Under the National Security Act, the DCI is personally responsible for protecting the sources and methods of U.S. intelligence. Helms found himself caught between that obligation and his obligation to testify fully and honestly before Congress. If Helms answered that the CIA had been involved in some way, he would have revealed operations in an open, public hearing. Alternatively, had he said that he would rather answer that in private, or in a closed session, it would also have been tantamount to admitting CIA involvement. After all, if the CIA was not involved, why not answer in public? Helms opted for a third choice, to view the question within very narrow bounds, preserve secrecy, and deny CIA involvement. There may have been a fourth choice, to answer as he did in public and then to visit the senators privately to discuss the realities of CIA activity in Chile. Helms apparently did not think of this choice, since in

Analysts' Options: A Cultural Difference

The two options for analysts who find they cannot compromise—fighting from within or quitting—tend to play out very differently in the bureaucracies of Britain and the United States. In Britain there is a strong tradition of quitting in protest. To cite a high-level example, Foreign Secretary Anthony Eden resigned in February 1938 when he disagreed with Neville Chamberlain's policy of appeasement toward Nazi Germany. In the United States resignation is more rare, with individuals opting instead to fight from within. There is no definitive way to account for this difference. Several U.S. civil servants did resign, however, during the early stages of the civil war in Bosnia to protest the lack of action by the United States.

1973 oversight of CIA activity was the prerogative of a small group of Senate Armed Services Committee members, not those on Foreign Relations.

Did Helms make the right choice? Should he have been prosecuted for perjury under these circumstances? How responsible were the senators (particularly Sen. Stuart Symington [D, Mo.], who knew the facts of the matter since he was also a member of the Senate Armed Services Committee, which then had oversight of the CIA), for asking such questions in open session?

THE TORRICELLI CASE.   In 1995 Rep. Robert Torricelli (D, N.J.), a member of the House Permanent Select Committee on Intelligence, wrote a letter to President Clinton accusing the CIA of having misled Congress about its activities in Guatemala and having had on its payroll a Guatemalan officer involved in human rights violations. Torricelli also made his letter available to the *New York Times*. Torricelli admitted that he had leaked the information to the press but argued that his duty as a member of Congress to preserve the integrity of government was greater than the oaths he had taken as a member of the House and of the Intelligence Committee to preserve secret information. Torricelli also argued that he had not violated committee rules, since he had received the information from a State Department officer in his personal office, and that it was not clear to him that the information had been properly classified.

The chairman of the Intelligence Committee filed charges against Torricelli, which were adjudicated by the House Ethics Committee. This committee decided that House rules concerning the handling of classified information were vague and ordered that in the future members would have a positive obligation to ascertain the true classification of information before releasing it. The committee went on to say that, had this ambiguity been resolved at the time he released the information, Torricelli would have been guilty of violating House rules.

Torricelli believed that the information provided by the State officer, a former employee of Torricelli's, revealed CIA duplicity. Having written to the president, was it necessary to release the information to the *New York Times* as well? Should he first have gone to the committee leadership or his party's leadership with his concerns?

Interestingly, the only person who was punished was the State officer who provided the information to Torricelli, Richard Nuccio. A panel appointed by DCI Deutch decided that Nuccio had provided the information without proper authorization. Nuccio lost his clearances and resigned from the State Department, eventually returning to work on Torricelli's staff. Ironically, Torricelli could have saved Nuccio by saying that he had asked Nuccio for the information. But, by saying that, Torricelli would have undercut his argument that he had been the innocent recipient.

In 1998 the Intelligence Community Whistleblower Protection Act became law, after much debate in Congress and the executive branch. The law established procedures by which intelligence community employees may report a complaint or urgent concern. They must first do so through channels in the intelligence community but are free to inform the Intelligence Committees if the community has taken no action by a specific time. Even then, the employees must inform executive branch officials that they are going to Congress and must handle their information in accordance with proper security procedures. Reflecting the Torricelli case, the whistleblower law states, "A member or employee of one of the intelligence committees who receives a complaint or information . . . does so in that member or employee's official capacity as a member or employee of that committee."

THE MEDIA

Reporters and their various media outlets exist to publish stories. The First Amendment to the Constitution offers the press broad freedom: "Congress shall make no law . . . abridging the freedom . . . of the press . . ."

The government has no way to prevent the media from reporting information that it has obtained. But freedom to publish is not the same as "the people's right to know," which is an interesting catch phrase but does not appear anywhere in the Constitution. The press's right to report also does not obligate government officials to provide information, especially classified information.

But what, if any, obligations does the press have when it obtains information with national security implications? Should press limits be self-imposed, or should the press operate on the premise of "finders keepers, losers weepers"? Just as ethics and morals change in other areas, so too they change in the media.

In the past, the press has come upon intelligence activities and agreed not to write about them for the sake of national security. For example, reporters discovered Cuban exile training camps in Florida prior to the Bay of Pigs and also learned about the construction of the *Glomar Explorer*, built by the Hughes Corporation for the CIA to retrieve a sunken Soviet submarine.

In the post-Watergate era of "investigative journalism" (a wonderful redundancy, as all journalism is investigative), it is difficult to imagine that many reporters or media outlets would be willing to suspend publication or to drop a story entirely. One has only to think about such scenes as U.S. television camera crews waiting onshore as the first U.S. troops landed in Somalia in 1993 to question the premise.

Still, the question remains. At what point, if any, should reporters put aside their professional and career interests for the sake of preserving the secrecy of some intelligence activity or information? What responsibilities, if any, does the press have for the results of a story it publishes?

CONCLUSION

Intelligence is not without its ethical and moral dilemmas, some of which can be excruciating. That these intelligence dilemmas exist also means that policy makers have choices to make that can have ethical and moral dimensions. Intelligence, perhaps more than any other government activity, operates on the edge of acceptable morality, occasionally dealing in techniques that would not be acceptable elsewhere in government or in private life. For most citizens, the trade-off between ethics and increased security is acceptable, provided that the intelligence community operates with rules, oversight, and accountability.

FURTHER READINGS

Barry, James A. "Covert Action Can Be Just." *Orbis* 37 (summer 1993): 375–390.
___. *The Sword of Justice: Ethics and Coercion in International Politics.* New York: Praeger Publishers, 1998.

Godfrey, E. Drexel. "Ethics and Intelligence." *Foreign Affairs* 56 (April 1978): 624–642; see also the response by Art Jacobs in the following issue.

Lauren, Paul Gordon. "Ethics and Intelligence." In *Intelligence: Policy and Process,* edited by Alfred C. Maurer et al. Boulder, Colo.: Westview Press, 1985.

Masters, Barrie P. "The Ethics of Intelligence Activities." National Security Affairs Forum, National War College, Washington, D.C., spring/summer 1976.

Powers, Thomas. *The Man Who Kept the Secrets: Richard Helms and the CIA.* New York: Alfred A. Knopf, 1979.

Sorel, Albert. *Europe Under the Old Regime.* Translated by Francis H. Herrick. New York: Harper and Row, 1947.

APPENDIX 1

Additional Bibliographic Citations and Web Sites

This bibliography, arranged topically, provides readings additional to those listed after each chapter. It is not a comprehensive bibliography of intelligence literature. Rather, the works have been chosen based on their relevance to and amplification of the themes developed in the book. Some works, although older, remain highly useful.

The list of Web sites was compiled by John Macartney, scholar in residence at American University's School of International Service.

REFERENCE

Lowenthal, Mark M. *The U.S. Intelligence Community: An Annotated Bibliography.* New York: Garland, 1994.

U.S. Congress. House Permanent Select Committee on Intelligence. *Compilation of Intelligence Laws and Related Laws and Executive Orders of Interest to the National Intelligence Community, as amended through January 3, 1998.* 105th Congress, 2d session. 1998.

Watson, Bruce W., et al., eds. *United States Intelligence: An Encyclopedia.* New York: Garland, 1990.

GENERAL WORKS

Dearth, Douglas H., and R. Thomas Goodden, eds. *Strategic Intelligence: Theory and Approach.* 2d ed. Washington, D.C.: Defense Intelligence Agency, Joint Military Intelligence Training Center, 1995.

Hilsman, Roger. *Strategic Intelligence and National Decisions.* Glencoe, Ill.: Greenwood, 1956.

Kent, Sherman. *Strategic Intelligence for American World Policy.* Princeton, N.J.: Princeton University Press, 1949.

Krizan, Lisa. *Intelligence Essentials for Everyone.* Washington, D.C.: Joint Military Intelligence College, 1999.

Laqueur, Walter. *A World of Secrets.* New York: Basic Books, 1985.

HISTORIES

Andrew, Christopher. *For the President's Eyes Only.* New York: Harper Perennial Library, 1995.

Montague, Ludwell Lee. *General Walter Bedell Smith as Director of Central Intelligence: October 1950–February 1953.* University Park: Pennsylvania State University Press, 1992.

Ranelagh, John. *The Agency: The Rise and Decline of the CIA.* New York: Simon and Schuster, 1987.

Troy, Thomas F. *Donovan and the CIA: A History of the Establishment of the Central Intelligence Agency.* Frederick, Md.: Greenwood, 1981.

U.S. Senate Select Committee to Study Governmental Operations with Respect to Intelligence Activities [Church Committee]. *Final Report,* Book IV: *Supplementary Detailed Staff Reports on Foreign and Military Intelligence.* 94th Congress, 2d session. 1976. [Also known as the Karalekas Report, after author Anne Karalekas.]

ANALYSIS—HISTORICAL

McAuliffe, Mary S., ed. *CIA Documents on the Cuban Missile Crisis 1962.* Washington, D.C.: Historical Staff, U.S. Central Intelligence Agency, 1992.

Price, Victoria S. *The DCI's Role in Producing Strategic Intelligence Estimates.* Newport, R.I.: U.S. Naval War College, 1980.

COVERT ACTION—HISTORICAL

Aguilar, Luis. *Operation Zapata.* Frederick, Md.: University Publications of America, 1981. [Bay of Pigs]

Bissell, Richard M., with Jonathan E. Lewis and Frances T. Pudlo. *Reflections of a Cold Warrior.* New Haven, Conn.: Yale University Press, 1996.

Blight, James G., and Peter Kornbluh, eds. *Politics of Illusion: The Bay of Pigs Invasion Reexamined.* Boulder, Colo.: Lynne Rienner Publishers, 1998.

Draper, Theodore. *A Very Thin Line: The Iran-Contra Affairs.* New York: Hill and Wang, 1991.

Persico, Joseph. *Casey: From the OSS to CIA.* New York: Viking, 1990.

Thomas, Ronald C., Jr. "Influences on Decisionmaking at the Bay of Pigs." *International Journal of Intelligence and Counterintelligence* 3 (winter 1989): 537–548.

U.S. Senate Select Committee to Study Governmental Operations with Respect to Intelligence Activities [Church Committee]. *Alleged Assassination Plots Involving Foreign Leaders.* 94th Congress, 1st session. 1975.

Wyden, Peter. *The Bay of Pigs: The Untold Story.* New York: Simon and Schuster, 1979.

INTELLIGENCE WEB SITES

SEARCHABLE DATABASES

- *http://intellit.muskingum.edu/intellsite/index.html*
- *http://webcom.com/%7Epinknoiz/covert/ciabasesearch.html*

MULTIPLE SITE LINKS

- *http://mprofaca.cro.net/kimirror.html*
- *http://www.loyola.edu/dept/politics/intel.html*
- *http://www.columbia.edu/cu/libraries/indiv/dsc/intell.html*
- *http://www.kimsoft.com/kim-spy.htm*

ARMED FORCES JOURNAL INTERNATIONAL

- *http://www.afji.com*

CENTRAL INTELLIGENCE AGENCY

- *http://www.odci.gov/csi* (Center for the Study of Intelligence)
- *http://www.foia.ucia.gov* (Freedom of Information Act documents)

NATIONAL SECURITY ARCHIVE

- *http://www.seas.gwu.edu/nsarchive* (declassified documents)

NEW YORK TIMES CIA PAGE

- *http://www.nytimes.com/library/national/cia-diningmain.html*

SENATE SELECT COMMITTEE ON INTELLIGENCE

- *http://www.senate.gov/committee/intelligence.html*

HUMINT

- *http://www.fas.org/irp/wwwspy.html* (Federation of American Scientists)
- *http://www3.theatlantic.com/issues/98feb/cia.htm* *(The Atlantic Monthly)*

IMINT

- *http://www.fas.org/irp/wwwimint.html* (Federation of American Scientists)
- *http://www.fas.org/irp/imint/kh-12.htm* (Federation of American Scientists)

MASINT

- *http://www.fas.org/irp/program/masint—evaluation—rep.htm* (Federation of American Scientists)
- *http://www.fas.org/irp/congress/1996—rpt/ic21/ic21007.htm* (Federation of American Scientists)

OSINT

- *http://www.oss.net* (Open Source Solutions)
- *http://www.fas.org/irp/eprint/oss980501.htm* (Federation of American Scientists)
- *http://www.fas.org/irp/wwwecon.html* (Federation of American Scientists)

SIGINT

- *http://www.fas.org/irp/wwwsigin.html* (Federation of American Scientists)

COUNTERINTELLIGENCE

- *http://www.nacic.gov* (National Counterintelligence Center)
- *http://www.fbi.gov/ansir/ansir.htm* (Federal Bureau of Investigation)
- *http://www.dtic.mil/dodsi/researc2.html* (Defense Security Service)
- *http://www.loyola.edu/dept/politics/hula/hitzrept.html* ("Abstract of Report of Investigation, the Aldrich H. Ames Case: An Assessment of CIA's Role in Identifying Ames as an Intelligence Penetration of the Agency," October 21, 1994)

COVERT ACTION

- *http://www.nytimes.com/library/national/cia-invismain.html* *(New York Times)*

INFORMATION OPERATIONS

- *http://www.infowar.com*

CURRENT NEWS ARTICLES

- *http://jya.com/crypto.htm*

INTELLIGENCE REFORM OF 1996

- *http://www.access.gpo.gov/int/report.html* ("Report of the Commission on the Roles and Capabilities of the United States Intelligence Community" [Les Aspin/Harold Brown])
- *http://www.access.gpo.gov/congress/house/intel/ic21/ic21—toc.html* ("The Intelligence Community in the 21st Century," Staff Study, Permanent Select Committee on Intelligence, House of Representatives, 104th Congress [IC21])

BUSINESS (COMPETITIVE) INTELLIGENCE

- *http://www.lookoutpoint.com/index.html* (Real-World Intelligence, Inc.)
- *http://www.scip.org* (Society of Competitive Intelligence Professionals)
- *http://www.stratfor.com* (Stratfor)
- *http://www.opsec.org* (Operations Security Professionals Society)
- *http://www.pcic.net* (Professional Connections in the Intelligence Community)
- *http://www.fas.org/irp/wwwecon.html* (Federation of American Scientists)

Foreign Intelligence Services

- *http://www.pro.gov.uk/releases/soe-europe.htm* (United Kingdom, Special Operations Executive)
- *http://www.mi5.gov.uk* (United Kingdom, MI-5)
- *http://www.gchq.gov.uk* (United Kingdom, Government Communications Headquarters)
- *http://www.csis-scrs.gc.ca* (Canadian Security Intelligence Service)
- *http://www.cse.dnd.ca/cse/english/home—1.html* (Canada, Communications Security Establishment)
- *http://www.asia-research.com/JI2000.html* (Japan)

Special Reports

- *http://www.carnegie.org/deadly/0697warning.htm* ("The Warning-Response Problem and Missed Opportunities in Preventive Diplomacy," Carnegie Commission on Preventing Deadly Conflict, 1997)
- *http://www.fas.org/irp/congress/1998_cr/s980731-rumsfeld.htm* ("The Rumsfeld Commission Report," *Congressional Record*, U.S. Senate, July 31, 1998)
- *http://www.seas.gwu.edu/nsarchive/news/19980222.htm* ("Inspector General's Survey of the Cuban Operation and Associated Documents," CIA report on Bay of Pigs)
- *http://www.fas.org/irp/cia/product/jeremiah.html* (Comments of Adm. David Jeremiah on his investigation into actions taken by the intelligence community leading up to the Indian nuclear test of 1998)
- *http://www.fas.org/irp/cia/product/cocaine2/index.html* ("Report of Investigation: Allegations of Connections between CIA and the Contras in Cocaine Trafficking to the United States," CIA inspector general)
- *http://www.washingtonpost.com/wp-srv/national/longterm/drugs/front.htm* ("Special Report: CIA, Contras and Drugs: Questions Linger," *Washington Post*)

Private Organizations

- *http://www.his.com/~afio* (Association of Former Intelligence Officers)
- *http://www.nmia.org* (National Military Intelligence Association)
- *http://www.xmission.com:80/~nip* (Naval Intelligence Professionals)
- *http://www.oss.net* (Open Source Solutions)
- *http://www.aochq.org* (Association of Old Crows)
- *http://www.opsec.org* (Operations Security Professionals Society)
- *http://www.afcea.com* (Association for Communications, Electronics, Intelligence and Information Systems Professionals)
- *http://www.cloakanddagger.com/dagger* (Cloak and Dagger Books)
- *http://intelligence-history.wiso.uni-erlangen.de* (International Intelligence History Study Group)

APPENDIX 2

Documents

THE NATIONAL SECURITY ACT (EXCERPTS)

The National Security Act is the fundamental legislation of the United States in terms of intelligence. It established the National Security Council, under which serves the director of central intelligence, who manages the Central Intelligence Agency. Although Congress has amended the National Security Act several times since enacting it in 1947, the intelligence community retains today the basic structure first envisaged by Ferdinand Eberstadt, an adviser to Secretary of the Navy James Forrestal and the act's principal architect.

The key provisions with regard to intelligence are:

SEC. 101:   The National Security Council
SEC. 102:   Office of the Director of Central Intelligence
SEC. 102A: Central Intelligence Agency
SEC. 103:   Responsibilities of the Director of Central Intelligence
                    (including the specific role of the CIA)
SEC. 104:   Authorities of the Director of Central Intelligence
SEC. 501:   Congressional oversight of intelligence
SEC. 502:   Reporting on intelligence activities, other than covert
                    action
SEC. 503:   Presidential approval and reporting of covert action
SEC. 504:   Funding of intelligence activities
SEC. 601:   Protection of identities of certain U.S. undercover intel-
                    ligence officers, agents, informants and sources
SEC. 701:   Exemption of certain CIA files from the Freedom of
                    Information Act
SEC. 801:   Procedures for access to classified information.

Other sections of the National Security Act concern the structure and roles of the Defense Department and its components and are not reproduced here.

NATIONAL SECURITY ACT OF 1947

ACT OF JULY 26, 1947

AN ACT To promote the national security by providing for a Secretary of Defense; for a National Military Establishment; for a Department of the Army, a Department of the Navy, and a Department of the Air Force; and for the coordination of the activities of the National Military Establishment with other departments and agencies of the Government concerned with the national security.

Be it enacted by the Senate and House of Representatives of the United States of America in Congress assembled,

SHORT TITLE

That [50 U.S.C. 401 note] this Act may be cited as the "National Security Act of 1947".

TABLE OF CONTENTS

---

[1] Item editorially inserted.

[2] This section was redesignated as section 108 by section 705(a)(2) of P.L. 102—496, but this entry in the table of contents was not repealed.

[3] Section repealed without amending table of contents.

---

[1] Section repealed without amending table of contents.

[2] Item editorially inserted.

DECLARATION OF POLICY

SEC. 2. [50 U.S.C. 401] In enacting this legislation, it is the intent of Congress to provide a comprehensive program for the future security of the United States; to provide for the establishment of integrated policies and procedures for the departments, agencies, and functions of the Government relating to the national security; to provide a Department of Defense, including the three military Departments of the Army, the Navy (including naval aviation and the United States Marine Corps), and the Air Force under the direction, authority, and control of the Secretary of Defense; to provide that each military department shall be separately organized under its own Secretary and shall function under the direction, authority, and control of the Secretary of Defense; to provide for their unified direction under civilian control of the Secretary of Defense but not to merge these departments or services; to provide for the establishment of unified or specified combatant commands, and a clear and direct line of command to such commands; to eliminate unnecessary duplication in the Department of Defense, and particularly in the field of research and engineering by vesting its overall direction and control in the Secretary of Defense; to provide more effective, efficient, and economical administration in the Department of Defense; to provide for the unified strategic direction of the combatant forces, for their operation under unified command, and for their integration into an efficient team of land, naval, and air forces but not to establish a single Chief of Staff over the armed forces nor an overall armed forces general staff.

DEFINITIONS

SEC. 3. [50 U.S.C. 401a] As used in this Act:

(1) The term "intelligence" includes foreign intelligence and counterintelligence.

(2) The term "foreign intelligence" means information relating to the capabilities, intentions, or activities of foreign governments or elements thereof, foreign organizations, or foreign persons.

(3) The term "counterintelligence" means information gathered and activities conducted to protect against espionage, other intelligence activities, sabotage, or assassinations conducted by or on behalf of foreign governments or elements thereof, foreign organizations, or foreign persons, or international terrorist activities.

(4) The term "intelligence community" includes—

(A) the Office of the Director of Central Intelligence, which shall include the Office of the Deputy Director of Central Intelligence, the National Intelligence Council (as provided for in section 105(b)(3)), and such other offices as the Director may designate;

(B) the Central Intelligence Agency;

(C) the National Security Agency;

(D) the Defense Intelligence Agency;

(E) the National Imagery and Mapping Agency;

(F) the National Reconnaissance Office;

(G) other offices within the Department of Defense for the collection of specialized national intelligence through reconnaissance programs;

(H) the intelligence elements of the Army, the Navy, the Air Force, the Marine Corps, the Federal Bureau of Investigation, the Department of the Treasury, and the Department of Energy;

(I) the Bureau of Intelligence and Research of the Department of State; and

(J) such other elements of any other department or agency as may be designated by the President, or designated jointly by the Director of Central Intelligence and the head of the department or agency concerned, as an element of the intelligence community.

(5) The terms "national intelligence" and "intelligence related to the national security"—

(A) each refer to intelligence which pertains to the interests of more than one department or agency of the Government; and

(B) do not refer to counterintelligence or law enforcement activities conducted by the Federal Bureau of Investigation except to the extent provided for in procedures agreed to by the Director of Central Intelligence and the Attorney General, or otherwise as expressly provided for in this title.

(6) The term "National Foreign Intelligence Program" refers to all programs, projects, and activities of the intelligence community, as well as any other programs of the intelligence community designated jointly by the Director of Central Intelligence and the head of a United States

department or agency by the President. Such term does not include programs, projects, or activities of the military departments to acquire intelligence solely for the planning and conduct of tactical military operations by United States Armed Forces.

TITLE I—COORDINATION FOR NATIONAL SECURITY

NATIONAL SECURITY COUNCIL

SEC. 101. [50 U.S.C. 402] (a) There is hereby established a council to be known as the National Security Council (thereinafter in this section referred to as the "Council").

The President of the United States shall preside over meetings of the Council: *Provided,* That in his absence he may designate a member of the Council to preside in his place.

The function of the Council shall be to advise the President with respect to the integration of domestic, foreign, and military policies relating to the national security so as to enable the military services and the other departments and agencies of the Government to cooperate more effectively in matters involving the national security.

The Council shall be composed of
  (1) the President;
  (2) the Vice President;
  (3) the Secretary of State;
  (4) the Secretary of Defense; . . .

(b) In addition to performing such other functions as the President may direct, for the purpose of more effectively coordinating the policies and functions of the departments and agencies of the Government relating to the national security, it shall, subject to the direction of the President, be the duty of the Council—

  (1) to assess and appraise the objectives, commitments, and risks of the United States in relation to our actual and potential military power, in the interest of national security, for the purpose of making recommendations to the President in connection therewith; and

  (2) to consider policies on matters of common interest to the departments and agencies of the Government concerned with the national security, and to make recommendations to the President in connection therewith. . . .

(d) The Council shall, from time to time, make such recommendations, and such other reports to the President as it deems appropriate or as the President may require.

(e) The Chairman (or in his absence the Vice Chairman) of the Joint Chiefs of Staff may, in his role as principal military adviser to the National Security Council and subject to the direction of the President, attend and participate in meetings of the National Security Council.

(f) The Director of National Drug Control Policy may, in his role as principal adviser to the National Security Council on national drug control policy, and subject to the direction of the President, attend and participate in meetings of the National Security Council. . . . [1]

(j) The Director of Central Intelligence (or, in the Director's absence, the Deputy Director of Central Intelligence) may, in the performance of the Director's duties under this Act and subject to the direction of the President, attend and participate in meetings of the National Security Council.

OFFICE OF THE DIRECTOR OF CENTRAL INTELLIGENCE

SEC. 102. [50 U.S.C. 403] (a) DIRECTOR OF CENTRAL INTELLIGENCE.—There is a Director of Central Intelligence who shall be appointed by the President, by and with the advice and consent of the Senate. The Director shall—

  (1) serve as head of the United States intelligence community;

  (2) act as the principal adviser to the President for intelligence matters related to the national security; and

  (3) serve as head of the Central Intelligence Agency.

---

[1] The amendment made by § 1003(a)(3) of P.L. 100-690 (102 Stat. 4182), redesignating subsection (f) as (g) and adding a new (f) is repealed by section 1009 of P.L. 100-690 (102 Stat. 4188), effective September 30, 1997, as amended by section 90208 of P.L. 103-322 (108 Stat. 1995).

(b) DEPUTY DIRECTORS OF CENTRAL INTELLIGENCE.—(1) There is a Deputy Director of Central Intelligence who shall be appointed by the President, by and with the advice and consent of the Senate.

(2) There is a Deputy Director of Central Intelligence for Community Management who shall be appointed by the President, by and with the advice and consent of the Senate.

(3) Each Deputy Director of Central Intelligence shall have extensive national security expertise.

(c) MILITARY STATUS OF DIRECTOR AND DEPUTY DIRECTORS.—(1)(A) Not more than one of the individuals serving in the positions specified in subparagraph (B) may be a commissioned officer of the Armed Forces, whether in active or retired status.

(B) The positions referred to in subparagraph (A) are the following:

(i) The Director of Central Intelligence.

(ii) The Deputy Director of Central Intelligence.

(iii) The Deputy Director of Central Intelligence for Community Management.

(2) It is the sense of Congress that, under ordinary circumstances, it is desirable that one of the individuals serving in the positions specified in paragraph (1)(B)—

(A) be a commissioned officer of the Armed Forces, whether in active or retired status; or

(B) have, by training or experience, an appreciation of military intelligence activities and requirements.

(3) A commissioned officer of the Armed Forces, while serving in a position specified in paragraph (1)(B)—

(A) shall not be subject to supervision or control by the Secretary of Defense or by any officer or employee of the Department of Defense;

(B) shall not exercise, by reason of the officer's status as a commissioned officer, any supervision or control with respect to any of the military or civilian personnel of the Department of Defense except as otherwise authorized by law; and

(C) shall not be counted against the numbers and percentages of commissioned officers of the rank and grade of such officer authorized for the military department of that officer.

(4) Except as provided in subparagraph (A) or (B) of paragraph (3), the appointment of an officer of the Armed Forces to a position specified in paragraph (1)(B) shall not affect the status, position, rank, or grade of such officer in the Armed Forces, or any emolument, perquisite, right, privilege, or benefit incident to or arising out of any such status, position, rank, or grade.

(5) A commissioned officer of the Armed Forces on active duty who is appointed to a position specified in paragraph (1)(B), while serving in such position and while remaining on active duty, shall continue to receive military pay and allowances and shall not receive the pay prescribed for such position. Funds from which such pay and allowances are paid shall be reimbursed from funds available to the Director of Central Intelligence.

(d) DUTIES OF DEPUTY DIRECTORS.—(1)(A) The Deputy Director of Central Intelligence shall assist the Director of Central Intelligence in carrying out the Director's responsibilities under this Act.

(B) The Deputy Director of Central Intelligence shall act for, and exercise the powers of, the Director of Central Intelligence during the Director's absence or disability or during a vacancy in the position of the Director of Central Intelligence.

(2) The Deputy Director of Central Intelligence for Community Management shall, subject to the direction of the Director of Central Intelligence, be responsible for the following:

(A) Directing the operations of the Community Management Staff.

(B) Through the Assistant Director of Central Intelligence for Collection, ensuring the efficient and effective collection of national intelligence using technical means and human sources.

(C) Through the Assistant Director of Central Intelligence for Analysis and Production, conducting oversight of the analysis and production of intelligence by elements of the intelligence community.

(D) Through the Assistant Director of Central Intelligence for Administration, performing community-wide management functions of the intelligence community, including the management of personnel and resources.

(3)(A) The Deputy Director of Central Intelligence takes precedence in the Office of the Director of Central Intelligence immediately after the Director of Central Intelligence.

(B) The Deputy Director of Central Intelligence for Community Management takes precedence in the Office of the Director of Central Intelligence immediately after the Deputy Director of Central Intelligence.

(e) OFFICE OF THE DIRECTOR OF CENTRAL INTELLIGENCE.—(1) There is an Office of the Director of Central Intelligence. The function of the Office is to assist the Director of Central Intelligence in carrying out the duties and responsibilities of the Director under this Act and to carry out such other duties as may be prescribed by law.

(2) The Office of the Director of Central Intelligence is composed of the following:

(A) The Director of Central Intelligence.

(B) The Deputy Director of Central Intelligence.

(C) The Deputy Director of Central Intelligence for Community Management.

(D) The National Intelligence Council.

(E) The Assistant Director of Central Intelligence for Collection.

(F) The Assistant Director of Central Intelligence for Analysis and Production.

(G) The Assistant Director of Central Intelligence for Administration.

(H) Such other offices and officials as may be established by law or the Director of Central Intelligence may establish or designate in the Office.

(3) To assist the Director in fulfilling the responsibilities of the Director as head of the intelligence community, the Director shall employ and utilize in the Office of the Director of Central Intelligence a professional staff having an expertise in matters relating to such responsibilities and may establish permanent positions and appropriate rates of pay with respect to that staff.

(4) The Office of the Director of Central Intelligence shall, for administrative purposes, be within the Central Intelligence Agency.

(f) ASSISTANT DIRECTOR OF CENTRAL INTELLIGENCE FOR COLLECTION.—(1) To assist the Director of Central Intelligence in carrying out the Director's responsibilities under this Act, there shall be an Assistant Director of Central Intelligence for Collection who shall be appointed by the President, by and with the advice and consent of the Senate.

(2) The Assistant Director for Collection shall assist the Director of Central Intelligence in carrying out the Director's collection responsibilities in order to ensure the efficient and effective collection of national intelligence.

(g) ASSISTANT DIRECTOR OF CENTRAL INTELLIGENCE FOR ANALYSIS AND PRODUCTION.—(1) To assist the Director of Central Intelligence in carrying out the Director's responsibilities under this Act, there shall be an Assistant Director of Central Intelligence for Analysis and Production who shall be appointed by the President, by and with the advice and consent of the Senate.

(2) The Assistant Director for Analysis and Production shall—

(A) oversee the analysis and production of intelligence by the elements of the intelligence community;

(B) establish standards and priorities relating to such analysis and production;

(C) monitor the allocation of resources for the analysis and production of intelligence in order to identify unnecessary duplication in the analysis and production of intelligence;

(D) identify intelligence to be collected for purposes of the Assistant Director of Central Intelligence for Collection; and

(E) provide such additional analysis and production of intelligence as the President and the National Security Council may require.

(h) ASSISTANT DIRECTOR OF CENTRAL INTELLIGENCE FOR ADMINISTRATION.—(1) To assist the Director of Central Intelligence in carrying out the Director's responsibilities under this Act, there shall be an Assistant Director of Central Intelligence for Administration who shall be appointed by the President, by and with the advice and consent of the Senate.

(2) The Assistant Director for Administration shall manage such activities relating to the administration of the intelligence community as the Director of Central Intelligence shall require.

CENTRAL INTELLIGENCE AGENCY

SEC. 102A. [50 U.S.C. 403–1] There is a Central Intelligence Agency. The function of the Agency shall be to assist the Director of Central Intelligence in carrying out the responsibilities referred to in paragraphs (1) through (5) of section 103(d) of this Act.

RESPONSIBILITIES OF THE DIRECTOR OF CENTRAL INTELLIGENCE

SEC. 103. [50 U.S.C. 403–3] (a) PROVISION OF INTELLIGENCE.—(1) Under the direction of the National Security Council, the Director of Central Intelligence shall be responsible for providing national intelligence—

(A) to the President;

(B) to the heads of departments and agencies of the executive branch;

(C) to the Chairman of the Joint Chiefs of Staff and senior military commanders; and

(D) where appropriate, to the Senate and House of Representatives and the committees thereof.

(2) Such national intelligence should be timely, objective, independent of political considerations, and based upon all sources available to the intelligence community.

(b) NATIONAL INTELLIGENCE COUNCIL.—(1)(A) There is established within the Office of the Director of Central Intelligence the National Intelligence Council (hereafter in this section referred to as the "Council"). The Council shall be composed of senior analysts within the intelligence community and substantive experts from the public and private sector, who shall be appointed by, report to, and serve at the pleasure of, the Director of Central Intelligence.

(B) The Director shall prescribe appropriate security requirements for personnel appointed from the private sector as a condition of service on the Council, or as contractors of the Council or employees of such contractors, to ensure the protection of intelligence sources and methods while avoiding, wherever possible, unduly intrusive requirements which the Director considers to be unnecessary for this purpose.

(2) The Council shall—

(A) produce national intelligence estimates for the Government, including, whenever the Council considers appropriate, alternative views held by elements of the intelligence community;

(B) evaluate community-wide collection and production of intelligence by the intelligence community and the requirements and resources of such collection and production; and

(C) otherwise assist the Director in carrying out the responsibilities described in subsection (a).

(3) Within their respective areas of expertise and under the direction of the Director, the members of the Council shall constitute the senior intelligence advisers of the intelligence community for purposes of representing the views of the intelligence community within the Government.

(4) Subject to the direction and control of the Director of Central Intelligence, the Council may carry out its responsibilities under this subsection by contract, including contracts for substantive experts necessary to assist the Council with particular assessments under this subsection.

(5) The Director shall make available to the Council such staff as may be necessary to permit the Council to carry out its responsibilities under this subsection and shall take appropriate measures to ensure that the Council and its staff satisfy the needs of policymaking officials and other consumers of intelligence. The Council shall also be readily accessible to policymaking officials and other appropriate individuals not otherwise associated with the intelligence community.

(6) The heads of elements within the intelligence community shall, as appropriate, furnish such support to the Council, including the preparation of intelligence analyses, as may be required by the Director.

(c) HEAD OF THE INTELLIGENCE COMMUNITY.—In the Director's capacity as head of the intelligence community, the Director shall—

(1) facilitate the development of an annual budget for intelligence and intelligence-related activities of the United States by—

(A) developing and presenting to the President an annual budget for the National Foreign Intelligence Program; and

(B) participating in the development by the Secretary of Defense of the annual budgets for the Joint Military Intelligence Program and the Tactical Intelligence and Related Activities Program;

(2) establish the requirements and priorities to govern the collection of national intelligence by elements of the intelligence community;

(3) approve collection requirements, determine collection priorities, and resolve conflicts in collection priorities levied on national collection assets, except as otherwise agreed with the Secretary of Defense pursuant to the direction of the President;

(4) promote and evaluate the utility of national intelligence to consumers within the Government;

(5) eliminate waste and unnecessary duplication within the intelligence community;

(6) protect intelligence sources and methods from unauthorized disclosure; and

(7) perform such other functions as the President or the National Security Council may direct.

(d) HEAD OF THE CENTRAL INTELLIGENCE AGENCY.—In the Director's capacity as head of the Central Intelligence Agency, the Director shall—

(1) collect intelligence through human sources and by other appropriate means, except that the Agency shall have no police, subpoena, or law enforcement powers or internal security functions;

(2) provide overall direction for the collection of national intelligence through human sources by elements of the intelligence community authorized to undertake such collection and, in coordination with other agencies of the Government which are authorized to undertake such collection, ensure that the most effective use is made of resources and that the risks to the United States and those involved in such collection are minimized;

(3) correlate and evaluate intelligence related to the national security and provide appropriate dissemination of such intelligence;

(4) perform such additional services as are of common concern to the elements of the intelligence community, which services the Director of Central Intelligence determines can be more efficiently accomplished centrally; and

(5) perform such other functions and duties related to intelligence affecting the national security as the President or the National Security Council may direct.

AUTHORITIES OF THE DIRECTOR OF CENTRAL INTELLIGENCE

SEC. 104. [50 U.S.C. 403–4] (a) ACCESS TO INTELLIGENCE.—To the extent recommended by the National Security Council and approved by the President, the Director of Central Intelligence shall have access to all intelligence related to the national security which is collected by any department, agency, or other entity of the United States.

(b) APPROVAL OF BUDGETS.—The Director of Central Intelligence shall provide guidance to elements of the intelligence community for the preparation of their annual budgets and shall approve such budgets before their incorporation in the National Foreign Intelligence Program.

(c) ROLE OF DCI IN REPROGRAMMING.—No funds made available under the National Foreign Intelligence Program may be reprogrammed by any element of the intelligence community without the prior approval of the Director of Central Intelligence except in accordance with procedures issued by the Director. The Secretary of Defense shall consult with the Director of Central Intelligence before reprogramming funds made available under the Joint Military Intelligence Program.

(d) TRANSFER OF FUNDS OR PERSONNEL WITHIN THE NATIONAL FOREIGN INTELLIGENCE PROGRAM.—(1) In addition to any other authorities available under law for such purposes, the Director of Central Intelligence, with the approval of the Director of the Office of Management and Budget, may transfer funds appropriated for a program within the National Foreign Intelligence Program to another such program and, in accordance with procedures to be developed by the Director and the heads of affected departments and agencies, may transfer personnel authorized for an element of the intelligence community to another such element for periods up to a year.

(2) A transfer of funds or personnel may be made under this subsection only if—

(A) the funds or personnel are being transferred to an activity that is a higher priority intelligence activity;

(B) the need for funds or personnel for such activity is based on unforeseen requirements;

(C) the transfer does not involve a transfer of funds to the Reserve for Contingencies of the Central Intelligence Agency;

(D) the transfer does not involve a transfer of funds or personnel from the Federal Bureau of Investigation; and

(E) the Secretary or head of the department which contains the affected element or elements of the intelligence community does not object to such transfer.

(3) Funds transferred under this subsection shall remain available for the same period as the appropriations account to which transferred.

(4) Any transfer of funds under this subsection shall be carried out in accordance with existing procedures applicable to reprogramming notifications for the appropriate congressional committees. Any proposed transfer for which notice is given to the appropriate congressional committees shall be accompanied by a report explaining the nature of the proposed transfer and how it satisfies the requirements of this subsection. In addition, the Select Committee on Intelligence of the Senate and the Permanent Select Committee on Intelligence of the House of Representatives shall be promptly notified of any transfer of funds made pursuant to this subsection in any case in which the transfer would not have otherwise required reprogramming notification under procedures in effect as of the date of the enactment of this section.

(5) The Director shall promptly submit to the Select Committee on Intelligence of the Senate and to the Permanent Select Committee on Intelligence of the House of Representatives and, in the case of the transfer of personnel to or from the Department of Defense, the Committee on Armed Services of the Senate and the Committee on National Security of the House of Representatives, a report on any transfer of personnel made pursuant to this subsection. The Director shall include in any such report an explanation of the nature of the transfer and how it satisfies the requirements of this subsection.

(e) COORDINATION WITH FOREIGN GOVERNMENTS.—Under the direction of the National Security Council and in a manner consistent with section 207 of the Foreign Service Act of 1980 (22 U.S.C. 3927), the Director shall coordinate the relationships between elements of the intelligence community and the intelligence or security services of foreign governments on all matters involving intelligence related to the national security or involving intelligence acquired through clandestine means.

(f) USE OF PERSONNEL.—The Director shall, in coordination with the heads of departments and agencies with elements in the intelligence community, institute policies and programs within the intelligence community—

(1) to provide for the rotation of personnel between the elements of the intelligence community, where appropriate, and to make such rotated service a factor to be considered for promotion to senior positions; and

(2) to consolidate, wherever possible, personnel, administrative, and security programs to reduce the overall costs of these activities within the intelligence community.

(g) TERMINATION OF EMPLOYMENT OF CIA EMPLOYEES.—Notwithstanding the provisions of any other law, the Director may, in the Director's discretion, terminate the employment of any officer or employee of the Central Intelligence Agency whenever the Director shall deem such termination necessary or advisable in the interests of the United States. Any such termination shall not affect the right of the officer or employee terminated to seek or accept employment in any other department or agency of the Government if declared eligible for such employment by the Office of Personnel Management.

RESPONSIBILITIES OF THE SECRETARY OF DEFENSE
PERTAINING TO THE NATIONAL FOREIGN INTELLIGENCE PROGRAM

SEC. 105. [50 U.S.C. 403–5] (a) IN GENERAL.—The Secretary of Defense, in consultation with the Director of Central Intelligence, shall—

(1) ensure that the budgets of the elements of the intelligence community within the Department of Defense are adequate to satisfy the overall intelligence needs of the Department of Defense, including the needs of the chairman of the Joint Chiefs of Staff and the commanders of the unified and specified commands and, wherever such elements are performing governmentwide functions, the needs of other departments and agencies;

(2) ensure appropriate implementation of the policies and resource decisions of the Director of Central Intelligence by elements of the Department of Defense within the National Foreign Intelligence Program;

(3) ensure that the tactical intelligence activities of the Department of Defense complement and are compatible with intelligence activities under the National Foreign Intelligence Program;

(4) ensure that the elements of the intelligence community within the Department of Defense are responsive and timely with respect to satisfying the needs of operational military forces;

(5) eliminate waste and unnecessary duplication among the intelligence activities of the Department of Defense; and

(6) ensure that intelligence activities of the Department of Defense are conducted jointly where appropriate.

(b) RESPONSIBILITY FOR THE PERFORMANCE OF SPECIFIC FUNCTIONS.—Consistent with sections 103 and 104 of this Act, the Secretary of Defense shall ensure—

(1) through the National Security Agency (except as otherwise directed by the President or the National Security Council), the continued operation of an effective unified organization for the conduct of signals intelligence activities and shall ensure that the product is disseminated in a timely manner to authorized recipients;

(2) through the National Imagery and Mapping Agency (except as otherwise directed by the President or the National Security Council), with appropriate representation from the intelligence community, the continued operation of an effective unified organization within the Department of Defense—

(A) for carrying out tasking of imagery collection;

(B) for the coordination of imagery processing and exploitation activities;

(C) for ensuring the dissemination of imagery in a timely manner to authorized recipients; and

(D) notwithstanding any other provision of law, for—

(i) prescribing technical architecture and standards related to imagery intelligence and geospatial information and ensuring compliance with such architecture and standards; and

(ii) developing and fielding systems of common concern related to imagery intelligence and geospatial information;

(3) through the National Reconnaissance Office (except as otherwise directed by the President or the National Security Council), the continued operation of an effective unified organization for the research and development, acquisition, and operation of overhead reconnaissance systems necessary to satisfy the requirements of all elements of the intelligence community;

(4) through the Defense Intelligence Agency (except as otherwise directed by the President or the National Security Council), the continued operation of an effective unified system within the Department of Defense for the production of timely, objective military and military-related intelligence, based upon all sources available to the intelligence community, and shall ensure the appropriate dissemination of such intelligence to authorized recipients;

(5) through the Defense Intelligence Agency (except as otherwise directed by the President or the National Security Council), effective management of Department of Defense human intelligence activities, including defense attaches; and

(6) that the military departments maintain sufficient capabilities to collect and produce intelligence to meet—

(A) the requirements of the Director of Central Intelligence;

(B) the requirements of the Secretary of Defense or the Chairman of the Joint Chiefs of Staff;

(C) the requirements of the unified and specified combatant commands and of joint operations; and

(D) the specialized requirements of the military departments for intelligence necessary to support tactical commanders, military planners, the research and development process, the acquisition of military equipment, and training and doctrine. . . .

(d) ANNUAL EVALUATION OF THE DIRECTOR OF CENTRAL INTELLIGENCE.—The Director of Central Intelligence, in consultation with the Secretary of Defense and the Chairman of the Joint Chiefs of Staff, shall submit each year to the Committee on Foreign Intelligence of the National Security Council and the appropriate congressional committees (as defined in section 109(c) of this Act) an evaluation of the performance and the responsiveness of the National Security Agency, the National Reconnaissance Office, and the National Imagery and Mapping Agency in meeting their national missions.

ASSISTANCE TO UNITED STATES LAW ENFORCEMENT AGENCIES

SEC. 105A. [50 U.S.C. 403–5a] (a) AUTHORITY TO PROVIDE ASSISTANCE.—Subject to subsection (b), elements of the intelligence community may, upon the request of a United States law enforcement agency, collect information outside the United States about individuals who are not United

States persons. Such elements may collect such information notwithstanding that the law enforcement agency intends to use the information collected for purposes of a law enforcement investigation or counterintelligence investigation.

(b) LIMITATION ON ASSISTANCE BY ELEMENTS OF DEPARTMENT OF DEFENSE.—(1) With respect to elements within the Department of Defense, the authority in subsection (a) applies only to the following:

(A) The National Security Agency.

(B) The National Reconnaissance Office.

(C) The National Imagery and Mapping Agency.

(D) The Defense Intelligence Agency.

(2) Assistance provided under this section by elements of the Department of Defense may not include the direct participation of a member of the Army, Navy, Air Force, or Marine Corps in an arrest or similar activity.

(3) Assistance may not be provided under this section by an element of the Department of Defense if the provision of such assistance will adversely affect the military preparedness of the United States.

(4) The Secretary of Defense shall prescribe regulations governing the exercise of authority under this section by elements of the Department of Defense, including regulations relating to the protection of sources and methods in the exercise of such authority.

(c) DEFINITIONS.—For purposes of subsection (a):

(1) The term "United States law enforcement agency" means any department or agency of the Federal Government that the Attorney General designates as law enforcement agency for purposes of this section.

(2) The term "United States person" means the following:

(A) A United States citizen.

(B) An alien known by the intelligence agency concerned to be a permanent resident alien.

(C) An unincorporated association substantially composed of United States citizens or permanent resident aliens.

(D) A corporation incorporated in the United States, except for a corporation directed and controlled by a foreign government or governments.

APPOINTMENT OF OFFICIALS RESPONSIBLE
FOR INTELLIGENCE-RELATED ACTIVITIES

SEC. 106. [50 U.S.C. 403–6] (a) CONCURRENCE OF DCI IN CERTAIN APPOINTMENTS.—(1) In the event of a vacancy in a position referred to in paragraph (2), the Secretary of Defense shall obtain the concurrence of the Director of Central Intelligence before recommending to the President an individual for appointment to the position. If the Director does not concur in the recommendation, the Secretary may make the recommendation to the President without the Director's concurrence, but shall include in the recommendation a statement that the Director does not concur in the recommendation.

(2) Paragraph (1) applies to the following positions:

(A) The Director of the National Security Agency.

(B) The Director of the National Reconnaissance Office.

(C) The Director of the National Imagery and Mapping Agency.

(b) CONSULTATION WITH DCI IN CERTAIN APPOINTMENTS.—(1) In the event of a vacancy in a position referred to in paragraph (2), the head of the department or agency having jurisdiction over the position shall consult with the Director of Central Intelligence before appointing an individual to fill the vacancy or recommending to the President an individual to be nominated to fill the vacancy.

(2) Paragraph (1) applies to the following positions:

(A) The Director of the Defense Intelligence Agency.

(B) The Assistant Secretary of State for Intelligence and Research.

(C) The Director of the Office of Nonproliferation and National Security of the Department of Energy.

(3) In the event of a vacancy in the position of the Assistant Director, National Security Division of the Federal Bureau of Investigation, the Director of the Federal Bureau of Investigation

shall provide timely notice to the Director of Central Intelligence of the recommendation of the
Director of the Federal Bureau of Investigation of an individual to fill the position in order that
the Director of Central Intelligence may consult with the Director of the Federal Bureau of Investigation before the Attorney General appoints an individual to fill the vacancy. . . .

ANNUAL REPORT ON INTELLIGENCE

SEC. 109. (a) IN GENERAL.—(1) Not later than January 31 each year, the President shall submit
to the appropriate congressional committees a report on the requirements of the United States for
intelligence and the activities of the intelligence community.

(2) The purpose of the report is to facilitate an assessment of the activities of the intelligence
community during the preceding fiscal year and to assist in the development of a mission and a
budget for the intelligence community for the fiscal year beginning in the year in which the report
is submitted.

(3) The report shall be submitted in unclassified form, but may include a classified annex.

(b) MATTERS COVERED.—(1) Each report under subsection (a) shall—

(A) specify the intelligence required to meet the national security interests of the United
States, and set forth an order of priority for the collection and analysis of intelligence required
to meet such interests, for the fiscal year beginning in the year in which the report is submitted; and

(B) evaluate the performance of the intelligence community in collecting and analyzing
intelligence required to meet such interests during the fiscal year ending in the year preceding
the year in which the report is submitted, including a description of the significant successes
and significant failures of the intelligence community in such collection and analysis during
that fiscal year.

(2) The report shall specify matters under paragraph (1)(A) in sufficient detail to assist Congress in making decisions with respect to the allocation of resources for the matters specified.

(c)[1] DEFINITION.—In this section, the term "appropriate congressional committees" means the
following:

(1) The Select Committee on Intelligence, the Committee on Appropriations, and the Committee on Armed Services of the Senate.

(2) The Permanent Select Committee on Intelligence, the Committee on Appropriations, and
the Committee on National Security of the House of Representatives.

(c)[1] TIME FOR SUBMISSION.—The report under this section for any year shall be submitted at the
same time that the President submits the budget for the next fiscal year pursuant to section 1105
of title 31, United States Code.

NATIONAL MISSION OF NATIONAL IMAGERY AND MAPPING AGENCY

SEC. 110. [50 U.S.C. 404e] (a) IN GENERAL.—In addition to the Department of Defense missions set forth in section 442 of title 10, United States Code, the National Imagery and Mapping
Agency shall support the imagery requirements of the Department of State and other departments
and agencies of the United States outside the Department of Defense.

(b) REQUIREMENTS AND PRIORITIES.—The Director of Central Intelligence shall establish
requirements and priorities governing the collection of national intelligence by the National
Imagery and Mapping Agency under subsection (a).

(c) CORRECTION OF DEFICIENCIES.—The Director of Central Intelligence shall develop and
implement such programs and policies as the Director and the Secretary of Defense jointly determine necessary to review and correct deficiencies identified in the capabilities of the National
Imagery and Mapping Agency to accomplish assigned national missions, including support to the
all-source analysis and production process. The Director shall consult with the Secretary of
Defense on the development and implementation of such programs and policies. The Secretary

---

[1] Two subsections (c) exist. Section 803(a) of P.L. 104–293 struck subsections (a) and (b) and
added new subsections (a), (b), and (c). The subsection (c) relating to time for submission probably should have been repealed.

shall obtain the advice of the Chairman of the Joint Chiefs of Staff regarding the matters on which the Director and the Secretary are to consult under the preceding sentence.

COLLECTION TASKING AUTHORITY

SEC. 111. [50 U.S.C. 404f] Unless otherwise directed by the President, the Director of Central Intelligence shall have authority (except as otherwise agreed by the Director and the Secretary of Defense) to—

(1) approve collection requirements levied on national imagery collection assets;
(2) determine priorities for such requirements; and
(3) resolve conflicts in such priorities.

RESTRICTIONS ON INTELLIGENCE SHARING WITH THE UNITED NATIONS

SEC. 112. [50 U.S.C. 404g] (a) PROVISION OF INTELLIGENCE INFORMATION TO THE UNITED NATIONS.—(1) No United States intelligence information may be provided to the United Nations or any organization affiliated with the United Nations, or to any officials or employees thereof, unless the President certifies to the appropriate committees of Congress that the Director of Central Intelligence, in consultation with the Secretary of State and the Secretary of Defense, has established and implemented procedures, and has worked with the United Nations to ensure implementation of procedures, for protecting from unauthorized disclosure United States intelligence sources and methods connected to such information.

(2) Paragraph (1) may be waived upon written certification by the President to the appropriate committees of Congress that providing such information to the United Nations or an organization affiliated with the United Nations, or to any officials or employees thereof, is in the national security interests of the United States.

(B) PERIODIC AND SPECIAL REPORTS.—(1) The President shall report semiannually to the appropriate committees of Congress on the types and volume of intelligence provided to the United Nations and the purposes for which it was provided during the period covered by the report. The President shall also report to the appropriate committees of Congress within 15 days after it has become known to the United States Government that there has been an unauthorized disclosure of intelligence provided by the United States to the United Nations.

(2) The requirement for periodic reports under the first sentence of paragraph (1) shall not apply to the provision of intelligence that is provided only to, and for the use of, appropriately cleared United States Government personnel serving with the United Nations.

(c) DELEGATION OF DUTIES.—The President may not delegate or assign the duties of the President under this section.

(D) RELATIONSHIP TO EXISTING LAW.—Nothing in this section shall be construed to—

(1) impair or otherwise affect the authority of the Director of Central Intelligence to protect intelligence sources and methods from unauthorized disclosure pursuant to section 103(c)(6) of this Act; or

(2) supersede or otherwise affect the provisions of title V of this Act.

(e) DEFINITION.—As used in this section, the term "appropriate committees of Congress" means the Committee on Foreign Relations and the Select Committee on Intelligence of the Senate and the Committee on Foreign Relations and the Permanent Select Committee on Intelligence of the House of Representatives. . . .

TITLE V—ACCOUNTABILITY FOR INTELLIGENCE ACTIVITIES

GENERAL CONGRESSIONAL OVERSIGHT PROVISIONS

SEC. 501. [50 U.S.C. 413] (a)(1) The President shall ensure that the intelligence committees are kept fully and currently informed of the intelligence activities of the United States, including any significant anticipated intelligence activity as required by this title.

(2) As used in this title, the term "intelligence committees" means the Select Committee on Intelligence of the Senate and the Permanent Select Committee on Intelligence of the House of Representatives.

(3) Nothing in this title shall be construed as requiring the approval of the intelligence committees as a condition precedent to the initiation of any significant anticipated intelligence activity.

(b) The President shall ensure that any illegal intelligence activity is reported promptly to the intelligence committees, as well as any corrective action that has been taken or is planned in connection with such illegal activity.

(c) The President and the intelligence committees shall each establish such procedures as may be necessary to carry out the provisions of this title.

(d) The House of Representatives and the Senate shall each establish, by rule or resolution of such House, procedures to protect from unauthorized disclosure all classified information, and all information relating to intelligence sources and methods, that is furnished to the intelligence committees or to Members of Congress under this title. Such procedures shall be established in consultation with the Director of Central Intelligence. In accordance with such procedures, each of the intelligence committees shall promptly call to the attention of its respective House, or to any appropriate committee or committees of its respective House, any matter relating to intelligence activities requiring the attention of such House or such committee or committees.

(e) Nothing in this Act shall be construed as authority to withhold information from the intelligence committees on the grounds that providing the information to the intelligence committees would constitute the unauthorized disclosure of classified information or information relating to intelligence sources and methods.

(f) As used in this section, the term "intelligence activities" includes covert actions as defined in section 503(e).

REPORTING OF INTELLIGENCE ACTIVITIES
OTHER THAN COVERT ACTIONS

SEC. 502. [50 U.S.C. 413a] To the extent consistent with due regard for the protection from unauthorized disclosure of classified information relating to sensitive intelligence sources and methods or other exceptionally sensitive matters, the Director of Central Intelligence and the heads of all departments, agencies, and other entities of the United States Government involved in intelligence activities shall—

(1) keep the intelligence committees fully and currently informed of all intelligence activities, other than a covert action (as defined in section 503(e)), which are the responsibility of, are engaged in by, or are carried out for or on behalf of, any department, agency, or entity of the United States Government, including any significant anticipated intelligence activity and any significant intelligence failure; and

(2) furnish the intelligence committees any information or material concerning intelligence activities, other than covert actions, which is within their custody or control, and which is requested by either of the intelligence committees in order to carry out its authorized responsibilities.

PRESIDENTIAL APPROVAL AND REPORTING OF COVERT ACTIONS

SEC. 503. [50 U.S.C. 413b] (a) The President may not authorize the conduct of a covert action by departments, agencies, or entities of the United States Government unless the President determines such an action is necessary to support identifiable foreign policy objectives of the United States and is important to the national security of the United States, which determination shall be set forth in a finding that shall meet each of the following conditions:

(1) Each finding shall be in writing, unless immediate action by the United States is required and time does not permit the preparation of a written finding, in which case a written record of the President's decision shall be contemporaneously made and shall be reduced to a written finding as soon as possible but in no event more than 48 hours after the decision is made.

(2) Except as permitted by paragraph (1), a finding may not authorize or sanction a covert action, or any aspect of any such action, which already has occurred.

(3) Each finding shall specify each department, agency, or entity of the United States Government authorized to fund or otherwise participate in any significant way in such action. Any employee, contractor, or contract agent of a department, agency, or entity of the United States Government other than the Central Intelligence Agency directed to participate in any way in a covert action shall be subject either to the policies and regulations of the Central Intelligence Agency, or to written policies or regulations adopted by such department, agency, or entity, to govern such participation.

(4) Each finding shall specify whether it is contemplated that any third party which is not an element of, or a contractor or contract agent of, the United States Government, or is not otherwise subject to United States Government policies and regulations, will be used to fund or otherwise participate in any significant way in the covert action concerned, or be used to undertake the covert action concerned on behalf of the United States.

(5) A finding may not authorize any action that would violate the Constitution or any statute of the United States.

(b) To the extent consistent with due regard for the protection from unauthorized disclosure of classified information relating to sensitive intelligence sources and methods or other exceptionally sensitive matters, the Director of Central Intelligence and the heads of all departments, agencies, and entities of the United States Government involved in a covert action—

(1) shall keep the intelligence committees fully and currently informed of all covert actions which are the responsibility of, are engaged in by, or are carried out for or on behalf of, any department, agency, or entity of the United States Government, including significant failures; and

(2) shall furnish to the intelligence committees any information or material concerning covert actions which is in the possession, custody, or control of any department, agency, or entity of the United States Government and which is requested by either of the intelligence committees in order to carry out its authorized responsibilities.

(c)(1) The President shall ensure that any finding approved pursuant to subsection (a) shall be reported to the intelligence committees as soon as possible after such approval and before the initiation of the covert action authorized by the finding, except as otherwise provided in paragraph (2) and paragraph (3).

(2) If the President determines that it is essential to limit access to the finding to meet extraordinary circumstances affecting vital interests of the United States, the finding may be reported to the chairmen and ranking minority members of the intelligence committees, the Speaker and minority leader of the House of Representatives, the majority and minority leaders of the Senate, and such other member or members of the congressional leadership as may be included by the President.

(3) Whenever a finding is not reported pursuant to paragraph (1) or (2) of this section, the President shall fully inform the intelligence committees in a timely fashion and shall provide a statement of the reasons for not giving prior notice.

(4) In a case under paragraph (1), (2), or (3), a copy of the finding, signed by the President, shall be provided to the chairman of each intelligence committee. When access to a finding is limited to the Members of Congress specified in paragraph (2), a statement of the reasons for limiting such access shall also be provided.

(d) The President shall ensure that the intelligence committees, or, if applicable, the Members of Congress specified in subsection (c)(2), are notified of any significant change in a previously approved covert action, or any significant undertaking pursuant to a previously approved finding, in the same manner as findings are reported pursuant to subsection (c).

(e) As used in this title, the term "covert action" means an activity or activities of the United States Government to influence political, economic, or military conditions abroad, where it is intended that the role of the United States Government will not be apparent or acknowledged publicly, but does not include—

(1) activities the primary purpose of which is to acquire intelligence, traditional counterintelligence activities, traditional activities to improve or maintain the operational security of United States Government programs, or administrative activities;

(2) traditional diplomatic or military activities or routine support to such activities;

(3) traditional law enforcement activities conducted by United States Government law enforcement agencies or routine support to such activities; or

(4) activities to provide routine support to the overt activities (other than activities described in paragraph (1), (2), or (3)) of other United States Government agencies abroad.

(f) No covert action may be conducted which is intended to influence United States political processes, public opinion, policies, or media.

FUNDING OF INTELLIGENCE ACTIVITIES

SEC. 504. [50 U.S.C. 414] (a) Appropriated funds available to an intelligence agency may be obligated or expended for an intelligence or intelligence-related activity only if—

(1) those funds were specifically authorized by the Congress for use for such activities; or

(2) in the case of funds from the Reserve for Contingencies of the Central Intelligence Agency and consistent with the provisions of section 503 of this Act concerning any significant anticipated intelligence activity, the Director of Central Intelligence has notified the appropriate congressional committees of the intent to make such funds available for such activity; or

(3) in the case of funds specifically authorized by the Congress for a different activity—

(A) the activity to be funded is a higher priority intelligence or intelligence-related activity;

(B) the need for funds for such activity is based on unforeseen requirements; and

(C) the Director of Central Intelligence, the Secretary of Defense, or the Attorney General, as appropriate, has notified the appropriate congressional committees of the intent to make such funds available for such activity;

(4) nothing in this subsection prohibits obligation or expenditure of funds available to an intelligence agency in accordance with sections 1535 and 1536 of title 31, United States Code.

(b) Funds available to an intelligence agency may not be made available for any intelligence or intelligence-related activity for which funds were denied by the Congress.

(c) No funds appropriated for, or otherwise available to, any department, agency, or entity of the United States Government may be expended, or may be directed to be expended, for any covert action, as defined in section 503(e), unless and until a Presidential finding required by subsection (a) of section 503 has been signed or otherwise issued in accordance with that subsection.

(d)(1) Except as otherwise specifically provided by law, funds available to an intelligence agency that are not appropriated funds may be obligated or expended for an intelligence or intelligence-related activity only if those funds are used for activities reported to the appropriate congressional committees pursuant to procedures which identify—

(A) the types of activities for which nonappropriated funds may be expended; and

(B) the circumstances under which an activity must be reported as a significant anticipated intelligence activity before such funds can be expended.

(2) Procedures for purposes of paragraph (1) shall be jointly agreed upon by the intelligence committees and, as appropriate, the Director of Central Intelligence or the Secretary of Defense.

(e) As used in this section—

(1) the term "intelligence agency" means any department, agency, or other entity of the United States involved in intelligence or intelligence-related activities;

(2) the term "appropriate congressional committees" means the Permanent Select Committee on Intelligence and the Committee on Appropriations of the House of Representatives and the Select Committee on Intelligence and the Committee on Appropriations of the Senate; and

(3) the term "specifically authorized by the Congress" means that—

(A) the activity and the amount of funds proposed to be used for that activity were identified in a formal budget request to the Congress, but funds shall be deemed to be specifically authorized for that activity only to the extent that the Congress both authorized the funds to be appropriated for that activity and appropriated the funds for that activity; or

(B) although the funds were not formally requested, the Congress both specifically authorized the appropriation of the funds for the activity and appropriated the funds for the activity. . . .

TITLE VI—PROTECTION OF CERTAIN NATIONAL SECURITY INFORMATION

PROTECTION OF IDENTITIES OF CERTAIN UNITED STATES UNDERCOVER INTELLIGENCE OFFICERS, AGENTS, INFORMANTS, AND SOURCES

SEC. 601. [50 U.S.C. 421] (a) Whoever, having or having had authorized access to classified information that identifies a covert agent, intentionally discloses any information identifying such covert agent to any individual not authorized to receive classified information, knowing that the information disclosed so identifies such covert agent and that the United States is taking affirmative measures to conceal such covert agent's intelligence relationship to the United States, shall be fined not more than $50,000 or imprisoned not more than ten years, or both.

(b) Whoever, as a result of having authorized access to classified information, learns the identity of a covert agent and intentionally discloses any information identifying such covert agent to any individual not authorized to receive classified information, knowing that the information disclosed so identifies such covert agent and that the United States is taking affirmative measures to conceal such covert agent's intelligence relationship to the United States, shall be fined not more than $25,000 or imprisoned not more than five years, or both.

(c) Whoever, in the course of a pattern of activities intended to identify and expose covert agents and with reason to believe that such activities would impair or impede the foreign intelligence activities of the United States, discloses any information that identifies an individual as a covert agent to any individual not authorized to receive classified information, knowing that the information disclosed so identifies such individual and that the United States is taking affirmative measures to conceal such individual's classified intelligence relationship to the United States, shall be fined not more than $15,000 or imprisoned not more than three years, or both.

DEFENSES AND EXCEPTIONS

SEC. 602. [50 U.S.C. 422] (a) It is a defense to a prosecution under section 601 that before the commission of the offense with which the defendant is charged, the United States had publicly acknowledged or revealed the intelligence relationship to the United States of the individual the disclosure of whose intelligence relationship to the United States is the basis for the prosecution.

(b)(1) Subject to paragraph (2), no person other than a person committing an offense under section 601 shall be subject to prosecution under such section by virtue of section 2 or 4 of title 18, United States Code, or shall be subject to prosecution for conspiracy to commit an offense under such section.

(2) Paragraph (1) shall not apply (A) in the case of a person who acted in the course of a pattern of activities intended to identify and expose covert agents and with reason to believe that such activities would impair or impede the foreign intelligence activities of the United States, or (B) in the case of a person who has authorized access to classified information.

(c) It shall not be an offense under section 601 to transmit information described in such section directly to the Select Committee on Intelligence of the Senate or to the Permanent Select Committee on Intelligence of the House of Representatives.

(d) It shall not be an offense under section 601 for an individual to disclose information that solely identifies himself as a covert agent.

REPORT

SEC. 603. [50 U.S.C. 423] (a) The President, after receiving information from the Director of Central Intelligence, shall submit to the Select Committee on Intelligence of the Senate and the Permanent Select Committee on Intelligence of the House of Representatives an annual report on measures to protect the identities of covert agents, and on any other matter relevant to the protection of the identities of covert agents.

(b) The report described in subsection (a) shall be exempt from any requirement for publication or disclosure. The first such report shall be submitted no later than February 1, 1983.

EXTRATERRITORIAL JURISDICTION

SEC. 604. [50 U.S.C. 424] There is jurisdiction over an offense under section 601 committed outside the United States if the individual committing the offense is a citizen of the United States or an alien lawfully admitted to the United States for permanent residence (as defined in section 101(a)(20) of the Immigration and Nationality Act).

PROVIDING INFORMATION TO CONGRESS

SEC. 605. [50 U.S.C. 425] Nothing in this title may be construed as authority to withhold information from the Congress or from a committee of either House of Congress.

DEFINITIONS

SEC. 606. [50 U.S.C. 426] For the purposes of this title:

(1) The term "classified information" means information or material designated and clearly marked or clearly represented, pursuant to the provisions of a statute or Executive order (or a regulation or order issued pursuant to a statute or Executive order), as requiring a specific degree of protection against unauthorized disclosure for reasons of national security.

(2) The term "authorized", when used with respect to access to classified information, means having authority, right, or permission pursuant to the provisions of a statute, Executive order, directive of the head of any department or agency engaged in foreign intelligence or counterintelligence activities, order of any United States court, or provisions of any Rule of the House of Representatives or resolution of the Senate which assigns responsibility within the respective House of Congress for the oversight of intelligence activities.

(3) The term "disclose" means to communicate, provide, impart, transmit, transfer, convey, publish, or otherwise make available.

(4) The term "covert agent" means—

(A) an officer or employee of an intelligence agency or a member of the Armed Forces assigned to duty with an intelligence agency—

(i) whose identity as such an officer, employee, or member is classified information, and

(ii) who is serving outside the United States or has within the last five years served outside the United States; or

(B) a United States citizen whose intelligence relationship to the United States is classified information, and

(i) who resides and acts outside the United States as an agent of, or informant or source of operational assistance to, an intelligence agency, or

(ii) who is at the time of the disclosure acting as an agent of, or informant to, the foreign counterintelligence or foreign counterterrorism components of the Federal Bureau of Investigation; or

(C) an individual, other than a United States citizen, whose past or present intelligence relationship to the United States is classified information and who is a present or former agent of, or a present or former informant or source of operational assistance to, an intelligence agency.

(5) The term "intelligence agency" means the Central Intelligence Agency, a foreign intelligence component of the Department of Defense, or the foreign counterintelligence or foreign counterterrorism components of the Federal Bureau of Investigation.

(6) The term "informant" means any individual who furnishes information to an intelligence agency in the course of a confidential relationship protecting the identity of such individual from public disclosure.

(7) The terms "officer" and "employee" have the meanings given such terms by section 2104 and 2105, respectively, of title 5, United States Code.

(8) The term "Armed Forces" means the Army, Navy, Air Force, Marine Corps, and Coast Guard.

(9) The term "United States", when used in a geographic sense, means all areas under the territorial sovereignty of the United States and the Trust Territory of the Pacific Islands.

(10) The term "pattern of activities" requires a series of acts with a common purpose or objective.

TITLE VII—PROTECTION OF OPERATIONAL FILES OF THE CENTRAL INTELLIGENCE AGENCY

EXEMPTION OF CERTAIN OPERATIONAL FILES FROM SEARCH, REVIEW, PUBLICATION, OR DISCLOSURE

SEC. 701. [50 U.S.C. 431] (a) Operational files of the Central Intelligence Agency may be exempted by the Director of Central Intelligence from the provisions of section 552 of title 5, United States Code (Freedom of Information Act), which require publication or disclosure, or search or review in connection therewith.

(b) For the purposes of this title the term "operational files" means—

(1) files of the Directorate of Operations which document the conduct of foreign intelligence or counterintelligence operations or intelligence or security liaison arrangements or information exchanges with foreign governments or their intelligence or security services;

(2) files of the Directorate for Science and Technology which document the means by which foreign intelligence or counterintelligence is collected through scientific and technical systems; and

(3) files of the Office of Personnel Security which document investigations conducted to determine the suitability of potential foreign intelligence or counterintelligence sources; except that files which are the sole repository of disseminated intelligence are not operational files.

(c) Notwithstanding subsection (a) of this section, exempted operational files shall continue to be subject to search and review for information concerning—

(1) United States citizens or aliens lawfully admitted for permanent residence who have requested information on themselves pursuant to the provisions of section 552 of title 5, United States Code (Freedom of Information Act), or section 552a of title 5, United States Code (Privacy Act of 1974);

(2) any special activity the existence of which is not exempt from disclosure under the provisions of section 552 of title 5, United States Code (Freedom of Information Act); or

(3) the specific subject matter of an investigation by the intelligence committees of the Congress, the Intelligence Oversight Board, the Department of Justice, the Office of General Counsel of the Central Intelligence Agency, the Office of Inspector General of the Central Intelligence Agency, or the Office of the Director of Central Intelligence for any impropriety, or violation of law, Executive order, or Presidential directive, in the conduct of an intelligence activity.

(d)(1) Files that are not exempted under subsection (a) of this section which contain information derived or disseminated from exempted operational files shall be subject to search and review.

(2) The inclusion of information from exempted operational files in files that are not exempted under subsection (a) of this section shall not affect the exemption under subsection (a) of this section of the originating operational files from search, review, publication, or disclosure.

(3) Records from exempted operational files which have been disseminated to and referenced in files that are not exempted under subsection (a) of this section and which have been returned to exempted operational files for sole retention shall be subject to search and review.

(e) The provisions of subsection (a) of this section shall not be superseded except by a provision of law which is enacted after the date of enactment of subsection (a), and which specifically cites and repeals or modifies its provisions.

(f) Whenever any person who has requested agency records under section 552 of title 5, United States Code (Freedom of Information Act), alleges that the Central Intelligence Agency has improperly withheld records because of failure to comply with any provision of this section, judicial review shall be available under the terms set forth in section 552(a)(4)(B) of title 5, United States Code, except that—

(1) in any case in which information specifically authorized under criteria established by an Executive order to be kept secret in the interest of national defense or foreign relations which is filed with, or produced for, the court by the Central Intelligence Agency, such information shall be examined ex parte, in camera by the court;

(2) the court shall, to the fullest extent practicable, determine issues of fact based on sworn written submissions of the parties;

(3) when a complainant alleges that requested records are improperly withheld because of improper placement solely in exempted operational files, the complainant shall support such allegation with a sworn written submission, based upon personal knowledge or otherwise admissible evidence;

(4)(A) when a complainant alleges that requested records were improperly withheld because of improper exemption of operational files, the Central Intelligence Agency shall meet its burden under section 552(a)(4)(B) of title 5, United States Code, by demonstrating to the court by sworn written submission that exempted operational files likely to contain responsive records currently perform the functions set forth in subsection (b) of this section; and

(B) the court may not order the Central Intelligence Agency to review the content of any exempted operational file or files in order to make the demonstration required under subparagraph (A) of this paragraph, unless the complainant disputes the Central Intelligence Agency's showing with a sworn written submission based on personal knowledge or otherwise admissible evidence;

(5) in proceedings under paragraphs (3) and (4) of this subsection, the parties shall not obtain discovery pursuant to rules 26 through 36 of the Federal Rules of Civil Procedure, except that requests for admission may be made pursuant to rules 26 and 36;

(6) if the court finds under this subsection that the Central Intelligence Agency has improperly withheld requested records because of failure to comply with any provision of this section, the court shall order the Central Intelligence Agency to search and review the appropriate exempted operational file or files for the requested records and make such records, or portions thereof, available in accordance with the provisions of section 552 of title 5, United States Code (Freedom of Information Act), and such order shall be the exclusive remedy for failure to comply with this section; and

(7) if at any time following the filing of a complaint pursuant to this subsection the Central Intelligence Agency agrees to search the appropriate exempted operational file or files for the requested records, the court shall dismiss the claim based upon such complaint. . . .

DECENNIAL REVIEW OF EXEMPTED OPERATIONAL FILES

SEC. 702. [50 U.S.C. 432] (a) Not less than once every ten years, the Director of Central Intelligence shall review the exemptions in force under subsection (a) of section 701 of this Act to determine whether such exemptions may be removed from any category of exempted files or any portion thereof.

(b) The review required by subsection (a) of this section shall include consideration of the historical value or other public interest in the subject matter of the particular category of files or portions thereof and the potential for declassifying a significant part of the information contained therein.

(c) A complainant who alleges that the Central Intelligence Agency has improperly withheld records because of failure to comply with this section may seek judicial review in the district court of the United States of the district in which any of the parties reside, or in the District of Columbia. In such a proceeding, the court's review shall be limited to determining (1) whether the Central Intelligence Agency has conducted the review required by subsection (a) of this section within ten years of enactment of this title or within ten years after the last review, and (2) whether the Central Intelligence Agency, in fact, considered the criteria set forth in subsection (b) of this section in conducting the required review.

TITLE VIII—ACCESS TO CLASSIFIED INFORMATION

PROCEDURES

SEC. 801. [50 U.S.C. 435] (a) Not later than 180 days after the date of enactment of this title, the President shall, by Executive order or regulation, establish procedures to govern access to classified information which shall be binding upon all departments, agencies, and offices of the executive branch of Government. . . .

REQUESTS BY AUTHORIZED INVESTIGATIVE AGENCIES

SEC. 802. [50 U.S.C. 436] (a)(1) Any authorized investigative agency may request from any financial agency, financial institution, or holding company, or from any consumer reporting agency, such financial records, other financial information, and consumer reports as may be necessary in order to conduct any authorized law enforcement investigation, counterintelligence inquiry, or security determination. Any authorized investigative agency may also request records maintained by any commercial entity within the United States pertaining to travel by an employee in the executive branch of Government outside the United States. . . .

EXECUTIVE ORDER 12333: UNITED STATES INTELLIGENCE ACTIVITIES

On December 4, 1981, President Ronald Reagan signed E.O. 12333, establishing the roles and responsibilities of the various intelligence agencies as well as rules for conducting intelligence activities. This was the third executive order on intelligence issued by as many presidents (President Gerald Ford, E.O. 11905; President Jimmy Carter, E.O. 12036). President Reagan's executive order has had much greater longevity; as of fall 1999, it remains the governing executive order for intelligence.

EXECUTIVE ORDER 12333 OF UNITED STATES INTELLIGENCE ACTIVITIES

(December 4, 1981, 46 F.R. 59941)

Timely and accurate information about the activities, capabilities, plans, and intentions of foreign powers, organizations, and persons, and their agents, is essential to the national security of the United States. All reasonable and lawful means must be used to ensure that the United States will receive the best intelligence available. For that purpose, by virtue of the authority vested in me by the Constitution and statutes of the United States of America, including the National Security Act of 1947, as amended, and as President of the United States of America, in order to provide for the effective conduct of United States intelligence activities and the protection of constitutional rights, it is hereby ordered as follows:

PART 1

Goals, Direction, Duties and Responsibilities With Respect to the National Intelligence Effort

1.1 *Goals.* The United States intelligence effort shall provide the President and the National Security Council with the necessary information on which to base decisions concerning the conduct and development of foreign, defense and economic policy, and the protection of United States national interests from foreign security threats. All departments and agencies shall cooperate fully to fulfill this goal.

(a) Maximum emphasis should be given to fostering analytical competition among appropriate elements of the Intelligence Community.

(b) All means, consistent with applicable United States law and this Order, and with full consideration of the rights of United States persons, shall be used to develop intelligence information for the President and the National Security Council. A balanced approach between technical collection efforts and other means should be maintained and encouraged.

(c) Special emphasis should be given to detecting and countering espionage and other threats and activities directed by foreign intelligence services against the United States Government, or United States corporations, establishments, or persons.

(d) To the greatest extent possible consistent with applicable United States law and this Order, and with full consideration of the rights of United States persons, all agencies and departments should seek to ensure full and free exchange of information in order to derive maximum benefit from the United States intelligence effort.

1.2 *The National Security Council.*

(a) *Purpose.* The National Security Council (NSC) was established by the National Security Act of 1947 to advise the President with respect to the integration of domestic, foreign and military policies relating to the national security. The NSC shall act as the highest Executive Branch entity that provides review of, guidance for and direction to the conduct of all national foreign intelligence, counterintelligence, and special activities, and attendant policies and programs.

(b) *Committees.* The NSC shall establish such committees as may be necessary to carry out its functions and responsibilities under this Order. The NSC, or a committee established by it, shall consider and submit to the President a policy recommendation, including all dissents, on each special activity and shall review proposals for other sensitive intelligence operations.

1.3 *National Foreign Intelligence Advisory Groups.*

(a) *Establishment and Duties.* The Director of Central Intelligence shall establish such boards, councils, or groups as required for the purpose of obtaining advice from within the Intelligence Community concerning:

(1) Production, review and coordination of national foreign intelligence;

(2) Priorities for the National Foreign Intelligence Program budget;

(3) Interagency exchanges of foreign intelligence information;

(4) Arrangements with foreign governments on intelligence matters;

(5) Protection of intelligence sources and methods;

(6) Activities of common concern; and

(7) Such other matters as may be referred by the Director of Central Intelligence.

(b) *Membership.* Advisory groups established pursuant to this section shall be chaired by the Director of Central Intelligence or his designated representative and shall consist of senior representatives from organizations within the Intelligence Community and from departments or agencies containing such organizations, as designated by the Director of Central Intelligence. Groups for consideration of substantive intelligence matters will include representatives of organizations involved in the collection, processing and analysis of intelligence. A senior representative of the Secretary of Commerce, the Attorney General, the Assistant to the President for National Security Affairs, and the Office of the Secretary of Defense shall be invited to participate in any group which deals with other than substantive intelligence matters.

1.4 *The Intelligence Community.* The agencies within the Intelligence Community shall, in accordance with applicable United States law and with the other provisions of this Order, conduct intelligence activities necessary for the conduct of foreign relations and the protection of the national security of the United States, including:

(a) Collection of information needed by the President, the National Security Council, the Secretaries of State and Defense, and other Executive Branch officials for the performance of their duties and responsibilities;

(b) Production and dissemination of intelligence;

(c) Collection of information concerning, and the conduct of activities to protect against, intelligence activities directed against the United States, international terrorist and international narcotics activities, and other hostile activities directed against the United States by foreign powers, organizations, persons, and their agents;

(d) Special activities;

(e) Administrative and support activities within the United States and abroad necessary for the performance of authorized activities; and

(f) Such other intelligence activities as the President may direct from time to time.

1.5 *Director of Central Intelligence.* In order to discharge the duties and responsibilities prescribed by law, the Director of Central Intelligence shall be responsible directly to the President and the NSC and shall:

(a) Act as the primary adviser to the President and the NSC on national foreign intelligence and provide the President and other officials in the Executive Branch with national foreign intelligence;

(b) Develop such objectives and guidance for the Intelligence Community as will enhance capabilities for responding to expected future needs for national foreign intelligence;

(c) Promote the development and maintenance of services of common concern by designated intelligence organizations on behalf of the Intelligence Community;

(d) Ensure implementation of special activities;

(e) Formulate policies concerning foreign intelligence and counterintelligence arrangements with foreign governments, coordinate foreign intelligence and counterintelligence relationships between agencies of the Intelligence Community and the intelligence or internal security services of foreign governments, and establish procedures governing the conduct of liaison by any department or agency with such services on narcotics activities;

(f) Participate in the development of procedures approved by the Attorney General governing criminal narcotics intelligence activities abroad to ensure that these activities are consistent with foreign intelligence programs;

(g) Ensure the establishment by the Intelligence Community of common security and access standards for managing and handling foreign intelligence systems, information, and products;

(h) Ensure that programs are developed which protect intelligence sources, methods, and analytical procedures;

(i) Establish uniform criteria for the determination of relative priorities for the transmission of critical national foreign intelligence, and advise the Secretary of Defense concerning the communications requirements of the Intelligence Community for the transmission of such intelligence;

(j) Establish appropriate staffs, committees, or other advisory groups to assist in the execution of the Director's responsibilities;

(k) Have full responsibility for production and dissemination of national foreign intelligence, and authority to levy analytic tasks on departmental intelligence production organizations, in consultation with those organizations, ensuring that appropriate mechanisms for competitive analysis are developed so that diverse points of view are considered fully and differences of judgment within the Intelligence Community are brought to the attention of national policymakers;

(l) Ensure the timely exploitation and dissemination of data gathered by national foreign intelligence collection means, and ensure that the resulting intelligence is disseminated immediately to appropriate government entities and military commands;

(m) Establish mechanisms which translate national foreign intelligence objectives and priorities approved by the NSC into specific guidance for the Intelligence Community, resolve conflicts in tasking priority, provide to departments and agencies having information collection capabilities that are not part of the National Foreign Intelligence Program advisory tasking concerning collection of national foreign intelligence, and provide for the development of plans and arrangements for transfer of required collection tasking authority to the Secretary of Defense when directed by the President;

(n) Develop, with the advice of the program managers and departments and agencies concerned, the consolidated National Foreign Intelligence Program budget, and present it to the President and the Congress;

(o) Review and approve all requests for reprogramming National Foreign Intelligence Program funds, in accordance with guidelines established by the Office of Management and Budget;

(p) Monitor National Foreign Intelligence Program implementation, and, as necessary, conduct program and performance audits and evaluations;

(q) Together with the Secretary of Defense, ensure that there is no unnecessary overlap between national foreign intelligence programs and Department of Defense intelligence programs consistent with the requirement to develop competitive analysis, and provide to and obtain from the Secretary of Defense all information necessary for this purpose;

(r) In accordance with law and relevant procedures approved by the Attorney General under this Order, give the heads of the departments and agencies access to all intelligence, developed by the CIA or the staff elements of the Director of Central Intelligence, relevant to the national intelligence needs of the departments and agencies; and

(s) Facilitate the use of national foreign intelligence products by Congress in a secure manner.

1.6 *Duties and Responsibilities of the Heads of Executive Branch Departments and Agencies.*

(a) The heads of all Executive Branch departments and agencies shall, in accordance with law and relevant procedures approved by the Attorney General under this Order, give the Director of Central Intelligence access to all information relevant to the national intelligence needs of the United States, and shall give due consideration to the requests from the Director of Central Intelligence for appropriate support for Intelligence Community activities.

(b) The heads of departments and agencies involved in the National Foreign Intelligence Program shall ensure timely development and submission to the Director of Central Intelligence by the program managers and heads of component activities of proposed national programs and budgets in the format designated by the Director of Central Intelligence, and shall also ensure that the Director of Central Intelligence is provided, in a timely and responsive manner, all information necessary to perform the Director's program and budget responsibilities.

(c) The heads of departments and agencies involved in the National Foreign Intelligence Program may appeal to the President decisions by the Director of Central Intelligence on budget or reprogramming matters of the National Foreign Intelligence Program.

1.7 *Senior Officials of the Intelligence Community.* The heads of departments and agencies with organizations in the Intelligence Community or the heads of such organizations, as appropriate, shall:

(a) Report to the Attorney General possible violations of federal criminal laws by employees and of specified federal criminal laws by any other person as provided in procedures agreed upon by the Attorney General and the head of the department or agency concerned, in a manner consistent with the protection of intelligence sources and methods, as specified in those procedures;

(b) In any case involving serious or continuing breaches of security, recommend to the Attorney General that the case be referred to the FBI for further investigation;

(c) Furnish the Director of Central Intelligence and the NSC, in accordance with applicable law and procedures approved by the Attorney General under this Order, the information required for the performance of their respective duties;

(d) Report to the Intelligence Oversight Board, and keep the Director of Central Intelligence appropriately informed, concerning any intelligence activities of their organizations that they have reason to believe may be unlawful or contrary to Executive order or Presidential directive;

(e) Protect intelligence and intelligence sources and methods from unauthorized disclosure consistent with guidance from the Director of Central Intelligence;

(f) Disseminate intelligence to cooperating foreign governments under arrangements established or agreed to by the Director of Central Intelligence;

(g) Participate in the development of procedures approved by the Attorney General governing production and dissemination of intelligence resulting from criminal narcotics intelligence activities abroad if their departments, agencies, or organizations have intelligence responsibilities for foreign or domestic narcotics production and trafficking;

(h) Instruct their employees to cooperate fully with the Intelligence Oversight Board; and

(i) Ensure that the Inspectors General and General Counsels for their organizations have access to any information necessary to perform their duties assigned by this Order.

1.8 *The Central Intelligence Agency.* All duties and responsibilities of the CIA shall be related to the intelligence functions set out below. As authorized by this Order; the National Security Act of 1947, as amended; the CIA Act of 1949, as amended; appropriate directives or other applicable law, the CIA shall:

(a) Collect, produce and disseminate foreign intelligence and counterintelligence, including information not otherwise obtainable. The collection of foreign intelligence or counterintelligence within the United States shall be coordinated with the FBI as required by procedures agreed upon by the Director of Central Intelligence and the Attorney General;

(b) Collect, produce and disseminate intelligence on foreign aspects of narcotics production and trafficking;

(c) Conduct counterintelligence activities outside the United States and, without assuming or performing any internal security functions, conduct counterintelligence activities within the United States in coordination with the FBI as required by procedures agreed upon by the Director of Central Intelligence and the Attorney General;

(d) Coordinate counterintelligence activities and the collection of information not otherwise obtainable when conducted outside the United States by other departments and agencies;

(e) Conduct special activities approved by the President. No agency except the CIA (or the Armed Forces of the United States in time of war declared by Congress or during any period covered by a report from the President to the Congress under the War Powers Resolution (87 Stat. 855)) may conduct any special activity unless the President determines that another agency is more likely to achieve a particular objective;

(f) Conduct services of common concern for the Intelligence Community as directed by the NSC;

(g) Carry out or contract for research, development and procurement of technical systems and devices relating to authorized functions;

(h) Protect the security of its installations, activities, information, property, and employees by appropriate means, including such investigations of applicants, employees, contractors, and other persons with similar associations with the CIA as are necessary; and

(i) Conduct such administrative and technical support activities within and outside the United States as are necessary to perform the functions described in sections (a) through (h) above, including procurement and essential cover and proprietary arrangements.

1.9 *The Department of State.* The Secretary of State shall:

(a) Overtly collect information relevant to United States foreign policy concerns;

(b) Produce and disseminate foreign intelligence relating to United States foreign policy as required for the execution of the Secretary's responsibilities;

(c) Disseminate, as appropriate, reports received from United States diplomatic and consular posts;

(d) Transmit reporting requirements of the Intelligence Community to the Chiefs of United States Missions abroad; and

(e) Support Chiefs of Missions in discharging their statutory responsibilities for direction and coordination of mission activities.

1.10 *The Department of the Treasury.* The Secretary of the Treasury shall:

(a) Overtly collect foreign financial and monetary information;

(b) Participate with the Department of State in the overt collection of general foreign economic information;

(c) Produce and disseminate foreign intelligence relating to United States economic policy as required for the execution of the Secretary's responsibilities; and

(d) Conduct, through the United States Secret Service, activities to determine the existence and capability of surveillance equipment being used against the President of the United States, the Executive Office of the President, and, as authorized by the Secretary of the Treasury, or the President, other Secret Service protectees and United States officials. No information shall be acquired intentionally through such activities except to protect against such surveillance, and those activities shall be conducted pursuant to procedures agreed upon by the Secretary of the Treasury and the Attorney General.

1.11 *The Department of Defense.* The Secretary of Defense shall:

(a) Collect national foreign intelligence and be responsive to collection tasking by the Director of Central Intelligence;

(b) Collect, produce and disseminate military and military-related foreign intelligence and counterintelligence as required for execution of the Secretary's responsibilities;

(c) Conduct programs and missions necessary to fulfill national, departmental and tactical foreign intelligence requirements;

(d) Conduct counterintelligence activities in support of Department of Defense components outside the United States in coordination with the CIA, and within the United States in coordination with the FBI pursuant to procedures agreed upon by the Secretary of Defense and the Attorney General;

(e) Conduct, as the executive agent of the United States Government, signals intelligence and communications security activities, except as otherwise directed by the NSC;

(f) Provide for the timely transmission of critical intelligence, as defined by the Director of Central Intelligence, within the United States Government;

(g) Carry out or contract for research, development and procurement of technical systems and devices relating to authorized intelligence functions;

(h) Protect the security of Department of Defense installations, activities, property, information, and employees by appropriate means, including such investigations of applicants, employees, contractors, and other persons with similar associations with the Department of Defense as are necessary;

(i) Establish and maintain military intelligence relationships and military intelligence exchange programs with selected cooperative foreign defense establishments and international organizations, and ensure that such relationships and programs are in accordance with policies formulated by the Director of Central Intelligence;

(j) Direct, operate, control and provide fiscal management for the National Security Agency and for defense and military intelligence and national reconnaissance entities; and

(k) Conduct such administrative and technical support activities within and outside the United States as are necessary to perform the functions described in sections (a) through (j) above.

1.12 *Intelligence Components Utilized by the Secretary of Defense.* In carrying out the responsibilities assigned in section 1.11, the Secretary of Defense is authorized to utilize the following:

(a) *Defense Intelligence Agency,* whose responsibilities shall include:

(1) Collection, production, or, through tasking and coordination, provision of military and military-related intelligence for the Secretary of Defense, the Joint Chiefs of Staff, other Defense components, and, as appropriate, non-Defense agencies;

(2) Collection and provision of military intelligence for national foreign intelligence and counterintelligence products;

(3) Coordination of all Department of Defense intelligence collection requirements;

(4) Management of the Defense Attache system; and

(5) Provision of foreign intelligence and counterintelligence staff support as directed by the Joint Chiefs of Staff.

(b) *National Security Agency,* whose responsibilities shall include:

(1) Establishment and operation of an effective unified organization for signals intelligence activities, except for the delegation of operational control over certain operations that are conducted through other elements of the Intelligence Community. No other department or agency may engage in signals intelligence activities except pursuant to a delegation by the Secretary of Defense;

(2) Control of signals intelligence collection and processing activities, including assignment of resources to an appropriate agent for such periods and tasks as required for the direct support of military commanders;

(3) Collection of signals intelligence information for national foreign intelligence purposes in accordance with guidance from the Director of Central Intelligence;

(4) Processing of signals intelligence data for national foreign intelligence purposes in accordance with guidance from the Director of Central Intelligence;

(5) Dissemination of signals intelligence information for national foreign intelligence purposes to authorized elements of the Government, including the military services, in accordance with guidance from the Director of Central Intelligence;

(6) Collection, processing and dissemination of signals intelligence information for counterintelligence purposes;

(7) Provision of signals intelligence support for the conduct of military operations in accordance with tasking, priorities, and standards of timeliness assigned by the Secretary of Defense. If provision of such support requires use of national collection systems, these systems will be tasked within existing guidance from the Director of Central Intelligence;

(8) Executing the responsibilities of the Secretary of Defense as executive agent for the communications security of the United States Government;

(9) Conduct of research and development to meet the needs of the United States for signals intelligence and communications security;

(10) Protection of the security of its installations, activities, property, information, and employees by appropriate means, including such investigations of applicants, employees, contractors, and other persons with similar associations with the NSA as are necessary;

(11) Prescribing, within its field of authorized operations, security regulations covering operating practices, including the transmission, handling and distribution of signals intelligence and communications security material within and among the elements under control of the Director of the NSA, and exercising the necessary supervisory control to ensure compliance with the regulations;

(12) Conduct of foreign cryptologic liaison relationships, with liaison for intelligence purposes conducted in accordance with policies formulated by the Director of Central Intelligence; and

(13) Conduct of such administrative and technical support activities within and outside the United States as are necessary to perform the functions described in sections (1) through (12) above, including procurement.

(c) *Offices for the collection of specialized intelligence through reconnaissance programs,* whose responsibilities shall include:

(1) Carrying out consolidated reconnaissance programs for specialized intelligence;

(2) Responding to tasking in accordance with procedures established by the Director of Central Intelligence; and

(3) Delegating authority to the various departments and agencies for research, development, procurement, and operations of designated means of collection.

(d) *The foreign intelligence and counterintelligence elements of the Army, Navy, Air Force, and Marine Corps,* whose responsibilities shall include:

(1) Collection, production and dissemination of military and military-related foreign intelligence and counterintelligence, and information on the foreign aspects of narcotics production and trafficking. When collection is conducted in response to national foreign intelligence requirements, it will be conducted in accordance with guidance from the Director of Central Intelligence. Collection of national foreign intelligence, not otherwise obtainable, outside the United States shall be coordinated with the CIA, and such collection within the United States shall be coordinated with the FBI;

(2) Conduct of counterintelligence activities outside the United States in coordination with the CIA, and within the United States in coordination with the FBI; and

(3) Monitoring of the development, procurement and management of tactical intelligence systems and equipment and conducting related research, development, and test and evaluation activities.

(e) *Other offices within the Department of Defense appropriate for conduct of the intelligence missions and responsibilities assigned to the Secretary of Defense.* If such other offices are used for intelligence purposes, the provisions of Part 2 of this Order shall apply to those offices when used for those purposes.

1.13 *The Department of Energy.* The Secretary of Energy shall:

(a) Participate with the Department of State in overtly collecting information with respect to foreign energy matters;

(b) Produce and disseminate foreign intelligence necessary for the Secretary's responsibilities;

(c) Participate in formulating intelligence collection and analysis requirements where the special expert capability of the Department can contribute; and

(d) Provide expert technical, analytical and research capability to other agencies within the Intelligence Community.

1.14 *The Federal Bureau of Investigation.* Under the supervision of the Attorney General and pursuant to such regulations as the Attorney General may establish, the Director of the FBI shall:

(a) Within the United States conduct counterintelligence and coordinate counterintelligence activities of other agencies within the Intelligence Community. When a counterintelligence activity of the

FBI involves military or civilian personnel of the Department of Defense, the FBI shall coordinate with the Department of Defense;

(b) Conduct counterintelligence activities outside the United States in coordination with the CIA as required by procedures agreed upon by the Director of Central Intelligence and the Attorney General;

(c) Conduct within the United States, when requested by officials of the Intelligence Community designated by the President, activities undertaken to collect foreign intelligence or support foreign intelligence collection requirements of other agencies within the Intelligence Community, or, when requested by the Director of the National Security Agency, to support the communications security activities of the United States Government;

(d) Produce and disseminate foreign intelligence and counterintelligence; and

(e) Carry out or contract for research, development and procurement of technical systems and devices relating to the functions authorized above.

PART 2

Conduct of Intelligence Activities

2.1 *Need.* Accurate and timely information about the capabilities, intentions and activities of foreign powers, organizations, or persons and their agents is essential to informed decisionmaking in the areas of national defense and foreign relations. Collection of such information is a priority objective and will be pursued in a vigorous, innovative and responsible manner that is consistent with the Constitution and applicable law and respectful of the principles upon which the United States was founded.

2.2 *Purpose.* This Order is intended to enhance human and technical collection techniques, especially those undertaken abroad, and the acquisition of significant foreign intelligence, as well as the detection and countering of international terrorist activities and espionage conducted by foreign powers. Set forth below are certain general principles that, in addition to and consistent with applicable laws, are intended to achieve the proper balance between the acquisition of essential information and protection of individual interests. Nothing in this Order shall be construed to apply to or interfere with any authorized civil or criminal law enforcement responsibility of any department or agency.

2.3 *Collection of Information.* Agencies within the Intelligence Community are authorized to collect, retain or disseminate information concerning United States persons only in accordance with procedures established by the head of the agency concerned and approved by the Attorney General, consistent with the authorities provided by Part 1 of this Order. Those procedures shall permit collection, retention and dissemination of the following types of information:

(a) Information that is publicly available or collected with the consent of the person concerned;

(b) Information constituting foreign intelligence or counterintelligence, including such information concerning corporations or other commercial organizations. Collection within the United States of foreign intelligence not otherwise obtainable shall be undertaken by the FBI or, when significant foreign intelligence is sought, by other authorized agencies of the Intelligence Community, provided that no foreign intelligence collection by such agencies may be undertaken for the purpose of acquiring information concerning the domestic activities of United States persons;

(c) Information obtained in the course of a lawful foreign intelligence, counterintelligence, international narcotics or international terrorism investigation;

(d) Information needed to protect the safety of any persons or organizations, including those who are targets, victims or hostages of international terrorist organizations;

(e) Information needed to protect foreign intelligence or counterintelligence sources or methods from unauthorized disclosure. Collection within the United States shall be undertaken by the FBI except that other agencies of the Intelligence Community may also collect such information concerning present or former employees, present or former intelligence agency contractors or their present or former employees, or applicants for any such employment or contracting;

(f) Information concerning persons who are reasonably believed to be potential sources or contacts for the purpose of determining their suitability or credibility;

(g) Information arising out of a lawful personnel, physical or communications security investigation;

(h) Information acquired by overhead reconnaissance not directed at specific United States persons;

(i) Incidentally obtained information that may indicate involvement in activities that may violate federal, state, local or foreign laws; and

(j) Information necessary for administrative purposes.

In addition, agencies within the Intelligence Community may disseminate information, other than information derived from signals intelligence, to each appropriate agency within the Intelligence Community for purposes of allowing the recipient agency to determine whether the information is relevant to its responsibilities and can be retained by it.

2.4 *Collection Techniques.* Agencies within the Intelligence Community shall use the least intrusive collection techniques feasible within the United States or directed against United States persons abroad. Agencies are not authorized to use such techniques as electronic surveillance, unconsented physical search, mail surveillance, physical surveillance, or monitoring devices unless they are in accordance with procedures established by the head of the agency concerned and approved by the Attorney General. Such procedures shall protect constitutional and other legal rights and limit use of such information to lawful governmental purposes. These procedures shall not authorize:

(a) The CIA to engage in electronic surveillance within the United States except for the purpose of training, testing, or conducting countermeasures to hostile electronic surveillance;

(b) Unconsented physical searches in the United States by agencies other than the FBI, except for:

(1) Searches by counterintelligence elements of the military services directed against military personnel within the United States or abroad for intelligence purposes, when authorized by a military commander empowered to approve physical searches for law enforcement purposes, based upon a finding of probable cause to believe that such persons are acting as agents of foreign powers; and

(2) Searches by CIA of personal property of non-United States persons lawfully in its possession.

(c) Physical surveillance of a United States person in the United States by agencies other than the FBI, except for:

(1) Physical surveillance of present or former employees, present or former intelligence agency contractors or their present of former employees, or applicants for any such employment or contracting; and

(2) Physical surveillance of a military person employed by a nonintelligence element of a military service.

(d) Physical surveillance of a United States person abroad to collect foreign intelligence, except to obtain significant information that cannot reasonably be acquired by other means.

2.5 *Attorney General Approval.* The Attorney General hereby is delegated the power to approve the use for intelligence purposes, within the United States or against a United States person abroad, of any technique for which a warrant would be required if undertaken for law enforcement purposes, provided that such techniques shall not be undertaken unless the Attorney General has determined in each case that there is probable cause to believe that the technique is directed against a foreign power or an agent of a foreign power. Electronic surveillance, as defined in the Foreign Intelligence Surveillance Act of 1978, shall be conducted in accordance with that Act, as well as this Order.

2.6 *Assistance to Law Enforcement Authorities.* Agencies within the Intelligence Community are authorized to:

(a) Cooperate with appropriate law enforcement agencies for the purpose of protecting the employees, information, property and facilities of any agency within the Intelligence Community;

(b) Unless otherwise precluded by law or this Order, participate in law enforcement activities to investigate or prevent clandestine intelligence activities by foreign powers, or international terrorist or narcotics activities;

(c) Provide specialized equipment, technical knowledge, or assistance of expert personnel for use by any department or agency, or, when lives are endangered, to support local law enforcement agencies. Provision of assistance by expert personnel shall be approved in each case by the General Counsel of the providing agency; and

(d) Render any other assistance and cooperation to law enforcement authorities not precluded by applicable law.

2.7 *Contracting.* Agencies within the Intelligence Community are authorized to enter into contracts or arrangements for the provision of goods or services with private companies or institutions in the United States and need not reveal the sponsorship of such contracts or arrangements for authorized intelligence purposes. Contracts or arrangements with academic institutions may be undertaken only with the contract of appropriate officials of the institution.

2.8 *Consistency With Other Laws.* Nothing in this Order shall be construed to authorize any activity in violation of the Constitution or statutes of the United States.

2.9 *Undisclosed Participation in Organizations Within the United States.* No one acting on behalf of agencies within the Intelligence Community may join or otherwise participate in any organization in the United States on behalf of any agency within the Intelligence Community without disclosing his intelligence affiliation to appropriate officials of the organization, except in accordance with procedures established by the head of the agency concerned and approved by the Attorney General. Such participation shall be authorized only if it is essential to achieving lawful purposes as determined by the agency head or designee. No such participation may be undertaken for the purpose of influencing the activity of the organization or its members except in cases where:

(a) The participation is undertaken on behalf of the FBI in the course of a lawful investigation; or

(b) The organization concerned is composed primarily of individuals who are not United States persons and is reasonably believed to be acting on behalf of a foreign power.

2.10 *Human Experimentation.* No agency within the Intelligence Community shall sponsor, contract for or conduct research on human subjects except in accordance with guidelines issued by the Department of Health and Human Services. The subject's informed consent shall be documented as required by those guidelines.

2.11 *Prohibition on Assassination.* No person employed by or acting on behalf of the United States Government shall engage in, or conspire to engage in, assassination.

2.12 *Indirect Participation.* No agency of the Intelligence Community shall participate in or request any person to undertake activities forbidden by this Order.

PART 3

General Provisions

3.1 *Congressional Oversight.* The duties and responsibilities of the Director of Central Intelligence and the heads of other departments, agencies, and entities engaged in intelligence activities to cooperate with the Congress in the conduct of its responsibilities for oversight of intelligence activities shall be as provided in title 50, United States Code, section 413. The requirements of section 662 of the Foreign Assistance Act of 1961, as amended (22 U.S.C. 2422), and section 501 of the National Security Act of 1947, as amended (50 U.S.C. 413), shall apply to all special activities as defined in this Order.

3.2 *Implementation.* The NSC, the Secretary of Defense, the Attorney General, and the Director of Central Intelligence shall issue such appropriate directives and procedures as are necessary to implement this Order. Heads of agencies within the Intelligence Community shall issue appropriate supplementary directives and procedures consistent with this Order. The Attorney General shall provide a statement of reasons for not approving any procedures established by the head of an agency in the Intelligence Community other than the FBI. The National Security Council may establish procedures in instances where the agency head and the Attorney General are unable to reach agreement on other than constitutional or other legal grounds.

3.3 *Procedures.* Until the procedures required by this Order have been established, the activities herein authorized which require procedures shall be conducted in accordance with existing procedures or requirements established under Executive Order No. 12036. Procedures required by this Order shall be established as expeditiously as possible. All procedures promulgated pursuant to this Order shall be made available to the congressional intelligence committees.

3.4 *Definitions.* For the purposes of this Order, the following terms shall have these meanings:

(a) *Counterintelligence* means information gathered and activities conducted to protect against espionage, other intelligence activities, sabotage, or assassinations conducted for or on behalf of foreign powers, organizations or persons, or international terrorist activities, but not including personnel, physical, document or communications security programs.

(b) *Electronic surveillance* means acquisitions of a nonpublic communication by electronic means without the consent of a person who is a party to an electronic communication or, in the case of a nonelectronic communication, without the consent of a person who is visibly present at the place of communication, but not including the use of radio direction-finding equipment solely to determine the location of a transmitter.

(c) *Employee* means a person employed by, assigned to or acting for an agency within the Intelligence Community.

(d) *Foreign intelligence* means information relating to the capabilities, intentions and activities of foreign powers, organizations or persons, but not including counterintelligence except for information on international terrorist activities.

(e) *Intelligence activities* means all activities that agencies within the Intelligence Community are authorized to conduct pursuant to this Order.

(f) *Intelligence Community and agencies within the Intelligence Community* refer to the following agencies or organizations:

(1) The Central Intelligence Agency (CIA);

(2) The National Security Agency (NSA);

(3) The Defense Intelligence Agency (DIA);

(4) The offices within the Department of Defense for the collection of specialized national foreign intelligence through reconnaissance programs;

(5) The Bureau of Intelligence and Research of the Department of State;

(6) The intelligence elements of the Army, Navy, Air Force, and Marine Corps, the Federal Bureau of Investigation (FBI), the Department of the Treasury, and the Department of Energy; and

(7) The staff elements of the Director of Central Intelligence.

(g) *The National Foreign Intelligence Program* includes the programs listed below, but its composition shall be subject to review by the National Security Council and modification by the President:

(1) The programs of the CIA;

(2) The Consolidated Cryptologic Program, the General Defense Intelligence Program, and the programs of the offices within the Department of Defense for the collection of specialized national foreign intelligence through reconnaissance, except such elements as the Director of Central Intelligence and the Secretary of Defense agree should be excluded;

(3) Other programs of agencies within the Intelligence Community designated jointly by the Director of Central Intelligence and the head of the department or by the President as national foreign intelligence or counterintelligence activities;

(4) Activities of the staff elements of the Director of Central Intelligence;

(5) Activities to acquire the intelligence required for the planning and conduct of tactical operations by the United States military forces are not included in the National Foreign Intelligence Program.

(h) *Special activities* means activities conducted in support of national foreign policy objectives abroad which are planned and executed so that the role of the United States Government is not apparent or acknowledged publicly, and functions in support of such activities, but which are not intended to influence United States political processes, public opinion, policies, or media and do not include diplomatic activities or the collection and production of intelligence or related support functions.

(i) *United States person* means a United States citizen, an alien known by the intelligence agency concerned to be a permanent resident alien, an unincorporated association substantially composed of United States citizens or permanent resident aliens, or a corporation incorporated in the United States, except for a corporation directed and controlled by a foreign government or governments.

3.5 *Purpose and Effect.* This Order is intended to control and provide direction and guidance to the Intelligence Community. Nothing contained herein or in any procedures promulgated hereunder is intended to confer any substantive or procedural right or privilege on any person or organization.

3.6 *Revocation.* Executive Order No. 12036 of January 24, 1978, as amended, entitled "United States Intelligence Activities," is revoked.

RONALD REAGAN
THE WHITE HOUSE,
December 4, 1981.

CONGRESSIONAL OVERSIGHT:
THE SENATE SELECT COMMITTEE ON INTELLIGENCE

The Senate established the Select Committee on Intelligence by Senate Resolution 400 (S. Res. 400), passed by the Senate in the 94th Congress (1976). Note that the committee has exclusive jurisdiction over only the director of central intelligence and the CIA, and that it shares jurisdiction over all other intelligence entities with other committees.

S. RES. 400 FROM THE 94TH CONGRESS

A RESOLUTION ESTABLISHING A
SELECT COMMITTEE ON INTELLIGENCE

Resolved, That it is the purpose of this resolution to establish a new select committee of the Senate, to be known as the Select Committee on Intelligence, to oversee and make continuing studies of the intelligence activities and programs of the United States Government, and to submit to the Senate appropriate proposals for legislation and report to the Senate concerning such intelligence activities and programs. In carrying out this purpose, the Select Committee on Intelligence shall make every effort to assure that the appropriate departments and agencies of the United States provide informed and timely intelligence necessary for the executive and legislative branches to make sound decisions affecting the security and vital interests of the Nation. It is further the purpose of this resolution to provide vigilant legislative oversight over the intelligence activities of the United States to assure that such activities are in conformity with the Constitution and laws of the United States.

SEC. 2. (a)(1) There is hereby established a select committee to be known as the Select Committee on Intelligence (hereinafter in this resolution referred to as the "select committee"). The select committee shall be composed of fifteen members appointed as follows:

    (A) two members from the Committee on Appropriations;

    (B) two members from the Committee on Armed Services;

    (C) two members from the Committee on Foreign Relations;

    (D) two members from the Committee on the Judiciary; and

    (E) seven members to be appointed from the Senate at large.

(2) Members appointed from each committee named in clauses (A) through (D) of paragraph (1) shall be evenly divided between the two major political parties and shall be appointed by the President pro tempore of the Senate upon the recommendations of the majority and minority leaders of the Senate. Four of the members appointed under clause (E) of paragraph (1) shall be appointed by the President pro tempore of the Senate upon the recommendation of the majority leader of the Senate and three shall be appointed by the President pro tempore of the Senate upon the recommendation of the minority leader of the Senate.

(3) The majority leader of the Senate and the minority leader of the Senate shall be ex officio members of the select committee but shall have no vote in the committee and shall not be counted for purposes of determining a quorum.

(b) No Senator may serve on the select committee for more than eight years of continuous service, exclusive of service by any Senator on such committee during the Ninety-fourth Congress. To the greatest extent practicable, one-third of the Members of the Senate appointed to the select committee at the beginning of the Ninety-seventh Congress and each Congress thereafter shall be Members of the Senate who did not serve on such committee during the preceding Congress.

(c) At the beginning of each Congress, the Members of the Senate who are members of the majority party of the Senate shall elect a chairman for the select committee, and the Members of the Senate who are from the minority party of the Senate shall elect a vice chairman for such committee. The vice chairman shall act in the place and stead of the chairman in the absence of the chairman. Neither the chairman nor the vice chairman of the select committee shall at the same time serve as chairman or ranking minority member of any other committee referred to in paragraph 6(f) of rule XXV of the Standing Rules of the Senate.

(d) For the purposes of paragraph 6(a) of rule XXV of the Standing Rules of the Senate, service of a Senator as a member of the select committee shall not be taken into account.

SEC. 3. (a) There shall be referred to the select committee all proposed legislation, messages, petitions, memorials, and other matters relating to the following:

    (1) The Central Intelligence Agency and the Director of Central Intelligence.

    (2) Intelligence activities of all other departments and agencies of the Government, including, but not limited to, the intelligence activities of the Defense Intelligence Agency, the National Security Agency, and other agencies of the Department of Defense; the Department of State; the Department of Justice; and the Department of the Treasury.

    (3) The organization or reorganization of any department or agency of the Government to the extent that the organization or reorganization relates to a function or activity involving intelligence activities.

(4) Authorization for appropriations, both direct and indirect, for the following:

(A) The Central Intelligence Agency and Director of Central Intelligence.

(B) The Defense Intelligence Agency.

(C) The National Security Agency.

(D) The intelligence activities of other agencies and subdivisions of the Department of Defense.

(E) The intelligence activities of the Department of State.

(F) The intelligence activities of the Federal Bureau of Investigation, including all activities of the Intelligence Division.

(G) Any department, agency, or subdivision which is the successor to any agency named in clause (A), (B), or (C); and the activities of any department, agency, or subdivision which is the successor to any department, agency, bureau, or subdivision named in clause (D), (E), or (F) to the extent that the activities of such successor department, agency, or subdivision are activities described in clause (D), (E), or (F).

(b) Any proposed legislation reported by the select committee, except any legislation involving matters specified in clause (1) or (4)(A) of subsection (a), containing any matter otherwise within the jurisdiction of any standing committee shall, at the request of the chairman of such standing committee, be referred to such standing committee for its consideration of such matter and be reported to the Senate by such standing committee within thirty days after the day on which such proposed legislation is referred to such standing committee; and any proposed legislation reported by any committee, other than the select committee, which contains any matter within the jurisdiction of the select committee shall, at the request of the chairman of the select committee, be referred to the select committee for its consideration of such matter and be reported to the Senate by the select committee within thirty days after the day on which such proposed legislation is referred to such committee. In any case in which a committee fails to report any proposed legislation referred to it within the time limit prescribed herein, such committee shall be automatically discharged from further consideration of such proposed legislation on the thirtieth day following the day on which such proposed legislation is referred to such committee unless the Senate provides otherwise. In computing any thirty-day period under this paragraph there shall be excluded from such computation any days on which the Senate is not in session.

(c) Nothing in this resolution shall be construed as prohibiting or otherwise restricting the authority of any other committee to study and review any intelligence activity to the extent that such activity directly affects a matter otherwise within the jurisdiction of such committee.

(d) Nothing in this resolution shall be construed as amending, limiting, or otherwise changing the authority of any standing committee of the Senate to obtain full and prompt access to the product of the intelligence activities of any department or agency of the Government relevant to a matter otherwise within the jurisdiction of such committee.

SEC. 4. (a) The select committee, for the purposes of accountability to the Senate, shall make regular and periodic reports to the Senate on the nature and extent of the intelligence activities of the various departments and agencies of the United States. Such committee shall promptly call to the attention of the Senate or to any other appropriate committee or committees of the Senate any matters requiring the attention of the Senate or such other committee or committees. In making such reports, the select committee shall proceed in a manner consistent with section 8(c)(2) to protect national security.

(b) The select committee shall obtain an annual report from the Director of the Central Intelligence Agency, the Secretary of Defense, the Secretary of State, and the Director of the Federal Bureau of Investigation. Such reports shall review the intelligence activities of the agency or department concerned and the intelligence activities of foreign countries directed at the United States or its interests. An unclassified version of each report may be made available to the public at the discretion of the select committee. Nothing herein shall be construed as requiring the public disclosure in such reports of the names of individuals engaged in intelligence activities for the United States or the divulging of intelligence methods employed or the sources of information on which such reports are based or the amount of funds authorized to be appropriated for intelligence activities.

(c) On or before March 15 of each year, the select committee shall submit to the Committee on the Budget of the Senate the views and estimates described in section 301(c) of the Congressional Budget Act of 1974 regarding matters within the jurisdiction of the select committee.

SEC. 5. (a) For the purposes of this resolution, the select committee is authorized in its discretion (1) to make investigations into any matter within its jurisdiction, (2) to make expenditures from the contingent fund of the Senate, (3) to employ personnel, (4) to hold hearings, (5) to sit and act at any time or place during the sessions, recesses, and adjourned periods of the Senate, (6) to require, by subpoena or otherwise, the attendance of witnesses and the production of correspondence, books, papers, and documents, (7) to take depositions and other testimony, (8) to procure the service of consultants or organizations thereof, in accordance with the provisions of section 202(i) of the Legislative Reorganization Act of 1946, and (9) with the prior consent of the Government department or agency concerned and the Committee on Rules and Administration, to use on a reimbursable basis the services of personnel of any such department or agency.

(b) The chairman of the select committee or any member thereof may administer oaths to witnesses.

(c) Subpoenas authorized by the select committee may be issued over the signature of the chairman, the vice chairman, or any member of the select committee designated by the chairman, and may be served by any person designated by the chairman or any member signing the subpoena.

SEC. 6. No employee of the select committee or any person engaged by contract or otherwise to perform service for or at the request of such committee shall be given access to any classified information by such committee unless such employee or person has (1) agreed in writing and under oath to be bound by the rules of the Senate (including the jurisdiction of the Select Committee on Standards and Conduct) and of such committee as to the security of such information during and after the period of his employment or contractual agreement with such committee; and (2) received an appropriate security clearance as determined by such committee in consultation with the Director of Central Intelligence. The type of security clearance to be required in the case of any such employee or person shall, within the determination of such committee in consultation with the Director of Central Intelligence, be commensurate with the sensitivity of the classified information to which such employee or person will be given access by such committee.

SEC. 7. The select committee shall formulate and carry out such rules and procedures as it deems necessary to prevent the disclosure, without the consent of the person or persons concerned, of information in the possession of such committee which unduly infringes upon the privacy or which violates the constitutional rights of such person or persons. Nothing herein shall be construed to prevent such committee from publicly disclosing any such information in any case in which such committee determines the national interest in the disclosure of such information clearly outweighs any infringement on the privacy of any person or persons.

SEC. 8. (a) The select committee may, subject to the provisions of this section, disclose publicly any information in the possession of such committee after a determination by such committee that the public interest would be served by such disclosure. Whenever committee action is required to disclose any information under this section, the committee shall meet to vote on the matter within five days after any member of the committee requests such a vote. No member of the select committee shall disclose any information, the disclosure of which requires a committee vote, prior to a vote by the committee on the question of the disclosure of such information or after such vote except in accordance with this section.

(b)(1) In any case in which the select committee votes to disclose publicly any information which has been classified under established security procedures, which has been submitted to it by the executive branch, and which the executive branch requests be kept secret, such committee shall notify the President of such vote.

(2) The select committee may disclose publicly such information after the expiration of a five-day period following the day on which notice of such vote is transmitted to the President, unless, prior to the expiration of such five-day period, the President, personally in writing, notifies the committee that he objects to the disclosure of such information, provides his reasons therefor, and certifies that the threat to the national interest of the United States posed by such disclosure is of such gravity that it outweighs any public interest in the disclosure.

(3) If the President, personally in writing, notifies the select committee of his objections to the disclosure of such information as provided in paragraph (2), such committee may, by majority vote, refer the question of the disclosure of such information to the Senate for consideration. The committee shall not publicly disclose such information without leave of the Senate.

(4) Whenever the select committee votes to refer the question of disclosure of any information to the Senate under paragraph (3), the chairman shall, not later than the first day on which the

Senate is in session following the day on which the vote occurs, report the matter to the Senate for its consideration.

(5) One hour after the Senate convenes on the fourth day on which the Senate is in session following the day on which any such matter is reported to the Senate or at such earlier time as the majority leader and the minority leader of the Senate jointly agree upon in accordance with section 133(f) of the Legislative Reorganization Act of 1946, the Senate shall go into closed session and the matter shall be the pending business. In considering the matter in closed session the Senate may—

(A) approve the public disclosure of all or any portion of the information in question, in which case the committee shall publicly disclose the information ordered to be disclosed,

(B) disapprove the public disclosure of all or any portion of the information in question, in which case the committee shall not publicly disclose the information ordered not to be disclosed, or

(C) refer all or any portion of the matter back to the committee, in which case the committee shall make the final determination with respect to the public disclosure of the information in question.

Upon conclusion of the consideration of such matter in closed session, which may not extend beyond the close of the ninth day on which the Senate is in session following the day on which such matter was reported to the Senate, or the close of the fifth day following the day agreed upon jointly by the majority and minority leaders in accordance with section 133(f) of the Legislative Reorganization Act of 1946 (whichever the case may be), the Senate shall immediately vote on the disposition of such matter in open session, without debate, and without divulging the information with respect to which the vote is being taken. The Senate shall vote to dispose of such matter by one or more of the means specified in clauses (A), (B), and (C) of the second sentence of this paragraph. Any vote of the Senate to disclose any information pursuant to this paragraph shall be subject to the right of a Member of the Senate to move for reconsideration of the vote within the time and pursuant to the procedures specified in rule XIII of the Standing Rules of the Senate, and the disclosure of such information shall be made consistent with that right.

(c)(1) No information in the possession of the select committee relating to the lawful intelligence activities of any department or agency of the United States which has been classified under established security procedures and which the select committee, pursuant to subsection (a) or (b) of this section, has determined should not be disclosed shall be made available to any person by a Member, officer, or employee of the Senate except in a closed session of the Senate or as provided in paragraph (2).

(2) The select committee may, under such regulations as the committee shall prescribe to protect the confidentiality of such information, make any information described in paragraph (1) available to any other committee or any other Member of the Senate. Whenever the select committee makes such information available, the committee shall keep a written record showing, in the case of any particular information, which committee or which Members of the Senate received such information. No Member of the Senate who, and no committee which, receives any information under this subsection, shall disclose such information except in a closed session of the Senate.

(d) It shall be the duty of the Select Committee on Standards and Conduct to investigate any unauthorized disclosure of intelligence information by a Member, officer or employee of the Senate in violation of subsection (c) and to report to the Senate concerning any allegation which it finds to be substantiated.

(e) Upon the request of any person who is subject to any such investigation, the Select Committee on Standards and Conduct shall release to such individual at the conclusion of its investigation a summary of its investigation together with its findings. If, at the conclusion of its investigation, the Select Committee on Standards and Conduct determines that there has been a significant breach of confidentiality or unauthorized disclosure by a Member, officer, or employee of the Senate, it shall report its findings to the Senate and recommend appropriate action such as censure, removal from committee membership, or expulsion from the Senate, in the case of Member, or removal from office or employment or punishment for contempt, in the case of an officer or employee.

SEC. 9. The select committee is authorized to permit any personal representative of the President, designated by the President to serve as a liaison to such committee, to attend any closed meeting of such committee.

SEC. 10. Upon expiration of the Select Committee on Governmental Operations With Respect to Intelligence Activities, established by Senate Resolution 21, Ninety-fourth Congress, all records, files, documents, and other materials in the possession, custody, or control of such committee, under appropriate conditions established by it, shall be transferred to the select committee.

SEC. 11. (a) It is the sense of the Senate that the head of each department and agency of the United States should keep the select committee fully and currently informed with respect to intelligence activities, including any significant anticipated activities, which are the responsibility of or engaged in by such department or agency: *Provided,* That this does not constitute a condition precedent to the implementation of any such anticipated intelligence activity.

(b) It is the sense of the Senate that the head of any department or agency of the United States involved in any intelligence activities should furnish any information or documentation in the possession, custody, or control of the department or agency, or person paid by such department or agency, whenever requested by the select committee with respect to any matter within such committee's jurisdiction.

(c) It is the sense of the Senate that each department and agency of the United States should report immediately upon discovery to the select committee any and all intelligence activities which constitute violations of the constitutional fights of any person, violations of law, or violations of Executive orders, Presidential directives, or departmental or agency rules or regulations; each department and agency should further report to such committee what actions have been taken or are expected to be taken by the departments or agencies with respect to such violations.

SEC. 12. Subject to the Standing Rules of the Senate, no funds shall be appropriated for any fiscal year beginning after September 30, 1976, with the exception of a continuing bill or resolution, or amendment thereto, or conference report thereon, to, or for use of, any department or agency of the United States to carry out any of the following activities, unless such funds shall have been previously authorized by a bill or joint resolution passed by the Senate during the same or preceding fiscal year to carry out such activity for such fiscal year:

(1) The activities of the Central Intelligence Agency and the Director of Central Intelligence.

(2) The activities of the Defense Intelligence Agency.

(3) The activities of the National Security Agency.

(4) The intelligence activities of other agencies and subdivisions of the Department of Defense.

(5) The intelligence activities of the Department of State.

(6) The intelligence activities of the Federal Bureau of Investigation, including all activities of the Intelligence Division.

SEC. 13. (a) The select committee shall make a study with respect to the following matters, taking into consideration with respect to each such matter, all relevant aspects of the effectiveness of planning, gathering, use, security, and dissemination of intelligence:

(1) the quality of the analytical capabilities of United States foreign intelligence agencies and means for integrating more closely analytical intelligence and policy formulation;

(2) the extent and nature of the authority of the departments and agencies of the executive branch to engage in intelligence activities and the desirability of developing charters for each intelligence agency or department;

(3) the organization of intelligence activities in the executive branch to maximize the effectiveness of the conduct, oversight, and accountability of intelligence activities; to reduce duplication or overlap; and to improve the morale of the personnel of the foreign intelligence agencies;

(4) the conduct of covert and clandestine activities and the procedures by which Congress is informed of such activities;

(5) the desirability of changing any law, Senate rule or procedure, or any Executive order, rule, or regulation to improve the protection of intelligence secrets and provide for disclosure of information for which there is no compelling reason for secrecy;

(6) the desirability of establishing a standing committee of the Senate on intelligence activities;

(7) the desirability of establishing a joint committee of the Senate and the House of Representatives on intelligence activities in lieu of having separate committees in each House of Congress, or of establishing procedures under which separate committees on intelligence activities of the two Houses of Congress would receive joint briefings from the intelligence

agencies and coordinate their policies with respect to the safeguarding of sensitive intelligence information;

(8) the authorization of funds for the intelligence activities of the Government and whether disclosure of any of the amounts of such funds is in the public interest; and

(9) the development of a uniform set of definitions for terms to be used in policies or guidelines which may be adopted by the executive or legislative branches to govern, clarify, and strengthen the operation of intelligence activities.

(b) The select committee may, in its discretion, omit from the special study required by this section any matter it determines has been adequately studied by the Select Committee To Study Governmental Operations With Respect to Intelligence Activities, established by Senate Resolution 21, Ninety-fourth Congress.

(c) The select committee shall report the results of the study provided for by this section to the Senate, together with any recommendations for legislative or other actions it deems appropriate, no later than July 1, 1977, and from time to time thereafter as it deems appropriate.

SEC. 14. (a) As used in this resolution, the term "intelligence activities" includes (1) the collection, analysis, production, dissemination, or use of information which relates to any foreign country, or any government, political group, party, military force, movement, or other association in such foreign country, and which relates to the defense, foreign policy, national security, or related policies of the United States, and other activity which is in support of such activities; (2) activities taken to counter similar activities directed against the United States; (3) covert or clandestine activities affecting the relations of the United States with any foreign government, political group, party, military force, movement or other association; (4) the collection, analysis, production, dissemination, or use of information about activities of persons within the United States, its territories and possessions, or nationals of the United States abroad whose political and related activities pose, or may be considered by any department, agency, bureau, office, division, instrumentality, or employee of the United States to pose, a threat to the internal security of the United States, and covert or clandestine activities directed against such persons. Such term does not include tactical foreign military intelligence serving no national policymaking function.

(b) As used in this resolution, the term "department or agency" includes any organization, committee, council, establishment, or office within the Federal Government.

(c) For purposes of this resolution, reference to any department, agency, bureau, or subdivision shall include a reference to any successor department, agency, bureau, or subdivision to the extent that such successor engages in intelligence activities now conducted by the department, agency, bureau, or subdivision referred to in this resolution.

SEC. 15. For the period from the date this resolution is agreed to through February 28, 1977, the expenses of the select committee under this resolution shall not exceed $275,000, of which amount not to exceed $30,000 shall be available for the procurement of the services of individual consultants, or organizations thereof, as authorized by section 202(i) of the Legislative Reorganization Act of 1946. Expenses of the select committee under this resolution shall be paid from the contingent fund of the Senate upon vouchers approved by the chairman of the select committee, except that vouchers shall not be required for the disbursement of salaries of employees paid at an annual rate.

SEC. 16. Nothing in this resolution shall be construed as constituting acquiescence by the Senate in any practice, or in the conduct of any activity, not otherwise authorized by law.

CONGRESSIONAL OVERSIGHT: THE HOUSE PERMANENT SELECT COMMITTEE ON INTELLIGENCE

The House of Representatives created the Permanent Select Committee on Intelligence by resolution in the 95th Congress (1977). The terms of the resolution are part of the Rules of the House. Each new Congress must adopt such a rule, since House select committees are not allowed to be permanent, and therefore the status of the House Permanent Select Committee on Intelligence is exceptional. The jurisdiction of the House committee is somewhat broader than that of the Senate Select Committee on Intelligence.

PERMANENT SELECT COMMITTEE ON INTELLIGENCE

11. (a)(1) There is established a Permanent Select Committee on Intelligence (hereafter in this clause referred to as the "select committee"). The select committee shall be composed of not more than 16 Members, Delegates, or the Resident Commissioner, of whom not more than nine be from the same party. The select committee shall include at least one Member, Delegate, or the Resident Commissioner from each of the following committees:

(A) the Committee on Appropriations;
(B) the Committee on Armed Services;
(C) the Committee on International Relations; and
(D) the Committee on the Judiciary.

(2) The Speaker and the Minority Leader shall be ex officio members of the select committee but shall have no vote in the select committee and may not be counted for purposes of determining a quorum thereof.

(3) The Speaker and Minority Leader each may designate a member of his leadership staff to assist him in his capacity as ex officio member, with the same access to committee meetings, hearings, briefings, and materials as employees of the select committee and subject to the same security clearance and confidentiality requirements as employees of the select committee under this clause.

(4)(A) Except as permitted by subdivision (B), a Member, Delegate, or Resident Commissioner, other than the Speaker or the Minority Leader, may not serve as a member of the select committee during more than four Congresses in a period of six successive Congresses (disregarding for this purpose any service for less than a full session in a Congress).

(B) A member of the select committee who served as either the chairman or the ranking minority member of the select committee in the immediately previous Congress and who did not serve in that respective capacity in an earlier Congress may serve as either the chairman or the ranking minority member of the select committee during one additional Congress.

(b)(1) There shall be referred to the select committee proposed legislation, messages, petitions, memorials, and other matters relating to the following:

(A) The Central Intelligence Agency, the Director of Central Intelligence, and the National Foreign Intelligence Program as defined in section 3(6) of the National Security Act of 1947.

(B) Intelligence and intelligence-related activities of all other departments and agencies of the Government, including the tactical intelligence and intelligence-related activities of the Department of Defense.

(C) The organization or reorganization of a department or agency of the Government to the extent that the organization or reorganization relates to a function or activity involving intelligence or intelligence-related activities.

(D) Authorizations for appropriations, both direct and indirect, for the following:

(i) The Central Intelligence Agency, the Director of Central Intelligence, and the National Foreign Intelligence Program as defined in section 3(6) of the National Security Act of 1947.

(ii) Intelligence and intelligence-related activities of all other departments and agencies of the Government, including the tactical intelligence and intelligence-related activities of the Department of Defense.

(iii) A department, agency, subdivision, or program that is a successor to an agency or program named or referred to in (i) or (ii).

(2) Proposed legislation initially reported by the select committee (other than provisions solely involving matters specified in subparagraph (1)(A) or subparagraph (1)(D)(i)) containing any matter otherwise within the jurisdiction of a standing committee shall be referred by the Speaker to that standing committee. Proposed legislation initially reported by another committee that con-

tains matter within the jurisdiction of the select committee shall be referred by the Speaker to the select committee if requested by the chairman of the select committee.

(3) Nothing in this clause shall be construed as prohibiting or otherwise restricting the authority of any other committee to study and review an intelligence or intelligence-related activity to the extent that such activity directly affects a matter otherwise within the jurisdiction of that committee.

(4) Nothing in this clause shall be construed as amending, limiting, or otherwise changing the authority of a standing committee to obtain full and prompt access to the product of the intelligence and intelligence-related activities of a department or agency of the Government relevant to a matter otherwise within the jurisdiction of that committee.

(c)(1) For purposes of accountability to the House, the select committee shall make regular and periodic reports to the House on the nature and extent of the intelligence and intelligence-related activities of the various departments and agencies of the United States. The select committee shall promptly call to the attention of the House, or to any other appropriate committee, a matter requiring the attention of the House or another committee. In making such report, the select committee shall proceed in a manner consistent with paragraph (g) to protect national security.

(2) The select committee shall obtain annual reports from the Director of the Central Intelligence Agency, the Secretary of Defense, the Secretary of State, and the Director of the Federal Bureau of Investigation. Such reports shall review the intelligence and intelligence-related activities of the agency or department concerned and the intelligence and intelligence-related activities of foreign countries directed at the United States or its interests.

An unclassified version of each report may be made available to the public at the discretion of the select committee. Nothing herein shall be construed as requiring the public disclosure in such reports of the names of persons engaged in intelligence or intelligence-related activities for the United States or the divulging of intelligence methods employed or the sources of information on which the reports are based or the amount of funds authorized to be appropriated for intelligence and intelligence-related activities.

(3) Within six weeks after the President submits a budget under section 1105(a) of title 31, United States Code, or at such time as the Committee on the Budget may request, the select committee shall submit to the Committee on the Budget the views and estimates described in section 301(d) of the Congressional Budget Act of 1974 regarding matters within the jurisdiction of the select committee.

(d)(1) Except as specified in subparagraph (2), clauses 6(a), (b), and (c) and 8(a), (b), and (c) of this rule, and clauses 1, 2, and 4 of rule XI shall apply to the select committee to the extent not inconsistent with this clause.

(2) Notwithstanding the requirements of the first sentence of clause 2(g)(2) of rule XI, in the presence of the number of members required under the rules of the select committee for the purpose of taking testimony or receiving evidence, the select committee may vote to close a hearing whenever a majority of those present determines that the testimony or evidence would endanger the national security.

(e) An employee of the select committee, or a person engaged by contract or otherwise to perform services for or at the request of the select committee, may not be given access to any classified information by the select committee unless such employee or person has—

(1) agreed in writing and under oath to be bound by the Rules of the House, including the jurisdiction of the Committee on Standards of Official Conduct and of the select committee concerning the security of classified information during and after the period of his employment or contractual agreement with the select committee; and

(2) received an appropriate security clearance, as determined by the select committee in consultation with the Director of Central Intelligence, that is commensurate with the sensitivity of the classified information to which such employee or person will be given access by the select committee.

(f) The select committee shall formulate and carry out such rules and procedures as it considers necessary to prevent the disclosure, without the consent of each person concerned, of information in the possession of the select committee that unduly infringes on the privacy or that violates the constitutional rights of such person. Nothing herein shall be construed to prevent the select committee from publicly disclosing classified information in a case in which it determines that national interest in the disclosure of classified information clearly outweighs any infringement on the privacy of a person.

(g)(1) The select committee may disclose publicly any information in its possession after a determination by the select committee that the public interest would be served by such disclosure. With respect to the disclosure of information for which this paragraph requires action by the select committee—

(A) the select committee shall meet to vote on the matter within five days after a member of the select committee requests a vote; and

(B) a member of the select committee may not make such a disclosure before a vote by the select committee on the matter, or after a vote by the select committee on the matter except in accordance with this paragraph.

(2)(A) In a case in which the select committee votes to disclose publicly any information that has been classified under established security procedures, that has been submitted to it by the executive branch, and that the executive branch requests be kept secret, the select committee shall notify the President of such vote.

(B) The select committee may disclose publicly such information after the expiration of a five-day period following the day on which notice of the vote to disclose is transmitted to the President unless, before the expiration of the five-day period, the President, personally in writing, notifies the select committee that he objects to the disclosure of such information, provides his reasons therefor, and certifies that the threat to the national interest of the United States posed by the disclosure is of such gravity that it outweighs any public interest in the disclosure.

(C) If the President, personally in writing, notifies the select committee of his objections to the disclosure of information as provided in subdivision (B), the select committee may, by majority vote, refer the question of the disclosure of such information, with a recommendation thereon, to the House. The select committee may not publicly disclose such information without leave of the House.

(D) Whenever the select committee votes to refer the question of disclosure of any information to the House under subdivision (C), the chairman shall, not later than the first day on which the House is in session following the day on which the vote occurs, report the matter to the House for its consideration.

(E) If the chairman of the select committee does not offer in the House a motion to consider in closed session a matter reported under subdivision (D) within four calendar days on which the House is in session after the recommendation described in subdivision (C) is reported, then such a motion shall be privileged when offered by a Member, Delegate, or Resident Commissioner. In either case such a motion shall be decided without debate or intervening motion except one that the House adjourn.

(F) Upon adoption by the House of a motion to resolve into closed session as described in subdivision (E), the Speaker may declare a recess subject to the call of the Chair. At the expiration of the recess, the pending question, in closed session, shall be, "Shall the House approve the recommendation of the select committee?".

(G) Debate on the question described in subdivision (F) shall be limited to two hours equally divided and controlled by the chairman and ranking minority member of the select committee. After such debate the previous question shall be considered as ordered on the question of approving the recommendation without intervening motion except one motion that the House adjourn. The House shall vote on the question in open session but without divulging the information with respect to which the vote is taken. If the recommendation of the select committee is not approved, then the question is considered as recommitted to the select committee for further recommendation.

(3)(A) Information in the possession of the select committee relating to the lawful intelligence or intelligence-related activities of a department or agency of the United States that has been classified under established security procedures, and that the select committee has determined should not be disclosed under subparagraph (1) or (2), may not be made available to any person by a Member, Delegate, Resident Commissioner, officer, or employee of the House except as provided in subdivision (B).

(B) The select committee shall, under such regulations as it may prescribe, make information described in subdivision (A) available to a committee or a Member, Delegate, or Resident Commissioner, and permit a Member, Delegate, or Resident Commissioner to attend a hearing of the select committee that is closed to the public. Whenever the select committee makes such information available, it shall keep a written record showing, in the case of particular information, which committee or which Member, Delegate, or Resident Commissioner received the information. A Member, Delegate, or Resident Commissioner who, and a committee that, receives information under this subdivision may not disclose the information except in a closed session of the House.

(4) The Committee on Standards of Official Conduct shall investigate any unauthorized disclosure of intelligence or intelligence-related information by a Member, Delegate, Resident Commissioner, officer, or employee of the House in violation of subparagraph (3) and report to the House concerning any allegation that it finds to be substantiated.

(5) Upon the request of a person who is subject to an investigation described in subparagraph (4), the Committee on Standards of Official Conduct shall release to such person at the conclusion of its investigation a summary of its investigation, together with its findings. If, at the conclusion of its investigation, the Committee on Standards of Official Conduct determines that there has been a significant breach of confidentiality or unauthorized disclosure by a Member, Delegate, Resident Commissioner, officer, or employee of the House, it shall report its findings to the House and recommend appropriate action. Recommendations may include censure, removal from committee membership, or expulsion from the House, in the case of a Member, or removal from office or employment or punishment for contempt, in the case of an officer or employee.

(h) The select committee may permit a personal representative of the President, designated by the President to serve as a liaison to the select committee, to attend any closed meeting of the select committee.

(i) Subject to the Rules of the House, funds may not be appropriated for a fiscal year, with the exception of a bill or joint resolution continuing appropriations, or an amendment thereto, or a conference report thereon, to, or for use of, a department or agency of the United States to carry out any of the following activities, unless the funds shall previously have been authorized by a bill or joint resolution passed by the House during the same or preceding fiscal year to carry out such activity for such fiscal year:

(1) The activities of the Central Intelligence Agency and the Director of Central Intelligence.

(2) The activities of the Defense Intelligence Agency.

(3) The activities of the National Security Agency.

(4) The intelligence and intelligence-related activities of other agencies and subdivisions of the Department of Defense.

(5) The intelligence and intelligence-related activities of the Department of State.

(6) The intelligence and intelligence-related activities of the Federal Bureau of Investigation, including all activities of the Intelligence Division.

(j)(1) In this clause the term "intelligence and intelligence-related activities" includes—

(A) the collection, analysis, production, dissemination, or use of information that relates to a foreign country, or a government, political group, party, military force, movement, or other association in a foreign country, and that relates to the defense, foreign policy, national security, or related policies of the United States and other activity in support of the collection, analysis, production, dissemination, or use of such information;

(B) activities taken to counter similar activities directed against the United States;

(C) covert or clandestine activities affecting the relations of the United States with a foreign government, political group, party, military force, movement, or other association;

(D) the collection, analysis, production, dissemination, or use of information about activities of persons within the United States, its territories and possessions, or nationals of the United States abroad whose political and related activities pose, or may be considered by a department, agency, bureau, office, division, instrumentality, or employee of the United States to pose, a threat to the internal security of the United States; and

(E) covert or clandestine activities directed against persons described in subdivision (D).

(2) In this clause the term "department or agency" includes any organization, committee, council, establishment, or office within the Federal Government.

(3) For purposes of this clause, reference to a department, agency, bureau, or subdivision shall include a reference to any successor department, agency, bureau, or subdivision to the extent that a successor engages in intelligence or intelligence-related activities now conducted by the department, agency, bureau, or subdivision referred to in this clause.

(k) Clause 12(a) of rule XXII does not apply to meetings of a conference committee respecting legislation (or any part thereof) reported by the Permanent Select Committee on Intelligence.

Author Index

Subject Index

b indicates a box reference; *f* indicates a figure reference

A

Abel, Rudolf, 185
Abrams, Elliot, 90
Acquired immunodeficiency syndrome (AIDS), 176–177
ADCI. *See* Assistant director of central intelligence
Afghanistan
  heroin poppies, 174
  paramilitary operation, 112
  as Soviet problem, 163, 164
  Taliban faction, 192
  use of narcotics by Soviet military, 191
  U.S. aid to Mujaheddin, 108, 115, 119, 164, 165, 191
  U.S. cruise missile attack, 118*b*
Africa, 168, 173, 176
Agencies. *See* Intelligence agencies
AIDS. *See* Acquired immunodeficiency syndrome
Alien and Sedition Acts (1798), 152
Allende, Salvador, 112, 113–114, 118–119, 186, 196
Allocation, appropriation, and authorization, 125, 136–137, 141
Ames, Aldrich
  effects of, 104, 147, 165
  effects on intelligence personnel information, 100–101
  intelligence shortcomings and, 22, 103, 134
  polygraph testing of, 99
Analysis and production, 7–8. *See also* Intelligence

competitive analysis, 13, 46, 89–90, 134, 158, 160
consensus on, 84–86, 194–195
covert action and, 116
crises, 77–78
current and long-term intelligence, 76–77
ethical and moral issues, 193–196
interpretation of images, 63–64
issues, 86–93
management, 79–80
measurement and signatures intelligence, 66
policy making and, 41, 127–128, 194, 195
post-cold war period, 169
redundancy of, 13
requirements, 76, 77
Soviet Union, 165
team exercises, 89, 134, 158, 160
traffic analysis, 65
value-added effect, 75–76
wheat versus chaff problem, 78
writing of intelligence products, 84
"Analysis, War, and Decision" (Betts), 2
Analysts. *See also* Kent, Sherman
  goals, knowledge, and mindset, 46–47, 80–86, 90–91, 93
  management of, 79–80
  objectivity, 78–79, 124
  options, 195–196, 197*b*
  policy making and, 90–91
  role of, 41
  training, 78–79
Angleton, James, 103
Angola, 163

251

intelligence oversight, 134
Iran-contra scandal, 110
members, 121
NSC-68, 156
role in policy making, 121
staff, 121–122
targeting of terrorist infrastructures,
118*b*
National Security Threat List, 103–104
NATO. *See* North Atlantic Treaty Organization
Navy, 11. *See also* Military
Neustadt, Richard, 109
"New World Order," 167
New York Times, 197, 198
NFIP. *See* National Foreign Intelligence
Program
NIC. *See* National Intelligence Council
Nicaragua. *See also* Iran-contra activities
Abrams, Elliot, and, 90
Boland, Edward, and, 138
intelligence community, 15
mining of Corinto, 147, 149
NICs. *See* National intelligence officers
NIEs. *See* National intelligence estimates
NIMA (National Imagery and Mapping
Agency). *See also* Department of
Defense
Nitze, Paul, 155–156
Nixon, Richard M., 121, 130
North, Oliver, 110
North Atlantic Treaty Organization
(NATO), 159, 178
NRO. *See* National Reconnaissance
Office
NSA. *See* National Security Agency
NSC. *See* National Security Council
Nuccio, Richard, 198
Nuclear testing, 58. *See also* Arms control

O

Office of Strategic Services (OSS), 11,
17, 61
Office of the Secretary of Defense
(OSD), 32
Office of the Secretary of Defense/Command, Control, Communications and
Intelligence (OSD/C3I), 32
Open-source intelligence (OSINT), 59,
60–61, 69–70, 72*f*, 177

OSD. *See* Office of the Secretary of
Defense
OSD/C3I. *See* Office of the Secretary of
Defense/Command, Control,
Communications and Intelligence
OSINT. *See* Open-source intelligence
OSS. *See* Office of Strategic Services
Oversight. *See* Congress, U.S.; Intelligence, U.S.

P

Pakistan, 173
Palestine, 124
Paramilitary. *See* Military
Patton, George S., 59
PDB (President's Daily Briefing). *See*
Presidents, U.S.
PDD. *See* Presidential decision directives
Peacekeeping operations, 178
Pearl Harbor, 12, 17–18, 80–81. *See also*
World War II
Pearl Harbor: Warning and Decision
(Wohlstetter), 55
Pelton, Ronald, 22, 100
Penkovsky, Oleg, 55, 165, 186
Pentagon Papers, 139
Peter the Great, 157
PFIAB. *See* President's Foreign Intelligence Advisory Board
Philby, Kim, 100*b*,103
Photo intelligence (PHOTINT), 61. *See
also* Imagery intelligence
Pinochet, Augusto, 119
PIOB. *See* President's Intelligence Oversight Board
Plausible deniability. *See* Covert action
Policy making. *See also* Congress, U.S.;
Ethical and moral issues; Political
issues
accountability and, 123
advocacy and, 3
behaviors of policy makers, 129–130
budget issues, 125
cold war, 169
environmental issues, 177
goals and agenda, 122, 123, 124–125
health issues, 176–177
loci of policy process, 120–123
narcotics trade, 174–175
post-cold war period, 169
setting priorities, 42–43, 55